# The Riddle
# of The New Testament

# THE RIDDLE
# OF THE NEW TESTAMENT

by
## SIR EDWYN HOSKYNS, BART.

and
## NOEL DAVEY

## FABER AND FABER LIMITED
### 24 Russell Square
### London

*First published in this edition mcmlviii
by Faber and Faber Limited
24 Russell Square London W.C.1
Printed in Great Britain by
Latimer Trend & Co Ltd Plymouth*

# Contents

5

# CONTENTS

# CONTENTS

# CONTENTS

## Introduction

The Christian Religion revolves round one central article of faith:

> Credo in unum Deum . . .
> Et in unum Dominum Jesum Christum . . .
> Qui propter nos homines,
> Et propter nostram salutem
> Descendit de coelis,
> Et incarnatus est . . . :
> Et homo factus est.
> Crucifixus etiam pro nobis:
> Sub Pontio Pilato passus,
> Et sepultus est.[1]

When the Catholic Christian kneels at the words *incarnatus est* or at the words *and was incarnate*, he marks with proper solemnity his recognition that the Christian religion has its origin neither in general religious experience, nor in some peculiar esoteric mysticism, nor in a dogma. He declares his faith to rest upon a particular event in history. Nor is the Catholic Christian peculiar in this concentration of faith. This is Christian ortho-

---

[1] I believe in one God . . .
And in one Lord Jesus Christ . . .
Who for us men, and for our salvation
Came down from heaven,
And was incarnate . . . . :
And was made man.
And was crucified also for us under Pontius Pilate.
He suffered and was buried.

THE NICENE CREED

In the modern Latin version *under Pontius Pilate* is taken with the verb *suffered* and not with the verb *crucified*. The English version is a correct translation of the original Greek.

9

doxy, both Catholic and Protestant. In consequence, the Christian religion is not merely open to historical investigation, but demands it, and its piety depends upon it. Inadequate or false reconstruction of the history of Jesus of Nazareth cuts at the heart of Christianity. The critical and historical study of the New Testament is therefore the prime activity of the church. The recognition of the paramount importance of a particular history and of the necessity of a critical reconstruction of it is not new in the life of the church. What is new is the emergence during the past two centuries of a precise method of handling historical evidence and an unshakable confidence in the adequacy of the new method.

It is commonly supposed that the modern method of historical investigation has been perfected outside the field of Biblical studies, and that it has then been applied to the Bible. The opposite is, however, nearer to the truth. The method emerged from the heart of Christian study, and was developed by Christian theologians in order to enable them to handle literary and historical problems presented by the Scriptures. The method thus evolved has exerted a creative influence upon the general study of history. Nor is this fortuitous. Christian theology has been creative in the field of historical investigation, because the theologian has been compelled to a delicate sense for the importance of history by a faith which is grounded upon a particular event.

The purpose of this book is to display the critical method at work upon the New Testament documents in the hope that some who are engaged elsewhere may be enabled to appreciate what has been and still is being achieved behind the scenes in the sphere of Christian historical theology. This purpose might at first seem to have been attained if the reader were provided with a number of assured critical results. But this would completely misrepresent the present situation. It is a strange paradox that precisely as the critic grows in confidence in the adequacy of his method, so he becomes increasingly diffident of his ability to catalogue 'assured results'. It is therefore difficult, if not impossible, to point to a number of critical achievements as though they were information to be handed out to the general reader. For example, the critic is unable with any confidence to date the New Testament documents precisely; nor can he, except in the case of the majority of the Pauline epistles, discover who wrote the various books. More serious is his inability to pronounce a final judgement as to whether isolated events happened or did not happen as they are recorded in the gospels. He is dealing almost wholly with anonymous books in which no reference is made to events familiar to the historian of the Roman Empire. (In the Lucan writings —the third Gospel and the Acts of the Apostles—the beginnings of the Christian religion are, it is true, set definitely within the framework of the history of the Roman Empire; but in this the Lucan writings are peculiar.) The problem of historicity is even more subtly elusive. Nowhere in the New Testament are events recorded or referred to simply as events. The events are set in a theological context and their record serves a theological purpose. This use of the word theological, however, raises the whole problem of the meaning of the Christian religion and, very particularly, of the historical events recorded in the Bible.

Consequently, if the general reader requires from the critic assured results concerning date, authorship, and historicity, set forth in tabulated form, he must be disappointed. The progress of critical historical investigation of the New Testament cannot be compared to a gradual mounting the steps of a ladder. One generation does not achieve a number of results which pass into the text-books, so that the next generation is enabled to mount a few steps higher. Rather, as each advance is made, the problem as a whole begins to look different; and the 'assured results' of the previous generation require constant reconsideration when seen in a new perspective. This does not, of course, mean that the modern critic stands aloof from the older criticism. He is completely dependent upon the work of his predecessors. But, where they supposed that they had reached definite and final conclusions, he sees new problems; and the older conclusions appear in their new context almost irrelevant, and, at times, trivial. It would therefore be to misrepresent the modern living criticism of the New Testament to catalogue a number of conclusions and present them as the fruits of the critical method. For this reason we have attempted to show the critical method at work; and to show it working not upon isolated problems of dates or authorship or historicity, but upon the main problem of the New Testament which lurks behind every fragment of it.

There is a riddle in the New Testament. And it is a riddle neither of literary criticism, nor of date and authorship, nor of the historicity of this or that episode. The riddle is a theological riddle, which is insoluble apart from the solution of an historical problem. What was the relation between Jesus of Nazareth and the primitive Christian church? That is the riddle. The New Testament documents, all of them, emerged from the primitive church. They reflected piety and encouraged faith. Was there, or was there not, a strict relationship between this rich piety and exuberant faith and the historical figure of Jesus of Nazareth? Did the life and death of Jesus of Nazareth control the life of the primitive church? or were his life and death submerged by a piety and faith wholly beyond his horizon? We know the primitive church from the New Testament documents. We do not as certainly know Jesus of Nazareth. The adequacy of the modern historical critical method is therefore finally tested by its success or failure in answering the problem of the Jesus of history. The authors of this book are confident that the critical method does survive this very severe test, and that it does disclose results, even assured results; but they are also persuaded that these results are very few, very surprising and very inconvenient. Inconvenient, because they do nothing to bring the New Testament within the orbit of modern humanitarian or humanistic teaching. Nothing, because the New Testament cannot speak of any human behaviour without first defining what men and women *are*.

Much that would properly have been included in a larger and more comprehensive work upon the New Testament has been omitted as not strictly relevant to the particular problem with which we are dealing. For example, the Acts of the Apostles would have been of prime importance had we been concerned to sketch the history of the primitive church. Since this is not our aim, the book has been almost wholly left out of account. The reader will, of course, notice many other glaring omissions. Questions of authorship and date have been dealt with, very inadequately, in an appendix. The reason for this is partly that no answer can be given to these questions, and partly that, even if answers could be given, very little would be gained thereby, since the further the critic advances in his work, the more certainly do these questions seem to be irrelevant, though the Christian status of the author is always supremely important. Yet it seemed desirable to give for reference some indication of the present position in regard to them. The names Matthew, Mark. Luke, John have been retained to denote the unknown authors of the final form of the four gospels, or to denote the books themselves. The use of these venerable names involves, however, no judgement upon the identification of Matthew and John with the Apostles, or of Luke with the companion of St. Paul, or of Mark with the interpreter of St. Peter.

We have not disturbed the reader by continuous references to current theological literature or to the works of famous critics of the last century. It has seemed more important to focus attention upon the New Testament documents and to illustrate the critical method, than to attach this or that theory to the critic who originated or developed it. Should this book fall into the hands of the expert, we ask him to forgive us when we have failed to assign due credit to the pioneers of New Testament criticism by omitting to name them or to give references to their books; and to forgive us also for having touched too lightly upon matters which will seem to him to be far more controversial then we have allowed. For example, we have not followed Dr. Streeter in his reconstruction of the stages in the literary composition of the third gospel. We regard Luke's editing of Mark to be still a prime fact in New Testament criticism, and we have judged that Professor Creed in his recent commentary upon St. Luke's Gospel has made Dr. Streeter's Proto-Luke theory untenable, at least in the form in which he stated it in Chapter VIII of his book on the Four Gospels. We have also treated the Epistle to the Ephesians as a Pauline epistle. The definite ascription of the Epistle to St. Paul is, of course, doubtful. But it seems to us legitimate to use it as, at least, throwing important light upon the theology of the Apostle, and as accurately representing what he had said and written.

A word is necessary to explain the form in which citations have been introduced from the Old and New Testaments. Normally, citations are taken from the Authorized Version. But we have quoted from the Revised Version or from the marginal readings in the Authorized or Revised Versions where they have seemed to us preferable; at times we have dared to translate from the Septuagint Greek version of the Old Testament, where it seemed important for the understanding of an allusion in the New Testament. Very rarely have we ventured upon our own translation of any portion of the Old Testament or of the New.

Should the reader desire to check in detail the argument in Chapters IV-VI of this book, he can do so the more easily if he has access to some modern synopsis of the first three Gospels, in which they are set out in parallel columns. For this we would recommend either *The Synoptic Gospels*, by J. M. Thompson, published by the Oxford University Press, where they are set out in English; or *A Synopsis of The First Three Gospels*, by A. Huck, published by J. C. B. Mohr, Tübingen, where they are set out in Greek.

Finally, we cannot allow this book to go to press without thanking our friend the Rev. Charles Smyth, sometime Fellow of Corpus Christi College, Cambridge, not only for his patience in looking through the proofs, but more particularly for his generous encouragement.

In preparing the third edition, the bibliography has been expanded, but otherwise, except for a few particularly necessary modifications, the text has been left as it was approved for the second edition by Sir Edwyn Hoskyns.

## Chapter I

## The Language: A Problem in Semasiology[1]

All the New Testament books were written within a period of one hundred years from the death of Jesus Christ, and they were all written in Greek, for Greek-speaking readers, by men who for the most part themselves lived in a Greek-speaking society. There can, then, be no accurate reconstruction of primitive Christian thought which does not rest upon an accurate study of the grammar and syntax of the Greek language during the first century A.D., and upon an accurate knowledge of the meaning which the Greek words used by the Christian writers had for their readers. Philology and lexicography form the essential groundwork of the interpretation of the New Testament.

Before, however, the specific problems presented by the Greek of the New Testament can be laid bare, it is necessary to recognize certain general problems which arise in the reconstruction of any thought from its expression in any tongue. There is an inevitable tension between the mind of a writer and the language at his disposal which, in itself, constitutes a problem. The two are mutually creative. On the one hand, a word, or even the lack of a word, may mould thought, because men think in words; on the other hand, the evolution of thought may twist the meaning of a word, because words are means of thought. So this moulding and twisting inevitably complicate expression, since they tend to increase the versatility of words at the expense of their

[1] 'That branch of philology which deals with the meanings of words, sense-development, and the like' (*New English Dictionary*).

precision. The mere sight of a common word will con-
jure up all kinds of associations; associations which, once
acquired, are hard to be rid of. Its etymological origin,
its past use in speech and in literature, the peculiar
vogue which it at present enjoys, are all liable to colour
the interpretation put upon it by writer and reader
alike; at any moment, indeed, it may be re-endowed
with an apparently extinct association by the design of
the one, or the preoccupation of the other. And so no
critic can afford to neglect this potentiality in the
material before him; least of all the critic of documents
of which the literary affinities show their writers to have
been themselves readers: men who read with a preoccupation, and wrote with a design. For New Testament study, neglect of it would be fatal.

Of all human languages, that of the Greek-speaking
peoples has probably been the least static. Both their
thought and their expression have been involved in a
vast, and, at times, rapidly changing process, which has
continued from many centuries before Christ until the
present day. Now, though one stage in this process may
be found to foreshadow or corroborate another, it can
never fully explain it. And so no relics of Greek thought
and expression can be so valuable for the understanding
of the New Testament as the records of the actual age in
which the writers lived. Formerly, exegesis suffered
greatly through lack of such contemporary records. In
their absence, the usage of the Classical period, preserved in a comparative profusion of documents, was
pressed to the interpretation of writings which originated
in a later and fundamentally different society, and sometimes proved more of a hindrance than a help. Particularly was this so where grammar or syntax was in question. It was difficult, without confirmatory evidence, to
realize that the nice precision of the Attic dialect was
no more, and that the method of thought which had
demanded and created such precision, but which was
itself dependent upon a certain phase of civilization, had

decayed with the city-state. But now much historical and archaeological research has made it possible to ascertain the nature of the language which bound together the eastern half of the Roman Empire. It is seen to have been pre-eminently a language of human experience, fitted to the mouths of ordinary men and women, whose logic moved in terms, not of scholarly argument, but of pictorial metaphor, and whose minds were occupied less with the meaning of life than with the living of it. This is not to deny that they were speculative. The popularity of the mystery religions, and, indeed, the spread of Christianity itself, show how deeply men were concerned with the problems of life and death, and death and life. It is rather to affirm that they did not separate speculation from the ordinary routine of living, or create a specialized vocabulary for its maintenance. As they attached superstitious importance to quite trivial actions, so they loaded the simplest words with the most far-reaching meaning, and were capable of using them diversely within the boundaries of a single sentence. Therefore, while the critic must beware of forcing a particular meaning upon every appearance of a word or phrase, he must be equally careful not to overlook an allusion because it may seem undefined. Here 'spirit' may be meant, there 'breath', for the same word serves for the two in Greek: misapprehension in either case ruins good exegesis. And so, since the writers themselves were not aware of any need to define terms, it is necessary, if they are to be rightly understood, to keep all their possible allusions constantly at hand, by tabulating examples of every diverse use. This is the object of lexicography, the tabulation of the different uses of words in the literature of a period or nation. It is an essential part of New Testament study.

During the last fifty years, the lexicography of the Greek language during the New Testament period has been made possible by the discovery of a great mass of contemporary inscriptions, records, and letters. Collation has followed collection, and it is now possible to find, in accessible form, illustrations of the contemporary use of almost every word in the New Testament. Consequently, much is now clear that was before obscure, and much certain that was hitherto in doubt. Perhaps the most significant result has been that many apparently vague expressions are now shown to have been capable of a more concrete and precise meaning. The Prodigal *Lk. xv. 13.* Son did not vaguely 'gather together' all his share of his father's substance: he 'realized' it, converted it into ready money. St. Paul had not heard that some of the Thessalonians were 'walking disorderly', but that they *2 Th. iii. 11.* were 'playing truant', not going to work, in expectation of the imminent end of the world. Judas carried the 'money-box', not the 'bag', and Jesus perhaps forbade *Jn. xii. 6.* the disciples to take with them, not, 'a leathern bag for *Mk. vi. 8* provisions', but a wallet such as mendicant friars of that *(A.V. 'scrip').* age used for collecting alms.

Important as these philological discoveries have been for the interpretation of the Greek of the New Testament, an exaggerated insistence upon them obscures its linguistic peculiarity. The New Testament documents were, no doubt, written in a language intelligible to the generality of Greek-speaking people; yet to suppose that they emerged from the background of Greek thought and experience would be to misunderstand them completely. There is a strange and awkward element in the language which not only affects the meanings of words, not only disturbs the grammar and syntax, but lurks everywhere in a maze of literary allusions which no ordinary Greek man or woman could conceivably have understood or even detected.

The truth is that behind these writings there lies an intractable Hebraic, Aramaic, Palestinian material. It is this foreign matter that complicates New Testament Greek. Each writer is to a greater or lesser degree struggling to interpret into Greek a non-Greek method of thought and a non-Greek terminology. There is, moreover, not merely a problem of language, but a problem also of literary background. No single New Testament author for one moment imagines that he can interpret his material apart from a knowledge of the Jewish sacred scriptures. The tension between the Jewish heritage and the Greek world vitally affects the language of the New Testament.

Whilst, then, our new knowledge of the spoken Greek of the first century A.D. undoubtedly clears up many grammatical and philological details, and makes the background of the New Testament more vivid and more human, nevertheless in the end these discoveries are for the most part unimportant, and they signally fail to resolve those more serious philological and lexicographical problems upon which an understanding of primitive Christianity ultimately rests.

It is obviously impossible here to illustrate difficulties of grammar and syntax which are capable of explanation only upon the background of Hebrew and Aramaic idiom. The philological problem that confronts the reader of the New Testament can be illustrated by reference to two words, both of which are important words in the New Testament—the Greek word *ekklesia*, translated in the English Authorized and Revised Versions by the word *church*, and the Greek word *aletheia*, which is rendered *truth*.

What did the New Testament writers mean when they made use of the Greek word *ekklesia*? In contemporary, as in classical, Greek its meaning was simple. Formed from a verb, 'call out', or 'call forth', in order to express a gathering of citizens summoned, by a herald, from their homes into some public place, it came later to be used of assemblies convoked for political purposes, and perhaps (cf. Acts xix. 41), in a weakened sense, of congregations of people without reference to their purpose. On the face of it, then, it would seem that Tyndale and Cranmer rightly substituted for Wycliffe's

*Acts xix. 41.*

'chirche' the more literal 'congregacion': yet, so unsatisfactory did their decision prove, that, before very long, it was reversed by the translators of the Authorized Version. And, indeed, the reason is not hard to find. In such a passage as:

'And at that tyme there was a great persecucion agaynst the *Acts viii. 1.* congregacion which was at Ierusalem, and they were all scattered abroade thorowout the regions of Iury and Samaria . . .',

it is evident that, if 'congregacion' is to fit the context, it must first be deprived of the very notion of assembling which the use of it was intended to secure, and then be read in an acquired sense as indicating a number of men and women who formed, in some way or another, a corporate body even when not assembled. For it is hardly likely that the writer meant that the persecutors swooped down upon them when they were all gathered together, any more than did St. Paul when he wrote: 'For I am the least of the apostles, that am not meet to *1 Cor. xv. 9.* be called an apostle, because I persecuted the *ekklesia* of God.'

But these passages which, by their meaning, show the inadequacy of rendering *ekklesia* 'assembly' or 'congregacion', prove, by their form, that classical and contemporary usage do not provide an interpretation of the *ekklesia* of the New Testament. For, that the writers refer to an *ekklesia* which is by its very nature exceptional, is evident from their use of the definite article. Yet the phrase, *the ekklesia*, used absolutely, though consistent in the New Testament, is never once found in secular writings. To a Greek who did not recognize in it some peculiar connotation, it must have been meaningless. Then how much more meaningless the further and equally unparalleled definition of peculiarity: *the ekklesia of God*!

Now, although classical and contemporary usage provides no analogy, there is one collection of Greek writings which abounds in references to an *ekklesia of*

*God*, or *of the Lord*. This is the Septuagint, the earliest Greek translation of the Hebrew scriptures. This book was the Bible of the Jews scattered throughout the Roman Empire. It was credited with a miraculous origin, and venerated as possessing divine inspiration. Were there no other evidence, it would be natural to look for its influence in the New Testament. But there is good reason for being sure that it had such influence. For instance, because it is almost impossible to transcribe manuscripts without making a certain number of errors, variations gradually crept into the Hebrew text of the Old Testament on the one hand, and into the Greek text on the other, which produced, by the time of Christ, considerable differences between them. The marked preference, in quotation, on the part of New Testament writers, for the readings of the Greek version, makes it certain that most of them were familiar with it.

A careful analysis of the books of the New Testament shows, not only that the authors tended to quote the Jewish scriptures from the Greek and to make use of Old Testament phrases in order to evoke their Jewish theological associations, but also that the writers were so completely impregnated by the Old Testament scriptures that they fell unconsciously into a scriptural turn of language. The Greek translation of the Hebrew scriptures was of prime importance to the New Testament writers precisely because they, like the men who produced the Septuagint, were faced with the problem of giving expression in Greek to ideas that had first taken form in a Semitic idiom. It is therefore natural to inquire whether Septuagint usage may, in part at least, account for the expression *the ekklesia of God*.

Two Hebrew words, which may be transliterated *edhah* and *qahal*, were used in the Old Testament to describe popular gatherings. Although by derivation far from synonymous, they were used fairly indiscriminately, and were both applied, in particular, to gatherings of all Israel.[1] In this connexion, properly speaking, *edhah* referred to 'the society itself, formed by the children of Israel or their representative heads, whether assembled or not assembled', while *qahal* denoted 'their actual meeting together'. But, after the Exile, *qahal* came to be used almost to the exclusion of *edhah*, and combined in itself the two shades of meaning which had formerly kept the words distinct. Meanwhile, Israel was becoming more and more conscious of being a peculiar nation, a chosen race, the elect people of God. And so the *qahal* of Jehovah was used to signify, not an assembly of Israel upon some particular occasion, but the people of Israel as God's people distinct from everybody else, whether assembled or unassembled, the chosen of Jehovah for his service.

The earliest translators[2] rendered both *edhah* and *qahal* by the Greek word *synagoge*, emphasizing the notion of 'assembling' by a word which, etymologically, meant 'lead together'. But later *synagoge* was generally reserved for *edhah*, and *ekklesia* for *qahal*. Probably this choice also was guided by etymology: *qahal* was formed from a verb meaning 'call' or 'summon' in precisely the same way as '*ekklesia*'. It is possible even that an identity of consonants enabled bilingual Jews to recognize the Hebrew *qahal* behind the Greek *ekklesia*. But, whatever the exact intention of the translators may have been, they caused *ekklesia of the Lord* to become a common scriptural phrase with exactly the same allusion to Israel's vocation as the *qahal of Jehovah*.[3]

Since Christians from a very early date regarded themselves as the 'Israel of God', the true elect race and 'holy nation', as opposed to the Jews who had *e.g.Gal.vi.16; 1 Pet. ii. 9.*

---

[1] This statement, and the quotations that follow, are taken from Dr. Hort's survey of the word *ekklesia* in the first chapter of his *Christian Ekklesia*.

[2] The Pentateuch was translated into Greek some time before the other books of the Old Testament.

[3] Jehovah is rendered 'the Lord' in the Septuagint.

rejected the Messiah, it might seem that, for that reason alone, *ekklesia* came to be their designation of themselves. By use of it they certainly claimed the Old Testament phrase, with the allusions of particularity and service just noted, as rightly descriptive of their function in the world. And no doubt this claim partly accounts for their choice of the phrase. Certainly, when *1 Cor. xi. 22.* St. Paul writes, 'What? Have ye not houses to eat and to drink in? or despise ye the *ekklesia of God*, and shame them that have not?' his use of the word *ekklesia* would not have surprised a non-Christian Jew. But when he defines the phrase it is clear that its background has *1 Cor. i. 2.* become even more complicated. For he writes to '*the ekklesia of God* which is at Corinth, to them that are sanctified in Christ Jesus, called to be saints, with all that call upon the name of our Lord'. Now, when it is remembered that the root of the word *ekklesia* is the same as that of the Greek participles 'called' and 'calling upon', it is impossible to suppose that its force is any longer dormant, as it had probably been in the Old Testament. It is as though he had written 'the *called-out* of God which is at Corinth, . . . *called* to be saints, with all that *call* upon the name of our Lord'. And, moreover, these two participles not only bring out this association in the word *ekklesia*, but re-define the genitive, 'of God'. They are called *by* God to be 'saints', that is, they are men who have been brought into a special relation *with* God. Thus the genitive, 'of God', implies that the *ekklesia* has both a subjective and an objective relation to God. All this was no doubt implicit in the Old Testament phrase. But here it is explicit, and here, too, in both respects, related to Jesus Christ. For the calling is *through* him, the sanctification *in* or *by* him. In fact, so intimately is he responsible for the foundation *Acts xx. 28.* and life of the *ekklesia*, that, in a passage in Acts, there appear the equally well attested variant readings, *ekklesia of God* and *ekklesia of the Lord*. And St. Paul does *Rom. xvi. 16.* not hesitate to write: 'All the *ekklesias of Christ* salute you.'

This last use adds to the difficulty of interpreting the word *ekklesia* solely in the light of the Old Testament. Hitherto it might have been supposed that the Old Testament idea of the people of God had simply been christianized by a reinterpretation of the relation to God in the light of the gospel. In that case *ekklesia* would still mean all the people of God assembled or unassembled, the new Israel, the whole Christian body. But here the plural appears, *ekklesias*, and not only here, but many times in the Pauline epistles. And these *ekklesias* may equally well be groups meeting in a house, or all the Christians of a great city. 'The *ekklesias* of Asia salute you. Aquila and Prisca salute you much in the Lord, with the *ekklesia* that is in their house.' Thus the name '*ekklesia*' can be given indiscriminately to the whole body of Christians, to local bodies of Christians, and even to smaller bodies of Christians within the local bodies. The corporate sense of *ekklesia* has not been lost in the emphasizing of the idea of calling. The word has been transformed to denote a body of men and women in which the unity of every part corresponds to, repeats, represents, and in fact *is* the unity of the whole. So *ekklesia* has one more association, which cannot be explained by its Old Testament history. The part is equal to the whole, because each part possesses, not a fragment of the Christ, but the whole Christ, and consequently, in accordance with the mathematical definition, the *ekklesia* is of the order of infinity.[1]

*So, e.g., in 1 Cor. xii. 28*

*1 Cor. xvi. 19.*

*cf. Maculal-Samma*

[1] It may be noted that the reproduction of the Biblical word *ekklesia* by the word *church* is almost entirely adequate. Etymologically it is derived from the Greek *kyriakon*, meaning 'that which belongs to the Lord'. The word therefore rightly emphasizes the primary significance which originally attached to the word *ekklesia*, and describes the Christians as a corporate body, who are the peculiar possession of God in the world. Moreover since the word *church* is in English a peculiar word used to reproduce *ekklesia* in the Authorized and Revised Versions of the New Testament, it has acquired the proper associations from its context in the New Testament. The word is, in

The examination of the word *ekklesia* has been comparatively simple because the word has no associations in modern thought to cloud the issue. For it is sometimes difficult to avoid reading the familiar English equivalents of the Greek in the light of their present use. Indeed, many words in common use to-day seem to mean nothing at all in their New Testament context. The very glibness of the translation baffles the reader. In particular, the Pauline and Johannine writings sometimes appear quite easy when actually read, yet fail to leave a clear impression upon the mind because the particular significance of apparently familiar words is missed. A remarkable illustration of the subtle change in the meaning of a word familiar in English is provided by the Greek word *aletheia*, rendered *truth*. This word cries for no particular philological investigation; and yet its use in the New Testament is strange and exceedingly awkward. Take, for example, the following passage:

*Eph. iv. 20-24.* 'But ye did not so learn Christ; if so be that ye heard him, and were taught in him, even as truth (A.V. the truth) is in Jesus: that ye put away as concerning your former manner of life, the old man, which waxeth corrupt after the lusts of deceit; and that ye be renewed in the spirit of your mind, and put on the new man which after God hath been created in righteousness and holiness of truth.'

It is only too easy to read the phrase 'as truth is in Jesus' without thinking clearly what it means. Yet the whole passage, and, indeed, much of St. Paul's teaching, depends upon a clear understanding of it. Does such an

---

fact, misleading only inasmuch as it has gathered other associations from later ecclesiastical history. But these can easily be corrected by referring it afresh to its scriptural setting. Whereas the northern races have turned to some variant of the Teutonic *kirika* or of the Slavonic *cerkov* to reproduce the Greek, *ekklesia* the southern races have retained the Greek word, e.g. *église*, *iglesia*, *chiesa*, etc. (Welsh, *eglwys*.) The late Mr. A. Hadrian Allcroft, however, set forth a new etymology for the word *church* (*The Circle and the Cross*, 2 vols., Macmillan).

expression as 'truth is in Jesus' make any sense at all to the modern reader? What conception of truth therefore justifies the statement that hearing (about) Jesus Christ, and being taught in him, will have, not an intellectual but a moral and spiritual effect upon them? Is truth connected with a manner of life? Finally, what has truth to do with righteousness and holiness?

Most men and women operate contentedly with a conception of truth which is bound up with their own conception of reality. That is true which is a fact, which is real, as opposed to that which is a fiction or an illusion. This conception, strictly speaking, has no moral or spiritual significance. Moreover, the imagination of a scientific age cherishes the dogma that truth is an ultimate standard although it recognizes no ultimate standard by which truth is itself determined. For a statement is commonly held to be true if it accords with the simplest explanation of the facts, with the experience of the race or of the individual, or with the supposed nature or fitness of things. A man is said to be true to his principles, to his religion, to type, or to himself. A musical note is true or false according to its relation to another note, or to an arbitrarily determined rate of vibration. The engineer 'trues up' the valve-face on a cylinder block.

Before it is possible to use the word 'true' without explicitly relating its subject to something else, a standard of truth has to be established in the minds of men, relationship to which will henceforth be implied. Now the Greek adjective *alethinos* in the spoken Greek of the first century A.D. did mean very much what the English adjective *true* means to the ordinary Englishman to-day. It meant something genuine and not counterfeit, without emphasis on any particular standard by which a statement or a thing may be judged true or false. When, however, the Greek noun *aletheia* and the Greek adjective *alethinos* were used to reproduce the Hebrew root 'MN, the whole emphasis was changed. The standard of truth not only took complete and manifest control of the noun *truth*, of the adjective *true*, and of the verb *to be true*, but also dominated the whole conception of knowledge. The Hebrew mind, in its certainty of a transcendent God, fixed upon him as the standard of truth. How this came about is not certain. It may be that the idea of steadfastness, 'truth to one's self', came naturally to be applied to him who was thought of, in no philosophical manner, as everlasting. It may be that the conception of a covenant relationship to which Jehovah would be true, even if Israel proved false, was actually responsible. At all events, the truth of Jehovah was regarded as an integral part of his character; in other words, he was conceived to be steadfast and consistent, in his nature, in his purpose, in his judgement, and in his dealings with men. A similar conception of steadfastness of purpose underlies the 'plighting of troth' in the English marriage service. The inability of the Hebrew mind to think of the character or nature of God apart from his actions in the world therefore caused them to think of his truth, not as static, but as active, or potentially active. God must, God would, manifest his truth to the world, for his nature demanded a vindication of itself. Present facts seemed to belie his consistency. He had promised to exalt the horn of David, yet Israel was in travail. He was holy and righteous, yet the righteous man was harassed and the holy man was mocked. So the truth of Jehovah came to be sighed for in exactly the same way as his mercy and his righteousness. When they were revealed, when he finally acted, the messianic age would be established.[1]

But if the Jews looked to the future for the final

[1] The Hebrew root 'MN is preserved in English in the liturgical *amen*, in which word the confidence that God will hear the prayers of his faithful people is formally expressed, and also, curiously enough, in the word *mammon*, meaning that in which the men of the world falsely trust (usually riches, of course), and implying a contrast with the living God who alone is the proper object of human confidence.

realization of the truth of God, they did so the more confidently because they believed that they had already experienced it. All God's dealings with men, all his judgements, had been true. So was his law, which he had given them through Moses. Indeed, it could itself be called the truth.

God was true. And God demanded that his servants should be like him. To know the truth, therefore, is to stand under the imperative of God, and so the object of knowledge has become the subject of action. 'Be ye holy as I am holy.' Thus the truth of Jehovah was the type and created the standard of human truth. Men must have truth in their hearts, and keep the law of truth; so shall they be said to walk in the way of truth, and so shall they be called 'true'. The last sentence sounds sentimental, but it is biblical throughout and in its biblical context there is no trace of sentimentality in it: it is entirely unmodern, and almost entirely un-Greek. Accordingly truth is not limited to rightness of knowledge. It is rightness of speech, of motive, and of action as well: rightness based, not upon concept nor upon convention, but upon the historical revelation of God. Hence, when this Hebraic background is recognized, the Johannine expression 'to do the truth', in spite of its apparent paradox to the modern reader, ought to occasion him no surprise. *1 Cor. i. 22, 23.*

*Jn. iii. 21; I Jn. i. 6; cf. Tobit xiii. 6.*

That such conceptions underlie the New Testament use of the word 'truth' is quite clear. The word embraces far more than the purely intellectual quality of modern thought. Otherwise the Pharisees and Herodians would hardly have said to Jesus: 'Teacher, we know that thou art true,' attributing to him truth of character as well as of speech and of doctrine. The truth which the New Testament writers are declaring is inseparable from the character and actions of God: *Mk. xii. 14.*

'For I say that Christ hath been made a minister of the circumcision for (the sake of) the truth of God, that he might *Rom. xv. 8, 9.*

confirm the promises given to the fathers, and that the Gentiles might glorify God for his mercy.'[1]

This passage helps to explain the phrase 'as truth is in Jesus'. When St. Paul wished to draw attention to the historical life of the Lord, he was accustomed to speak of Jesus without adding 'Christ'. Consequently 'as truth is in Jesus' means that his life, death and resurrection are 'truth'. This identification is confirmed by the general and frequent New Testament use of 'the truth', unqualified, for 'the gospel'. The gospel, which is the truth, is not limited to the teaching of Christ, for apprehension of it consists in 'hearing him and being taught in him', a hearing which could not be in the flesh, since the Ephesians had never seen Jesus. This 'hearing' and 'being taught' refer not only to the witness borne in the primitive church to the historical Jesus, but also to the creative insight which proceeded from acceptance of and surrender to that witness. The Old Testament conception of truth is thus disturbed by a new historical event, in which the power and the wisdom of God are manifested and also his fidelity and mercy. Jesus

*Rom. xv. 8, 9.* 'was made a minister of the circumcision for the sake of the truth of God, that he might confirm the promises given to the fathers, and that the Gentiles might glorify God for his mercy'.

Jesus is the occurrence in which God confirmed his promises and for this reason he is also the place of understanding—*locus intelligentiae*. Truth, the truth of God, is in him. This is what St. Paul means when he says 'As truth is in Jesus', but he means more than this. The inevitable result of learning the history of Jesus Christ is a reaction upon the learners. Here is a further echo of the Old Testament conception. This truth of life, this truth in the moral and spiritual sphere, is the

[1] St. Paul more often reiterates the Old Testament conception of the truth or consistency of God in the phrase, 'God is faithful, who . . .', e.g. 1 Cor. x. 13; cf. 1 Cor. i. 9; 2 Cor. i. 18; 2 Th. iii. 3.

action of God. The new man is created by God in righteousness and holiness of truth. But the agent is Christ, since the apprehension is 'in him' and it is he who is 'heard'.

The conception of truth in the New Testament is therefore based on that of the Old. Truth is a quality of God, and for this reason he is less an object of inquiry than a subject of action. He is the living God. His truth is revealed in and through a particular history, and his truth must be imitated and realized not merely in the sphere of knowledge, but in every sphere of life, by those who stand in a peculiar relationship to this particular history. So far the Old and New Testaments agree. But, whereas the Old is still looking for the full revelation of the truth of God, the New sees it in the present, as an efficacious reality controlling the lives of men and women, on the basis of a new, and even more particular, series of past historical facts; for it is wholly and completely focused in the life, death and resurrection of Jesus Christ.

This conception of truth is not peculiar to St. Paul. It underlies the fourth Gospel in such statements as 'And the Word was made flesh and dwelt among us *Jn. i. 14.* (and we beheld his glory, glory as of the only begotten of the Father), full of grace and truth'; 'I am the way, *Jn. xiv. 6.* the truth, and the life: no one cometh unto the Father, but by me'. Truth, in short, is knowledge of God through Jesus; such knowledge of God as through Jesus makes men veritably sons of God.

It remains, on the basis of the preceding illustrations, to indicate the direction in which modern New Testament philology and lexicography are moving. To discover the exact meaning and associations of New Testament words is by no means simple. Merely to collect their various uses, throughout scripture and other relevant records, is not sufficient. It is necessary to trace the evolution through which the words have passed, and to mark the important moments in this process. Mere lexicography must pass into semasiology before the remarkable features of the language of the New Testament become clear.

Although the accurate study of the implications of New Testament philology is still in its infancy, because its precise scope has not as yet been adequately defined, it is, however, even now possible to summarize in general terms certain philological conclusions. The language of the New Testament directs our attention to quite ordinary Greek-speaking men and women who lived in the great cities of the eastern Mediterranean during the first century A.D. But the particular men and women for whom the New Testament books were written were not moving in terms of Greek thought and experience. In so far as they were Christians they were being uprooted from their Greek soil by contact with a peculiarly Hebraic material which for their benefit was being translated very inadequately into Greek forms. This inadequacy was not a failure in translation. It marked the importance of the Hebraic material, and forcibly directed the attention of the Christians to it. To escape into a Greek method of thought was to deny the truth of the Christian religion. At first sight it might seem that the Hebraic material was simply the Jewish Old Testament scriptures, and that the inadequacy of translation was simply the inadequacy of the Septuagint translation of the Old Testament scriptures into Greek. But this is not the case. The peculiarity of the language of the New Testament is the result of a new Hebraic-Aramaic-Palestinian history, by which the Old Testament scriptures have emerged with a new emphasis. This whole creative process has taken place in a particular history which lies behind the Greek speaking Christians and behind the writers of the New Testament books. The radical change which has affected the language of the New Testament writers is not primarily the result of a new spiritual experience bubbling up in the Greek-speaking communities of Christians, nor does it proceed from the moral or religious experience of this or of that outstanding Christian. The highly significant twisting of the language has taken place behind all this Christian moral and spiritual experience: it has taken place in a purely Hebraic-Aramaic environment. But more than this, the actual creative element which is at work in the New Testament language is everywhere due to a vigorous recognition that the living God has acted in a particular history, and that Christian moral and spiritual experience depends entirely upon that history. Further, it is also clear that the New Testament language is unintelligible unless the events took place in the heart of Judaism and on the background of the Old Testament scriptures. Everywhere the peculiarly Christian usage of a word proceeds from a remoulding of the meaning which it had borne in the Old Testament.

So long as the modern New Testament reader is consciously or unconsciously interpreting it in terms of a humanitarian ethic or of a humanitarian spiritual experience, he is sinning against the meaning of words. If we are to understand the Greek of the New Testament we can be satisfied neither with a lexicon of Classical Greek, nor with a lexicon of the spoken Greek of the first century A.D., nor even with a lexicon of the Greek of the Septuagint, even if one could be procured which noted carefully the Hebrew words which underlie the Greek of the translation. We can be satisfied only with a lexicon devoted wholly to the New Testament itself, in which the specifically Christian associations which became attached to each word are carefully detected and set forth.

In conclusion, when the science of semasiology is applied to the New Testament in Greek, the problems which arise serve only to raise in a peculiarly acute form the problem, first, of the life and death of a single, concrete, historical, flesh-and-blood figure—Jesus of Nazareth, and, secondly, of the emergence of the church on the basis of that particular history. They also suggest that no understanding of that particular history or of the emergence of the church is possible unless the critic is prepared to pass beyond that which is most characteristic in modern thought, to think of God as the living and active God, and to move freely in terms not only of revelation in general, but of the revelation of the power of the living God in a particular history.

## NOTE

When this chapter was originally written, there was in existence no comprehensive lexicon containing a scientific treatment of the changes in the meanings of words that took place as a consequence of the emergence of primitive Christianity. There was, of course, the *Biblico-Theological Lexicon of New Testament Greek* by Cremer, tr. into English in 1878, 4th edition 1895, and published by T. & T. Clark. But so much has come to light since then that the work is out of date. Now, however, a lexicon is in course of publication edited by Dr. Gerhard Kittel under the title *Theologisches Worterbuch zum Neuen Testament* and published by W. Kohlhammer at Stuttgart. The purpose of this lexicon is to define as precisely as possible the new weight, emphasis and energy that Greek words acquired as a result of the peculiar theological setting in which they were used by Christian speakers and writers. Almost every German theologian has contributed to the first four volumes, which contain many famous articles.

A similar treatment in another field is evident in *Verbal Scholarship and the Growth of some Abstract Terms*, an inaugural lecture by Dr. A. C. Pearson, Cambridge 1922.

## Chapter II
## The Text

If the examination of the meaning of the important Greek words which recur again and again in the New Testament documents raises an acute historical problem, since it points to a particular historical occurrence in Palestine; if there can be no understanding of the New Testament apart from the possibility of delineating the significance of that particular history, at least in its main outlines; and further, if that history must be reconstructed from the New Testament documents, since we have no other available sources of information; it is at once evident that no reconstruction of the history is possible unless the critical historian has reasonable confidence that the text of the New Testament has not suffered serious corruption during the fourteen centuries when it was transmitted by scribes. No serious historical work can be undertaken on the basis of texts which may be suspected of being radically corrupt.

The work of the textual critics during the past two centuries has given the historian precisely that general confidence which he requires, and has provided him with at least an adequate text of the New Testament in Greek. This is a very remarkable achievement, in which English scholarship has played a major part. Since, however, textual criticism leaves a number of problems still unsolved, it is essential to summarize the main results of this long and patient investigation of the manuscripts in order to make clear what conclusions have, in fact, emerged. In theory, the aim of textual criticism has been to lay bare what the authors of the New

Testament documents actually wrote. In practice, the aim has been, first to test the value of the printed text upon which all the older commentators worked, known as the *Textus Receptus*—the text 'received by all', as the printer of the 1633 Elzevir edition boldly announced in his preface—and, secondly, to trace the pedigrees of variant readings, which appear scattered about in the extant Greek, Latin, Syriac, Coptic, Armenian, Georgian, Gothic and Abyssinian manuscripts of the New Testament, and which were known to the early fathers of the church.

We now know exactly upon what the *Textus Receptus* was based. It was based upon a twelfth-century Greek manuscript which Erasmus sent to be printed at Froben's press in Basle in 1515. In the margin of this manuscript Erasmus substituted in his own hand a few variant readings from another twelfth-century manuscript also accessible to him in Basle. Since, however, neither of these manuscripts contained the book of the Revelation of St. John, Erasmus procured another, which seems to have been formerly at Basle but is now preserved in the Oettlingen-Wallerstein Library at Mayhingen, a village not far from Ulm, and which contains only the text of the Revelation and a commentary upon it. Erasmus was thus able to fill up what was lacking in his other Basle manuscripts. His procedure is illustrated by the fact that, since the Mayhingen manuscript lacks the last six verses, Erasmus, having no other manuscript of the book at hand, himself translated them into Greek from the Latin. The Greek text published by Froben in March 1516, side by side with the new translation into Latin which Erasmus had made, was therefore issued with all the prestige of his name. But it was, in fact, substantially the text of a single manuscript now known by the Arabic numeral 2. The Erasmus Greek Testament was, however, to gain further prestige. The famous Greek Testament issued by Robert Stephanus from the Royal Press at Paris in 1550 was based upon it. Stephanus had, it is true, introduced quite a large number of corrections from the magnificent Greek text printed at Alcala under the patronage of Cardinal Ximenes in 1520, usually known as the Complutensian (from the Latin place-name of Alcala), and in addition he introduced in the interior margins of the text a number of variant readings from the Complutensian and also from fifteen other manuscripts including codex Bezae and codex Regius, which had been collated for him by his son Henry. Finally Elzevir reprinted the first edition of Theodore Beza's text, which did not differ essentially from the text of Robert Stephanus, and this was the *Textus Receptus* upon which all work upon the New Testament in Greek was principally grounded until quite modern times. Thus we may almost say that a single twelfth-century manuscript provided the text upon which our English post-Reformation knowledge of the primitive church rested until Westcott and Hort published their Greek Testament in 1881. The discovery of the manuscript authority behind the printed *Textus Receptus*, however, tells us nothing, unless a judgement be possible concerning the value of the readings contained in manuscript 2. But it is impossible to test the readings contained in this manuscript unless the critic can trace, not only their pedigrees but also the pedigrees of competing variant readings which are found in other manuscripts. It is evident that if the birth of a particular variant reading can be detected in the course of the transmission of the text, that reading must be removed from the authentic text, since its origin will have been exposed. It is evident also that if the purpose of textual criticism be to track the pedigrees of readings, this pedigree hunting is possible only if the pedigrees of the manuscripts themselves can be discovered, and their provenance disclosed. Textual criticism cannot move safely without the help of palaeography. It will be seen then that we are in the presence of a very delicate and absorbing science. Yet, in spite of its difficulty, quite definite conclusions have been reached.

Of the hundreds of manuscripts of the New Testament in Greek at present in existence, it would be hard to find two in all respects alike. Variations in spelling, variations in order, variations in actual words and even in whole verses, make each more or less distinct. This lack of identity springs from the very nature of transcription by hand. No copyist, however lavish of his care or skilful in his craft, can avoid occasional error in the spelling and ordering of words: no subsequent copyist noticing a consequent nonsense, is likely to resist giving it meaning by correction. And so, not errors only, but erroneous reconstructions as well, are incorporated in the text and handed on in every fresh transcription. The original is left further and further behind; contradictions between manuscripts of different traditions multiply, and presently attempts are made to reconcile them. The result is chaos. In the midst of this chaos, the textual critic sets to work.

Until the publication of the *Chester Beatty Biblical Papyri* in 1933 there was no codex known to scholars that was older than the fourth century. The Chester Beatty fragments are considerable fragments of papyrus codices and are dated with some confidence by Sir Frederic Kenyon in the third century. There do, of course, exist tiny papyrus fragments of an earlier date. Even so, no text has been preserved that is not the result of several transcriptions. Although a certain number may be singled out as less corrupt than others, when these disagree none has established sufficient confidence in itself to justify its unquestioned adoption.

Careful comparison of the manuscripts has shown that many of them agree in their choice of a certain proportion of the disputed readings. These may therefore be grouped together. This is the starting point of textual criticism. For, in the first place, it makes possible rough pedigrees of manuscripts. If all the copies of the New Testament ever made were extant to-day, it would be simple to discover how they stood in relation to each other and to the original autographs. For each copyist, though he corrected perhaps a certain number of more obvious slips, must have handed on many of the errors of the transcription before him. And so, as the text was copied by scribe after scribe, there came into being distinct traditions, recognizable by the peculiar colour of their variant readings. Therefore, if all the manuscripts of a group which generally agree preserve a particular reading not found elsewhere, it is evident, either that the reading was original and that all other transcriptions are in that respect erroneous; or that the copyist of some particular manuscript, from which the whole group descended, introduced this variant into the text. Conversely, if two or three manuscripts of such a group have readings unknown to the earlier members of the group, it will be probable that the responsible error was made in some manuscript later than these earlier members. In this way, some variant readings are shown to be late and irrelevant, others to be early and quite possibly original.

But the chief purpose of trying to ascertain the pedigrees of manuscripts and their place in the traditions of the text is to discover distinct textual traditions. For, where it can be proved that the agreements of two manuscripts are due to a common ancestor, those agreements are only guaranteed as far back as the common ancestor. But where manuscripts that represent an independent transmission of the text agree in a whole series of readings, this agreement warrants the assumption that these readings were current in very early days, precisely because their birth eludes detection.

The process of tracking the pedigrees of readings reveals the existence in the fourth and fifth centuries of distinct lines of textual tradition. As soon as the books of the New Testament began to be valued, copies were made and distributed among churches. At first, no doubt, the autographs were copied; then the copies themselves. During the first five centuries, the life of the church revolved round great cities such as Rome, Lyons, and Carthage in the west, Antioch, Ephesus, Caesarea and Alexandria in the middle east, and Edessa on the eastern border of the Roman Empire. These centres must presumably have possessed important manuscripts of the New Testament, and these manuscripts may well have exerted an influence upon the books used in surrounding districts, since, whenever new copies were needed, recourse would be had to the nearest great city.

With the reign of Constantine and the peace of the church there began a new era, marked by the emergence of the growing prestige of Rome and of Constantinople. Not only was it necessary to replace the scriptures destroyed during the great persecutions, but also there was far closer intercourse between the various churches, which produced both a mixing of the texts and important authorized revisions of the whole New Testament. The aim of these revisions was partly to introduce a generally accepted text, and partly to remove those unliterary features of the earlier manuscripts which were not fitted to the new respectability of the church, and shocked the delicate sensibilities of men and women accustomed to the classical literature of Greece and Rome. It was during this period that a whole series of readings appeared of which the early fathers had known nothing: during this period also the text of the New Testament became more or less fixed both in Greek and in Latin. The most epoch-making revision seems to have been made at Antioch at the beginning of the fourth century by a certain Lucian. In making his revision he was not only concerned to produce an elegant, easily running text, but amalgamated or conflated variant readings already in existence. It is probable that during the next four hundred years his revision of the text lay behind the gradual standardization of the official text of Byzantium, the political centre of the Eastern Empire. The Byzantine text became the authorized version of the Greek church. Nearly all extant Greek manuscripts are therefore either founded upon it, or more or less corrected into conformity with it; and, since MS. 2 represents this text, it formed the basis of the *Textus Receptus*. What happened in the east happened also in the west. Damasus, bishop of Rome during the second half of the fourth century, instructed Jerome to undertake a revision of the old Latin versions. Jerome produced his revision, and this revision, known as the Vulgate, gradually submerged the old Latin versions, took control of the transmission of the Latin text, and became the authorized version of the western church.

The effect of these authoritative revisions was that manuscripts representing the state of the text before these revisions fell into disuse, and, with certain significant exceptions, disappeared. Nearly all existing Greek and Latin manuscripts have been influenced by these revisions. Yet, even so, because the older traditions were firmly rooted in many parts of the church, and because it was more easy to correct the obvious variants than to obtain fresh copies, many older readings have been preserved. It is therefore possible to distinguish in the first place between revised and unrevised readings. Where manuscripts depart from the text of the revision by which they have been influenced, and their variants are not obviously later corruptions, the variant may be said to be unrevised. These unrevised readings, unless they can be explained in some way or other as obvious corruptions, have to be taken seriously, since it is impossible to detect their birth.

It is now possible to define precisely the critical procedure in handling variant readings. Where a variant came into being with one of the great revisions and was unknown before that revision, it must be put on one side, for its origin has been discovered. The whole interest now centres in variant readings known to have existed before the great revisions. Here a canon of criticism emerges. If it be clear that a variant reading was current in more than one of the textual traditions of the second and third centuries, its pedigree escapes detection, and from the point of view of pure textual criticism it cannot be removed. The textual critic can only say that it was current in the second century.

The detection of variant readings which existed before the great revisions is assisted by a study of the Egyptian and Syriac versions, and of those existing Latin manuscripts which are wholly or in part uninfluenced by the Vulgate. The New Testament was translated from Greek into Coptic, Latin and Syriac, before the fourth century. Thus the Egyptian versions reflect the form of the older text of Alexandria from which they were probably made. The old Latin manuscripts represent versions made from the Greek before the Byzantine revision. The Syriac versions, and very particularly the two surviving manuscripts of the old Syriac version, also represent the Greek text before, or apart from, the Byzantine revision. The text used by the early fathers is of course all-important here.

Hitherto, readings current behind the two great revisions have been called unrevised readings, but there is evidence that a revision of the Greek text had in fact already been undertaken in Alexandria at the end of the second century or at the beginning of the third. Alexandrian scholars had long been familiar with the difficulties of manuscript tradition and were skilled textual critics, for similar problems had arisen in the transcription of the classical authors. Alexandria, indeed, was of all centres of early Christianity the place where a skilled judgement upon variant readings in the New Testament manuscripts might be expected, and this expectation is in fact borne out by the survival of a series of manuscripts, some of them with a clear Egyptian provenance. The most important manuscripts in this connexion are codex Vaticanus, codex Sinaiticus, the Paris palimpsest (C), codex Regius, minuscule 33, manuscripts of the Egyptian versions, especially the Sahidic version, and of the Ethiopic (Abyssinian) version, and also the texts used by Origen while he lived at Alexandria. These manuscripts contain a large number of readings not found elsewhere. It is important to remember, however, that if these readings are the result of a revision, they rest upon a scholarly judgement and there is no evidence whatever that this judgement was based upon a knowledge of the autographs. Moreover, the Alexandrian scholars were possessed of a nice sense for correct literary Greek, and there is every reason to suppose that they tended to smooth out the roughness of the earlier tradition and to substitute, so far as this was possible, a greater literary elegance. Yet, at the same time, they undoubtedly rid the text of obvious errors and preserved many venerable readings which might otherwise have been lost.

A recent analysis of the readings contained in a number of manuscripts has drawn attention to another centre of distribution of readings, if not, indeed, of another revision of the text. Caesarea during the fourth century was a very important centre of Christian erudition. It was there that Eusebius wrote his history of the church, a work which could not have been composed had Eusebius not had a library behind him. And that there was a library there we know because he tells us that Pamphilus, the admirer of Origen, added to the library of Caesarea the works of Origen and of other ecclesiastical writers (Eusebius, *Ecclesiastical History* VI, 32). Pamphilus founded at Caesarea a school of sacred learning and spent much time in transcribing and correcting manuscripts of the scriptures and especially of the Septuagint as it had been edited in the Hexapla of Origen (see Lawlor and Oulton, *Eusebius Ecclesiastical History*, Vol. II, pp. 331 f.). Codex Koridethi, Mark v. 31—xvi. 8 in the Washington codex, minuscules 28,

565, 700, and family 1 and family 13, and also the most
ancient surviving manuscripts of the old Georgian version, although nearly all influenced by the Byzantine
text, nevertheless contain a series of remarkable variant
readings, readings which seem, moreover, to have been
known to Origen when he was at Caesarea. It is therefore not unnatural to see in their agreements a common
influence. This does not, of course, mean that these
readings originated in Caesarea; indeed, they are at
times supported by the Chester Beatty papyrus codex
and were therefore, as Kenyon has pointed out, already
current in Egypt at an earlier period. They may well,
however, have circulated from Caesarea.

It is possible, then, to distinguish, behind the great
Byzantine and Vulgate revisions, several distinct traditions of the text. This is of great importance. For it
means that the agreement of any two of these fairly
independent traditions, in any variant reading, places
it beyond the judgement of the textual critic, and that
even a reading found in one of them only cannot safely
be dismissed. Nevertheless, it is difficult to give a pre-
eminent authority to any of these traditions, or to agreements between any particular two of them. None is
infallible, and each on occasion seems to preserve the
right reading by itself. When all is said and done, each
reading has to be examined on its individual merits.
Therefore textual criticism is at this point merged in the
general interpretation of the New Testament, and ceases
to be a distinct branch of New Testament study.

The great labour spent during the past two centuries
in collating manuscripts, and in tracing their pedigrees
in order to track the pedigrees of variant readings, has
enabled scholars to arrive at confident conclusions upon
a very large number of variant readings. For example,
a conclusion seems to be reached by pure textual critical
methods on the variant reading to Mark i. 2. Mark

wrote either: 'as has been written in the prophets', or
'as has been written in Isaiah the prophet'. He follows
up his statement with two Old Testament quotations,
one from the book of Malachi, the other from Isaiah.
The question is whether, knowing that he was quoting
from the prophets, he said so, and subsequently a scribe
blundered, or whether the blunder was his.

*Mk. i. 2.*

*Mal. iii. 1.*

*Is. xl. 3.*

External evidence—The manuscript evidence is as
follows: the reading *in the prophets* is supported by the
vast majority of the Greek manuscripts and was therefore the reading adopted in the Byzantine text. Did the
Byzantine text initiate this reading, or merely establish
it? It is also the reading in the Washington codex, in
minuscule 28, in family 13, in the text of the Harklean
Syriac version, in one manuscript of the Egyptian
Bohairic version, in the Armenian and Ethiopic versions, and is known in one manuscript of the old Latin
version. Moreover the passage is also thus quoted once
in the Latin translation of Irenaeus. Were it not for
these two Latin readings and the Ethiopic version it
would seem that at no point does the evidence necessarily go behind the Byzantine text. The evidence is
therefore weak, but it is not yet possible to say with
certainty that the Byzantine text did more than establish
an already existing reading.

The manuscript evidence for the reading *in Isaiah the
prophet* is as follows: it is supported by codex Vaticanus,
codex Alexandrinus, codex Bezae, codex Regius, codex
Koridethi, by nine Greek minuscules including 33, 565,
700, and by family 1. The whole Latin manuscript
evidence, old Latin and Vulgate, with the exceptions
already mentioned, confirms this reading. So also do
the Syriac, Coptic, and Georgian versions, and four
manuscripts of the Armenian version. In addition it is
supported by three out of the four occasions upon which
Irenaeus refers to the passage, by Origen, Epiphanius,
Basil of Caesarea, Jerome and Augustine. Owing to the
wide geographical distribution of this evidence it would

almost seem that this must have been the original reading. Since, however, there may still be some uncertainty the internal evidence must also be taken into account.

Internal evidence—Let it be supposed that *in the prophets* was the original reading. Can the emergence of the reading *in Isaiah the prophet* be explained, either by carelessness in transcription or by a conscious alteration? There would seem to be no possible explanation of this alteration on either ground. Let it be supposed, on the other hand, that Mark wrote *in Isaiah the prophet*. The correction to *in the prophets* is almost demanded, not by carelessness of transcription, but in order to avoid ascribing the quotation from Malachi to the prophet Isaiah.

The conclusion is inevitable. Mark made the blunder, and it was finally removed. But there is more than this. If it be assumed that Mark did write *in Isaiah the prophet* the procedure of Matthew and Luke, who delete the quotation from Malachi while preserving the name *Isaiah*, is intelligible. Thus they remedy Mark's blunder by very drastic methods. A comparison of the three gospels therefore shows Mark's eagerness to open his gospel with impressive Old Testament quotations. But it also shows the accurate knowledge of the Old Testament possessed by both his editors. - *i.e. Matthew & Luke.*

Textual criticism has shown that there was no serious corruption of the text of the New Testament between the fourth century and the invention of printing, and that even the *Textus Receptus* would not lead the theologian or the historian far astray. None the less, of the large number of interesting variant readings already current during the second and third centuries, the original reading cannot be determined by textual criticism alone. The very subtle problems which they present can be handled, but only by the New Testament historian who is beginning to reach conclusions in other branches of New Testament critical study.

A discussion of the Matthaean parable of the Ten Vir- *Mt. xxv. 1-13.*
gins, which contains two interesting and important variant readings, illustrates this merging of textual criticism in
the general field of New Testament exegesis. In the first
verse most manuscripts read, 'Then shall the kingdom
of heaven be likened unto ten virgins, which took their
lamps and went forth to meet the bridegroom.' But
several manuscripts read 'went forth to meet the bridegroom and the bride'. The textual evidence is as follows:

The longer reading, containing the words *and the
bride*, is found in the Vulgate and in the old Latin versions, in the Greek of the codex Bezae, in one of the
manuscripts representing the old Syriac version, in
some later Syriac manuscripts and in the Armenian
versions. It is found also in certain interesting Greek
manuscripts headed by codices Monacensis and Koridethi. The vast majority of the Greek manuscripts and
of the other versions have the shorter reading.

Everything, then, points to the fact that both readings
were current in the second century. That is to say, the
birth of neither of these readings can be detected in the
transmission of the text. Having established this, textual
criticism can do no more. The decision as to which
reading is to be adopted must be handed over to the
historian. The longer reading is easily intelligible. It
rivets the parable to the ancient custom of the bridegroom going forth to meet the bride, and bringing her
back to his own house. But on this basis it is possible to
argue in diametrically opposite fashions. On the one
hand, it may be supposed that the sight of an actual
wedding gave form to the parable, and that Jesus
simply took the incidents as they appeared, and gave
them further meaning. By this reasoning, the procession
of the bride and bridegroom, and the group of virgins
at the door of the house, owe their existence to wedding
custom. It is true that the bride plays no part in the
story. But why should she? Jesus is telling a story to
illustrate a spiritual truth; the details of the story have

no further special significance. On the other hand, if the shorter reading be adopted, the parable is an eschatological parable, and the isolation of the bridegroom emphasizes the final coming of the messiah at the end. The absence of the bride is then essential, and an illustration from common custom is manipulated in order to secure the eschatological significance. We are then faced by a clear alternative. Either the bride's presence is original, and omission of her is due to the pressure of the eschatology and to a desire to trim the original text so that it may more clearly display the eschatological significance and emphasize Jesus as the coming judge; or the isolation of the bridegroom is original, and the bride is added in order to bring the parable into harmony with known wedding customs, and to make the story more vivid to those readers who were familiar with such scenes.

It is clear that we are here in the presence of an historical problem of the first magnitude. It concerns the nature of the teaching of Jesus, or at least the emphasis in the Matthaean record of that teaching. Did the evangelist preserve hints that Jesus taught moral and spiritual truths by means of simple stories reflecting common occurrences in the experience of his hearers; or did he preserve in his record evidence that common occurrences were in the parabolic teaching of Jesus twisted out of their context in order to express the gospel of God which in its essence could be interpeted only by the use of eschatological language and imagery? In other words, did the manipulation of wedding custom take place in the mind of Jesus or in the course of Christian interpretation of his teaching?

The same parable contains another variant reading of subtle significance. At the crucial moment in the story the foolish virgins beg some oil from their prudent companions. How, in fact, do the wise virgins answer this request? According to one reading, which is supported by the uncial codices, Sinaiticus, Regius,

Dublinensis, and by a few minuscules including the Paris manuscript numbered 33, they refuse the request more or less politely: 'Perhaps there will not be enough for us and you.' According to another reading, which is supported by the vast majority of the Greek manuscripts headed by codex Vaticanus and codex Bezae, they answer, with almost incredible brutality: 'Never! there will certainly not be enough for us and you.' According to the first reading, there is no particular emphasis upon the answer of the wise virgins, and the reader moves on undisturbed. If the second reading be adopted, the whole point of the parable lies in the roughness of the answer. The oil which enables the wise to enter with the bridegroom is untransferable oil; there can be no loan or gift of that which secures salvation. Here is a terrible sternness; here is no easy humanitarianism, no brotherly or sisterly tenderness; here, when ultimate salvation is at stake, there emerges what to the modern reader seems arbitrary cruelty. Again the historical problem arises in the midst of a delicate problem in textual criticism. On which side did the Jesus of history stand? Did his parables follow the natural course of a story, or was the story broken by a terrible moral earnestness challenging the hearers to a decision upon which hung an ultimate issue? Was he a kind philanthropist, whose teaching has been complicated by the intrusion of a harsh eschatological supernaturalism, or does the grim eschatology belong to the original history, and is the tenderness precisely the intrusion? This is the historical problem raised in one form or another by the whole of the New Testament material, and it is raised by the existence of variant readings between which the textual critic cannot decide. The decision is therefore handed over to the historian. The issue which underlies so many of the variant readings is just the same issue as was found to underlie the problem of the meaning of New Testament words. Once again the problem is the Jesus of history and the origin of the church.

Vide supra, p. 12.

## NOTE

An admirable introduction to the textual criticism of the New Testament has been written by Léon Vaganay, *Introduction to the Textual Criticism of the New Testament*, London 1937, a translation of one of the volumes of the *Bibliothèque Catholique des Sciences Religieuses*. Dr. Souter added to his Greek text of the New Testament, published at the Clarendon Press, a selection of variant readings. However, for a compendium of variant readings the eighth edition of Tischendorf's text has hitherto been indispensable. Since this edition was published between 1869 and 1872, it of course contained no reference to manuscripts discovered since that time, nor to the groups of minuscules such as family 1 and family 13, which have been seen to be so important. The work of Tischendorf is now being brought up to date. The publication of Westcott and Hort's text with a complete critical apparatus has been undertaken by the Clarendon Press, and the first two volumes, the Gospel of Mark, and the Gospel of Matthew, both edited by S. C. E. Legg, were published in 1935 and 1940 respectively, C. R. Gregory's Prolegomena, printed as Vol. III of the eighth edition of Tischendorf's Novum Testamentum Graece from 1884 to 1894, is still the most complete and elaborate and indispensable description of the material relevant to textual criticism. It was separately published in German, corrected and expanded, under the title *Textkritik des Neuen Testamentes*, Leipzig, 1900-1909. The relevant evidence for the textual criticism of the Acts of the Apostles is accessible in *The Text of Acts* by J. H. Ropes, Vol. III of *The Beginnings of Christianity*, ed. by Foakes Jackson and Kirsopp Lake, London, 1926.

## Chapter III

## The History

The peculiar difficulties which beset the philologist and the textual critic in handling the language and text of the New Testament are occasioned by an acute historical problem. It is necessary, before proceeding further, to state the problem as it is presented in the subject matter of the New Testament itself: that is, to state the problem with which the critical historian is faced before ever he applies technical critical methods to its solution.

In the First Epistle General of Peter the elect are exhorted to endure suffering for conscience' sake, on the grounds that it is acceptable to God. For:

'Hereunto were ye called: because Christ also suffered for you, leaving you an example, that ye should follow his steps: who did no sin, neither was guile found in his mouth: who, when he was reviled, reviled not again; when he suffered, threatened not: but committed his cause to him that judgeth righteously: who his own self bare our sins in his body upon the tree, that we, having died unto sins, might live unto righteousness; by whose bruise ye were healed. For ye were going astray like sheep; but are now returned unto the Shepherd and Bishop of your souls.' *1 Pet. ii. 21-25.*

This appeal to the passion of Jesus Christ is the culmination of an argument and is not lightly chosen, for the writer returns to it again and again. Nor is the close association of the death of Jesus with human salvation peculiar to this epistle. It is emphasized in the writings of St. Paul, in the speeches in the Acts, in the Epistle to the Hebrews, in the book of the Revelation, and in the Gospel and Epistles of John. In fact, so usual is it, *cf. e.g., iii, 18 ff., and chs. i and iv.*

*e.g. 1 Cor. xv. 1-5; Acts ii. 22-42; xx. 28.*

51

Heb. xii. 1-4;
Rev. i. 4-7;
Jn. i. 29;
vi. 51; xix. 30;
1 Jn. i. 7;
ii. 1, 2.
and therefore so familiar to the reader of the New Testament, that its strangeness is easily missed. But it is strange indeed. Why should the sufferings of a man some years before be the example of behaviour to which men who never knew him are uniquely called? Why should his death upon a tree be considered a bearing of their sins? Why should this bearing of sins enable the same men to die unto sins and to live unto righteousness, so that they are healed by his bruise? And why can it be affirmed that this example and this bearing of sins are responsible for the entirely new life which they are living?

It is an appeal to history, to certain events which are said to have taken place, not in the distant but in the immediate past, and which may well have taken place, since they are not, from one point of view, outside the common experience of mankind. But when allusion is made to these events or when they are definitely re-counted, a significance is given to them which lies wholly beyond ordinary human experience. Someone suffered and was reviled, was hung on a tree, and died. So much explains itself: such things have happened a thousand times. He was, moreover, completely patient and meek throughout his ordeal, and commended his cause to God. That too, though less usual, can be understood. Because such occurrences are self-explanatory; because they are understandable; if they were to happen again they would be described in much the same way. But if they *were* to happen again: if a sinless man *were* to suffer and die nailed to a tree, it would be by no means obvious that, in so doing, he was bearing the sins of other men in his body, and that the manner of his death was, not only an example for their own bearing of suffering, but an efficacious assurance that they, being dead unto sins, might live unto righteousness.

And yet, all this is stated as if it were self-evident from the event. Christ did all these things in his passion, and, far from proving them, the author simply appeals to the doing of them as the culminating proof of his argument. How is he led to make such a statement? And what validity can such a statement have for his modern readers?

Suffering, reviling, being patient, dying, are descriptions of various human experiences. But they are tolerable descriptions of such experiences only when these are isolated and examined by themselves. When such experiences play a significant part in a whole context of events, they are better and more definitely expressed in terms of that context. 'X scored a goal' is a description of an event isolated from its context. 'X won the Cup for the Corinthians' might equally describe the same event, and more adequately, since it places it in its proper context. Actually, indeed, X kicked a leather ball between two posts, and the reader never doubts that he did so. But, because it was the critical moment in a critical match in a Cup Tie, his action is truly, and indeed, more truly, described as 'winning the Cup'. The historian writes history best when he examines the whole context of events, and describes them according to their proper significance. And so this Petrine description of the death of Jesus will be better history than a bare record of the same event, if it is rightly founded on a knowledge of a larger context of events which showed him to be a unique person, and his actions to have a unique significance for other men and women.

This larger context is therefore a primary object of critical investigation. The events described in the New Testament must be examined, and their true significance discovered. But it may not be possible to reconstruct the whole context of these events in detail. A large part of the New Testament is not simple narration of facts, but expression of judgements upon facts. Judgements, however, are themselves highly important material. Most football enthusiasts to-day learn about their sport from written reports which consist largely of judgements. A good report is one which fastens upon the significant points of the play, and indicates them so as to give a true impression of a match. A bad report, on the other hand, is one which either misses the significant points, or misinterprets them so as to give a false impression. The critical demands made upon a journalist are made also upon all investigators and explorers: 'In every great discoverer there is a dual passion—the passion to see and the passion to report; and in the greatest this duality is fused into one—a passion to see and to report truly' (*The Exploration of the Pacific*, J. C. Beaglehole, p. 3). So the value of a report depends partly upon the person and ability of the reporter and partly upon the singleness of his judgement. A false impression may arise from the subconscious influence of irrelevant events, from partiality to some pet theory, from a bee in a bonnet, from a personal antipathy, or even, perhaps, from some quite extraneous accident. And so it is with the reports and judgements in the New Testament. The first task of criticism is, therefore, to explain the material as it now exists. For some reason or another, perhaps for many various reasons, the story of the life and death of Jesus came to be recounted in its present form. The judgements responsible for this form may have been true or false. In either case the fact that they were made has to be explained. And the second task of criticism is to discover at what point, and if possible, by whom, these judgements were made. For if it can be ascertained who first fastened larger significances upon the events of the life and death of Jesus, and if any irrelevant motives which induced them to do so can be isolated, much will have been done to enable the modern reader in his turn to form a judgement for himself. And that is the ultimate purpose of the exposition of the New Testament. The business of the commentator is to 'set forth the meaning of holy scripture itself, to extract truths from, not to import them into it.' (Liddon, *Life of Pusey*, Vol. III, p. 150.)

The selected verses of the First Epistle General of

Peter illustrate how fearlessly the writers of the books
of the New Testament riveted a particular significance
to the history of Jesus. The problem, then, is to discover
whether there is evidence that they were led to do so
by some extraneous influence; or whether there is evidence that the significance was embedded in the concrete, historical living of the life and in the concrete,
historical dying of the death, and, moreover, actually
conditioned the course of the one and the fact of the
other. In the latter case, the primitive church, far from
imposing its own interpretation upon these events, extracted, and exposed, and bore witness to their proper
significance. So these verses illustrate the real problem
with which all New Testament exegesis is ultimately
faced.

The verses form a culmination of an argument. They
are therefore inserted with a particular purpose. The
author is not content to achieve that purpose by depicting the suffering of Christ as a type of what Christians
must expect of their vocation, and his bearing of it as
an example of how they must perform it; he adds,
gratuitously it may seem at first sight, that the passion
was not only typical and exemplary, but that it was so
because it was redemptive and sacrificial. Not only does
the author refer to historical events for a purpose, but
he regards them as having taken place because of that
purpose. That is to say, he is not attaching a significance
to historical events; he is claiming that the purpose
produced the events. So often has he proclaimed, or
heard proclaimed, the passion of Jesus as the basis of
salvation, that he quite naturally recalls that significance
of it when appealing to it in another connexion. 'By
whose bruise ye were healed.' This is a forcible reminder
that many events in the Life of Jesus were preserved in
the tradition because they served a purpose. They were
edifying or reassuring, controversial or comforting. And
the fact that the early church needed to be edified and
reassured, to controvert and be comforted, caused them

to be handed down until evangelists were moved to collect them together, again for a purpose. But, as this passage shows, the same events could be used for various purposes. Moreover, varying use, and a constant demand for a precedent in any novel problem that confronted the church, may have given some of the stories a completely unhistorical significance. We are all familiar even to-day, perhaps indeed supremely to-day, with the facility with which a biblical episode or a biblical saying is twisted out of its context in order that it may be applied to an urgent modern need, and set in a context wholly foreign to its original setting. This procedure has an important bearing on New Testament criticism, for a precisely similar procedure may underlie the New Testament as it stands. It may be that even in the primitive church 'men were accustomed to wrest and pervert the language of scripture, by adapting it to modern events.' (Sir Walter Scott, *Woodstock*, Chapter I.) Each incident must be examined for signs of a motive and, if a motive is evident which emphasizes a significance incompatible with the ministry of Jesus but explained by the needs of a later date, the particular turn given by it to the incident must be discounted, if the aim of the historian be to recover the Jesus of history, and not merely to record the beliefs of the primitive Christians. The incident may indeed quite well have taken place, but it is bad history to describe it in relation to a context to which it does not belong. In this case, therefore, since the passion of Jesus is used as a type, as an example, and as an assurance of redemption, reasons must be found for concluding that the events which occurred in Palestine were occasioned by an exemplary and redemptive purpose, or else it must follow that this description of them rests on a false interpretation, induced, perhaps, by the influence of those religions that were satisfying at that time the craving of the Hellenic world for assurance of salvation. If this be so, the exemplary and redemptive gospel of the church rests historically upon the spiritual needs of the primitive Christians, and not upon the life and death of Jesus of Nazareth, as the authors of the New Testament books would have us suppose.

Now, what is the context in which the author of the First Epistle General of Peter did in fact place the passion of Jesus? At first sight the verses read quite naturally as a piece of description which appears neither conventional nor forced. As far as the description of actual events is concerned, it might well be the first impression of an eye-witness. A surprising element is, however, introduced into the interpretation of these verses when they are compared with the Greek version of the fifty-third chapter of Isaiah. The language is so similar that the resemblance cannot be fortuitous.

| *1 Peter ii. 21 ff.* | *Isaiah liii.* |
|---|---|
| 21. (Christ) also suffered for you leaving you an example that ye should follow his steps. | 4. he . . . is pained for us. |
| 22. who did no sin neither was guile found in his mouth. | 9. he did no sin nor guile was in his mouth. |
| 23. who, when he was reviled, reviled not again; when he suffered, threatened not; but committed himself to him that judgeth righteously; | (cf. 7. as a lamb before his shearers is dumb, so opens he not his mouth) (cf. 11. the Lord also is pleased to justify the just one) |
| 24. who his own self bare our sins | 11. and he shall bear their sins (cf. 4-6 he bears our sins he was wounded on account of our sins and was bruised because of our iniquities the Lord gave him up for our sins) |
| in his body | |
| upon the tree, that we, having died unto sin, might live unto righteousness; by whose bruise ye were healed. | 5. by his bruise we were healed |

| *1 Peter ii. 21 ff.* | *Isaiah liii.* |
|---|---|
| 25. For ye were going astray like sheep; but are now returned unto the Shepherd and Bishop of your souls.[1] | 6. all we like sheep have gone astray |

How is this similarity to be explained? Clearly the writer was picturing Christ in terms taken from the suffering of the faithful slave of God in the Prophecy of Isaiah. But this passage and other parts of the epistle show that the author quite consciously sets the passion of Jesus, not primarily in the context of Christian piety, but in the context of the Old Testament scriptures. A clear problem therefore arises. Did this conception of the fulfilment of the Old Testament in the concrete history of Jesus of Nazareth cause the author of this epistle and the other New Testament writers both to set down as history details not actually true and also to introduce in the process a context foreign to the actual history? In any case, what right had he and they to apply this language to Jesus? Was the need for finding in Old Testament scripture a prophecy of the passion so great that Christian apologists invented the identification of Jesus with the suffering servant, or did the course of the ministry itself demand this identification? In other words, are we confronted with a process that took the spiritual experience of the Christians to be fundamental and found in Old Testament prophecy the saction for it? Or, alternatively, did the Old Testament provide the context which in fact occasioned the ministry and death of Jesus, and did the author of this epistle rightly set him firmly in that context, and rightly declare the spiritual and moral life of the Christians to

[1] For the sake of clarity only parallels from Isaiah liii are set out. But verse 23 seems to echo the language of Psalm xxii. 7: 'All they that see me laugh me to scorn. . . .' Moreover, the attribution to God, in verse 25, of the title 'Shepherd', while explicable from the context, has other Old Testament precedent, as for example Psalm xxiii. 1.

be dependent upon their recognition of the passion of Jesus as the fulfilment of the word of God revealed to Israel? Or, to put it in another way, does the New Testament ultimately rest upon human spiritual and mystical experience, or does it rest upon a particular individual history which gave a peculiar direction to the knowledge and behaviour of the primitive Christtians? Or, lastly, to put the problem in yet a different form, is the Jesus of history wholly submerged in the New Testament, or does that history rigorously control all our New Testament documents?

## NOTE

The problem raised in this chapter has been dealt with recently by Professor Rudolf Bultmann in his book *Jesus*, English translation *Jesus and the Word*, London, 1935. Also by Professor Gerhard Kittel in his essay in *Mysterium Christi*, London, 1930.

## Chapter IV

## The Evangelists

*1 Pet. ii. 21-65* The description of the passion in the First Epistle of Peter shows that in the church at the end of the first century the life and death of Jesus were recounted in the context of the Old Testament scriptures; it shows also that it was this that gave to the Christians their assurance of salvation and redemption, and imposed upon them a peculiarly intense moral demand. It is clear also from this passage and from others in the Pauline epistles, in the Epistle to the Hebrews, and in the Johannine writings, that the outstanding men in the primitive church found no difficulty in using the Old Testament to interpret the life, death and resurrection of Jesus and to explain to the Christians what was involved in their calling. In fact, Old Testament conceptions, once adopted, lent themselves admirably for this purpose.

If, therefore, it was the Old Testament context that gave redemptive significance to the life and death of Jesus, it is obviously the duty of the historian to trace back this close interweaving of Old and New, in order to discover whether there is any evidence in the New Testament of a period when nothing was known of this interweaving. Such evidence would suggest that the historical Jesus was unencumbered with this heavy significance. The claim has been made that it is precisely this discovery which results from the application to the gospels of modern methods of historical and literary criticism. It is claimed that historical criticism rids the Jesus of history of any redemptive significance, and in particular rids his death of that peculiar importance which primitive Christian piety attached to it. This removal of the encumbrance with which the writers of the New Testament or the church are supposed to have loaded the Jesus of history gave the sanction of critical scholarship to the modern distinction between Jesus and the church, and set modern writers and modern preachers free to place him in the context of humanitarian idealism or in the context of popular ideas about evolution. This whole procedure is justifiable only if Jesus can be detached from the Old Testament background, since the Old Testament writers are completely controlled by belief in the particular historical revelation of the living God. Modern humanitarian idealism is not only foreign to the Old Testament, but is incompatible with it. So great a weight has been placed upon the 'assured results' of the older criticism that it is necessary to test these results and to call attention to the direction in which more recent criticism is moving. Work upon the first three gospels is here all-important; for the reconstruction of the Jesus of history must be grounded upon a critical investigation of these documents.

As they stand, the synoptic gospels portray the life and death of Jesus in the context of the Old Testament scriptures exactly as they are portrayed in the other New Testament books. The subtlety of this Old Testament penetration is not usually recognized. A most striking illustration is found in the influence of the twenty-second psalm upon the passion narratives. This *Ps. xxii.* psalm is in itself a remarkable poem, treating of the affliction of 'the afflicted'; his rejection by men, and apparent forsaking by God. The Psalm ends[1] with a declaration of faith in God, and an assurance of justification by him, attended with a consequent penitent conversion of mankind. It treats, in fact, of an idea very similar to that found in the sufferings of the slave of God in Isaiah, and may be closely connected with it.

[1] It is of no present importance that the Psalm is composite: it was so long before the time of Jesus.

In the first place the Psalm is used several times by
Mark. 'They that passed by railed on him, wagging
their heads', just as those that saw the sufferer of the
Psalm 'shook the head'. The soldiers 'part his garments
among them, casting lots upon them, what each should
take', just as in the Psalm 'they parted my garments
among them, and cast lots upon my raiment'. The
author of the fourth Gospel elaborates the episode and
makes the fulfilment of the Psalm explicit:

*Mk. xv. 29.*

*Ps. xxii. 7.*

*Mk. xv. 24.*

*Ps. xxii. 18.*

*Jn. xix. 23 f.*

'The soldiers therefore, when they had crucified Jesus, took
his garments, and made four parts, to every soldier a part; and
also the coat: now the coat was without seam, woven from the
top throughout. They said therefore one to another, Let us not
rend it, but cast lots for it, whose it shall be: that the scripture
might be fulfilled, which saith, They parted my garments
among them and upon my vesture did they cast lots.'

In the first Gospel it is further recorded that the
Scribes taunted Jesus, saying, 'He trusted in God; let
him deliver him now, if he desireth him!' just as in the
Psalm the bystanders cried out, 'He hoped in the Lord;
let him deliver him now, because he desireth him!' And
Luke adds: 'All the people stood beholding, and the
rulers also scoffed at him,' using the same words as the
Psalm: 'All they that beheld me scoffed at me,' thereby
declaring him evidently to be 'a reproach of men, and
despised of the people'. This consistent tendency to
describe events of the passion in the language of the
Psalm in four different documents presents a problem
which is brought to a head when Mark and Matthew
record that 'at the ninth hour Jesus cried with a loud
voice, Eloi eloi, lama sabachthani?', the actual opening
verse of the Psalm: 'My God, my God . . . why hast thou
forsaken me?' The problem is capable of precise for-
mulation. Did Jesus set his passion in the context of Old
Testament scripture? And did an intention of fulfilment
condition his words and actions? If this be so, the
evangelists are merely drawing out the implications of
his passion and emphasizing them clearly in their

*Mt. xxvii. 43.*

*Ps. xxii. 8.*

*Lk. xxiii. 35.*

*Ps. xxii. 7.*

*Ps. xxii. 6.*

*Mk. xv. 34.*

*Ps. xxii. 1.*

narratives. Or does the initiative lie rather with the church, in which case it must be supposed that the evangelists, moved by the needs of the faithful Christians, attached a peculiar significance to the death of the Lord, and placed in his mouth words that sanctioned their procedure?

Old Testament allusions are, however, not found only in the passion narratives: they are woven into the whole Gospel material in various ways and in a very subtle manner. They are found most obviously in the first Gospel, in which a number of stories are recorded with the addition of a pendant in order to show that they fulfilled this or that Old Testament prediction. The author, for instance, remarks that the events connected with the miraculous birth of Jesus 'came to pass, *Mt. i. 22, 23.* that it might be fulfilled which was spoken by the Lord through the prophet, saying:

> Behold a virgin shall be with child *cf. Is. vii. 14.*
> And shall bring forth a son,
> And they shall call his name Emmanuel'.

Sometimes the relevance of the prophecy is not obvious, as when it is shown that Jesus came and dwelt in a city called Nazareth: 'that it might be fulfilled *Mt. ii. 23.* which was spoken through the prophets, that he should be called a Nazarene', and that, later, 'he came and *Mt. iv. 13-16.* dwelt in Capernaum, which is by the sea, in the borders of Zebulon: that it might be fulfilled which was spoken through Isaiah the prophet, saying:

> The land of Zebulon and the land of Naphtali, *cf. Is. ix. 1, 2.*
> The way of the sea, beyond Jordan,
> Galilee of the Gentiles,
> The people which sat in darkness
> Saw a great light,
> And to them which sat in the region
>     and shadow of death,
> To them did light spring up.'

So far the uneasiness of the argument does not affect the narrative to which it is fastened. But in at least one instance the history is disturbed in order to approximate it more closely to an Old Testament passage. *Mk. xi. 1-8.* Mark and Luke both relate that, when Jesus made his *Lk. xix. 29-* entry into Jerusalem he sent disciples to borrow a colt *35.* for him to ride upon. According to the first Gospel, *Mt. xxi. 1-7.* however, two animals were brought—an ass and her colt. And this 'came to pass that it might be fulfilled which was spoken through the prophet saying:

*Zech. ix. 9.*
> Tell ye the daughter of Zion,
> Behold, thy King cometh unto thee,
> Meek, and riding upon an ass,
> And upon a colt the foal of an ass.'

In the original prophecy the duplication of the animals is due merely to the parallelism of Semitic poetry.[1] The prophet therefore never intended his readers to understand that the king would enter the city riding in triumph upon two asses. In order, however, to make clear that Jesus did fulfil this particular prophecy the evangelist soberly introduces the second animal. But it must not for one moment be imagined that the evangelist created the connexion between the prophecy of Zechariah and an episode in the life of Jesus. Mark and Luke also clearly had this prophecy in mind when they described the incident. The historical problem lies behind the evangelists. Did Jesus enter Jerusalem riding upon an ass in order to draw attention to an ancient prophecy? And if so, what was involved in this public action?

[1] A convenient illustration of a similar parallel occurs in Ps. viii. 4:

> What is man, that thou art mindful of him?
> And the son of man, that thou visitest him?

'Man' and 'son of man' both represent mankind; they do not differentiate between two classes of people. Whatever subtle distinction of emphasis there may be, the variation is primarily due to the idiom of Hebrew poetry.

The argument from the Old Testament is by no means confined to Matthew, though there it is most crudely obvious. It conditions also the gospel of Luke, in which it is made plain that Jesus is the Christ foretold by prophecy: the evangelist states the thesis openly in the narrative of the birth, and confirms it repeatedly in the stories of the post-resurrection appearances. Moreover, this intention is so subtle that it affects the actual language in which the gospel is written. When Luke passes from his preface to his narrative, he passes abruptly from literary Greek into Old Testament idiom and phraseology. The story is filled with Old Testament allusions, as, for instance, when he writes: 'And Jesus, advanced in wisdom and stature, and in favour with God and man', echoing 'And the child Samuel grew on, and was in favour both with the Lord, and also with men'. The Greek reader is at once removed from the Greek world and is set firmly within the sphere of Jewish messianic hope. This is not mere literary artistry, the geographical and historical sympathy of a sensitive author: it is a declaration to his cultured Greek readers that salvation is of the Jews.

*e.g.*
*Lk. i. 33, 35; xxiv, 25, 44.*

*Lk. i. 1-4.*

*Lk. ii. 52.*

*1 Sam. ii. 26.*

Both Matthew and Luke are concerned to show that the life and death of Jesus are properly intelligible only in the context of the Old Testament scriptures. The same characteristic, however, controls the Marcan narrative also. If it were merely a question of noticing actual quotations from the Old Testament scriptures it would only be necessary to draw attention to the different type used for this purpose in the Westcott and Hort Greek text of the gospel, or, indeed, to the marginal references provided in the more elaborate editions of the Authorized and Revised English Versions. Westcott and Hort in the short gospel of Mark note 71 quotations from the Old Testament. But, impressive as this list is, it may be misleading, for passages containing no direct quotations may prove, on further examination, to be pregnant with Old Testament allusions. The tracking

c

down of such allusions is not an unprofitable piece of work, but one that must be done if the Marcan gospel is to speak to us as it spoke to those who did not look up Old Testament allusions but had the Old Testament in their constitution. For where such allusions are implicit in the narrative, failure to recognize them may seriously damage interpretation. Thus there is an indispensable allusion to the prophecy of Zechariah in the Marcan version of the entry into Jerusalem, although no word of it is actually quoted. Again, in the midst of a great storm at sea, Jesus lies in a boat asleep upon a cushion: 'And they rouse him, and say to him, Master, carest thou not that we perish?' A reader familiar with the Old Testament can hardly fail to be reminded of the tense sense of affliction and yearning for salvation which permeates so much of the Old Testament literature and in particular the Psalter, and which is voiced in such a cry as 'Awake, why sleepest thou, O Lord? Arise, cast us not off for ever. Wherefore hidest thou thy face? And forgettest our affliction and oppression. . . .' The cry of the disciples rests, in the Marcan story, upon the same general background, even though it may not be an echo of the psalmist's words.

*Mk. xi. 1-8.*
*cf. Zech. ix. 9.*

*Mk. iv. 38.*

*Ps. xliv. 23 f.*

Sometimes this method of analysis produces results that seem to be outrageous. For example, Mark alone records that, after the arrest in Gethsemane,

*Mk. xiv. 51 f.*

'A certain young man followed with him, having a linen cloth cast about him, over his naked body: and they lay hold on him; but he left the linen cloth, and fled naked.'

This statement has often been explained on the supposition that the author is referring to himself. Only one who had experienced it, it is said, would record such an insignificant detail. Taken in connexion with the tradition that St. Mark wrote the gospel, it is deduced that this passage is a reminiscence by the author of an event in his own life. And so, indeed, it may have been. But other commentators are impatient of such a

network of suppositions, and suggest different reasons
for its inclusion. Loisy follows Keim in recalling a verse
of Amos:[1]

'He that is courageous among the mighty shall flee away *Amos. ii. 16.*
naked in that day, saith the Lord.'

Far from agreeing that the incident is an historical
reminiscence, Loisy suggests that it has actually been
created by the application of this Old Testament
prophecy interpreted messianically. Just when the
reader seems to be standing firmly on palpably historical ground, his position is thrown into question by
an interpretation which he may well dismiss as fantastic,
but which remains none the less disquieting.

Again, it has often been said of Mark's brief account
of the temptation that the mention of wild beasts is
merely a homely detail based upon the reminiscence of
one who had heard Jesus describe his ordeal. Mark
wrote:

'And he was in the wilderness forty days, tempted of Satan; *Mk. i. 13.*
and he was with the wild beasts; and the angels ministered
unto him.'

The psalter, however, contains the following passage:

> 'He shall give his angels charge over thee,        *Ps. xci. 11-13.*
> To keep thee in all thy ways.
> They shall bear thee in their hands,
> Lest thou dash thy foot against a stone.
> Thou shalt tread upon the lion and adder:
> The young lion and the serpent
> Shalt thou trample under thy feet.'

Could there be a better summary of these lines than
the few words of Mark? But if Mark's words are a summary, are they not also an allusion to the theme of the
Psalm, evoked because the theme of the Psalm is pre-

---

[1] Loisy A. F., *Les Évangiles synoptiques*, vol. 2. pp. 589-91.
Loisy points out that the Hebrew text, as against the Greek
of the Septuagint, reads *shall flee* naked. He cites Rev. xvi. 15 as
another possible allusion to the same passage of Amos.

cisely that of the evangelist? For the Psalm treats of
one who has confident trust in God, and of the afflictions, physical and spiritual, which he shall overcome
if God be his refuge and strength. To recall such a
Psalm fills out the Marcan narrative of the temptation.
Moreover, it is perhaps possible that the careful linking
of the temptation to the story of the descent of the Spirit
as a dove upon Jesus echoes the confident assurance of
the same psalmist, who prefaces the trials of the
righteous with the words:

*Ps. xci. 4.*          'He shall cover thee with his pinions,
              And under his wings shalt thou take refuge.'

Here again, is it entirely satisfactory either to dismiss
such allusions as absurd, or to aver that the beasts and
the angels are purely historical and insignificant reminiscences? Is it not preferable to conclude—perhaps
even in the case of the young man who fled naked—that
those who formed the synoptic tradition were so steeped
in the prophets and the psalms, and so conscious that
in the history of Jesus the prophets and the psalms find
their realization, so convinced that the day of the Lord
has come, that they slipped, half consciously, half unconsciously, into a biblical phraseology when relating
what they without doubt accepted as historical events?
They, at any rate, could not speak of insignificant details, for to them every detail re-echoed their theme and
invited them to use the language of the prophets and
the psalmists. It is therefore necessary to read the gospels
with ears as open for Old Testament allusion as were
theirs who wrote them. Doubtless it will sometimes be
concluded that the allusion is too nebulous to be conscious—as for instance in the former of the cases just
considered—but it may none the less be there. And even
if both the cases that have just been considered are
wrong illustrations it is none the less important that
readers of the New Testament should risk being called
fantastic in order that their ears may be opened to these

Old Testament echoes when they are not irrelevant but essential.

At times the Old Testament allusion lies nearer the surface and recognition of it is vital for the understanding of the gospel. For instance, the story of the storm is closely linked with the healing of the Gerasene De- *Mk. iv. 35-* moniac. The psalmists frequently used the metaphor of *v. 20.* a storm or of great waters to express the tribulation of the righteous, from which only the intervention of God can save them.

'Save me, O Lord, for the waters are come in unto my soul.' *Ps. lxix. 1.*

And God alone can save, for

> 'Thou rulest the raging of the sea: *Ps. lxxxix. 9.*
> When the waves thereof arise, thou stillest them.'

Or again:

> 'The floods have lifted up, O Lord, *Ps. xciii. 3 f.*
> The floods have lifted up their voice;
> The floods lift up their waves.
> Above the voices of many waters,
> The mighty breakers of the sea,
> The Lord on high is mighty.'

And so He can save from the tumult of evil and oppression:

'He sent from on high, he took me; *Ps. xviii. 16 f.*
He drew me out of great waters.
He delivered me from my strong enemy,
And from them that hated me, for they were too mighty for
    me.'

'By terrible things thou wilt answer us in righteousness, *Ps. lxv. 5-8.*
   O God of our salvation;
Thou that art the confidence of all the ends of the earth,
And of them that are afar off upon the sea:
Which by his strength setteth fast the mountains;
Being girded about with might:
Which stilleth the roaring of the seas, the roaring of their
    waves,
And the tumult of the peoples.
They also that dwell in the uttermost parts are afraid at thy
    tokens.'

It was, perhaps, familiarity with this metaphor which led the priestly historian to elaborate the story of Noah as a type of Israel overwhelmed, as it were, in their captivity, by the 'great floods' of Gentile oppression. *Test. Naph. vi.* And it certainly inspired a later writer to picture the dispersion of the Jews in the same fashion. In the Testament of Naphthali, Naphthali and his brother patriarchs enter a boat. And suddenly there come a storm and a great whirlwind, and their father Jacob is whirled away from the helm and separated from them. The boat fills, is smashed by the waves, and the patriarchs are scattered on planks to the ends of the earth. Then Levi puts on sackcloth and prays to the Lord. Immediately the storm ceases, and the boat, now once more seaworthy, makes the land in peace. And there they find Jacob and rejoice together. So a simple hope that God will cause the stormy dispersion of Israel among the nations to cease, and will gather all the tribes together once more, finds expression in this same metaphor of a storm. The sequence is precisely that of the Psalms. Tumult and oppression pictured as a storm—intervention by God—peace.

*Mk. iv. 35-v. 20.* Exactly the same sequence occurs in Mark in two consecutive miracles. First of all the scene is the sea. Jesus and the disciples enter a boat. A whirlwind springs up, the sea rages, and the boat fills. Jesus, however, is asleep in the bow. In fear they wake him and call upon him. He rebukes the wind and the sea, and immediately both are calm. And thereupon they come to the other side and meet a man possessed, whose frenzy, like that of the storm, cannot be tamed or fettered by man. Jesus drives the devil out, and the man is left clothed and in his right mind, sitting at his feet.

The close sequence of these two miracles and the movement of the narrative from the storm of the sea to the tumult of the man, and from the calm of the sea to the peace of the man, reproduces the sequence and the movement of the passages cited from the Psalms. Jesus

stills the troubled waters and the tribulation of the
people. It is difficult to think that this general Old
Testament background was absent from the mind of
the author of the gospel, and that he did not expect his
readers to be aware that the hope of Israel is here being
fulfilled. There is more here than a mere record of two
episodes in the life of Jesus in their correct chronological
order. For, though the literary critic has no reason to
dismiss either or both of these miracles as unhistorical
and to regard them as allegories or myths, and no
reason even to doubt that they may have happened in
close sequence, he has good reason to suppose that
they belong together not primarily because of an interest in chronological sequence, but because their significance lies in this conjunction. Mark is not here arguing
about the fulfilment of Old Testament prophecy; he is
simply setting down in writing a material which itself
contains the answer to the quesion of the disciples:
'Who then is this, that even the wind and the sea obey
him?' But the answer is intelligible only if the Old
Testament context be recognized, and the conjunction
of these two episodes makes this possible.

Indeed, not these miracles only, but the whole gospel
of Mark provokes that question, and suggests with it
the answer to it. The opening words of the gospel are
a bold and provocative proclamation of a thesis. 'The *Mk. i. 1.*
beginning of the gospel of Jesus Christ, the Son of
God.'[1] The narrative is knit together so that it supports,
still more provocatively, the same thesis. It begins by *Mk. i. 2-8.*
showing that John was a prophet, preparing the way of
the Lord by prophesying that a mightier than he will
baptize with the Holy Ghost. The Holy Ghost descends *Mk. i. 10.*
upon Jesus, and his words and actions declare the presence in the midst of the Jewish people of the mighty
one to whose advent John had borne witness. He resists

[1] 'the Son of God' is omitted in some manuscripts. The Marcan gospel is the record of Jesus as the Christ, the Son of God,
whether or no the words 'Son of God' are authentic.

Satan in the wilderness, drives him out of his possessions,

*Mk. i. 13.*

*Mk. i. 26, 34.* restores freedom to those who have been his prey. His

*Mk. i. 22, 27.* teaching and his powers alike reveal his authority,

*Mk. i. 24; iii.* which puzzles those that witness it, but is no puzzle

*11; v. 7.* either to the evangelist or to the powers of evil. He

*Mk. ii. 5, 27 f.* forgives sins, and exercises authority over the sabbath.
But his power is misconstrued and his authority doubted.
Accordingly, various misconstructions are illustrated
one after another, and immediately refuted. A leper

*Mk. i. 40.* takes him to be an arbitrary wonder-worker—'If you
like, you can cleanse me'—and, although indeed
cleansed, is roundly rebuked and then sent to show him-

*Mk. iii. 21 f.* self to the priest. Some think that Jesus is beside himself,
others that he is possessed, and he immediately in their
presence indicates his authority both by word and by

*Mk. iii. 23-29.* action. Can Satan drive out Satan? To credit Jesus with
evil power is blasphemy against the Holy Spirit. He is

*Mk. vi. 14 f;* neither John the Baptist, nor Elijah, nor yet one of the

*viii, 28.* prophets returned from the powers of death. He is not

*Mk. viii. 29,* the worldly messiah of Peter's inadequate confession, or

*33; xii. 35-37.* the successor of King David expected by the scribes.
Indeed, his works testify as much. The messiah of

*Mk. v. 27-29.* common expectation might have healed with the hem

*Mk. iv. 39.* of his garment, have stilled the waves of the sea with a

*Mk. ii. 8.* word, have penetrated the thoughts of men, but would

*Mk. xii. 9;* he have dared to reject the chosen race? Even the dis-

*xi. 14.* ciples of Jesus fail to understand him, although he sets

*Mk. viii. 31;* before them the humiliation imposed upon him by

*ix. 12 f.; x. 38;* divine necessity and revealed in the Old Testament

*xiv. 21, 49.* scriptures. So the people reject him; the rulers reject

*Mk. xiv. 1;* him; the disciples forsake him and flee. And then, in the

*xv. 11;* depth of rejection, when God too seems to have for-

*xiv. 50; xv.* saken him, faith was born. When the centurion, which

*34.* stood over against him, saw that he so gave up the

*Mk. xv. 39.* ghost, he said, 'Truly this man was Son of God'.[1]

---

[1] Son of God is in the original Greek anarthrous. It is, however, doubtful whether it is for that reason capable of being
translated 'a son of God' as in the R.V. margin, since other-

If this is to any extent a right impression of the Marcan gospel, the forces that were working upon the author clearly need further investigation. Mark had been led to write, neither simply by a desire to recount the life of Jesus as a bare chronological record, nor yet by a demand for a facsimile of his ministry and passion. The chronology of the Gospel may be, roughly at least, correct, and events may have happened much as he described, yet the narrative is primarily conditioned by the definite intention of proclaiming the gospel of Jesus Christ. It was this intention which led the evangelist to give form and order to the material and to emphasize and clarify the tradition which he had received. But why this particular form? And why this particular emphasis and clarification? These are the primary questions to which the critical historian must give an answer. Did the needs of the primitive church, its preaching, its manner of apologetic, its spiritual experience, the innate conceptions of its non-Jewish converts or the peculiar theologizing of St. Paul, cause him to complicate the simple story of the vigorous life and tragic death of a Jewish reformer, and to invest them with this heavy significance? Or was there a complication in the material itself which drove him so to order it that clearer expression might be given to the interpretation which it inevitably and unmistakably demanded? Why, for instance, did he again and again, in portraying his subject, use the medium of Old Testament aspiration? Was it because the apostolic age had been driven to do so in the hope of compelling the attention of the Jewish world? Or was it that Old Testament aspiration did in fact condition the teaching and action of Jesus, so that he went to his death consciously in order that the scripture might be fulfilled, and ordered his ministry to that end? In other words, is the particular Marcan ordering an imposition upon the

wise the anarthrous phrase πνεῦμα θεοῦ in the Matthaean account of the baptism might be translated 'a spirit of God'. *Mt. iii. 16.*

73

original history, or the very essence of it? Why, above all, was the evangelist occupied primarily with the person of Jesus, rather than with his teaching; or, at least, why did he regard the teaching as intelligible only to those who perceived the significance of his person? Was it because the religious needs of early converts, and in particular of Gentile converts, had already distorted the life of a humane moralist, or of a fanatic proclaiming that the end of the world is at hand in order that they might have an assurance of salvation and so indulge their longing for eternal life? Or was it because the moral demands of Jesus were occasioned by the peculiarity of his relation to God, and were therefore final, ultimate and eschatological? And was it because the peculiarity of this relation and the ultimate character of his demands were fully manifested only in his death and resurrection?

These are some of the problems raised by the gospel of Mark, and raised even more clearly by the authors of the gospels of Matthew and Luke when they prefaced the story of the ministry of Jesus by the stories of the *Phil. ii. 5-11.* nativity, and by St. Paul and the authors of the fourth *Jn. i. 1-14.* Gospel and of the Epistle to the Hebrews when they *Heb. i. 1-3.* set Jesus on a cosmological and almost mystical background.

The result, then, of an examination of the gospels *as they stand* is that they were written with a clear and unmistakable purpose. They were written in order to declare that the life and death of Jesus were the fulfilment of the promises made by the living God through the prophets and psalmists of Israel. They were written in order to bear witness to the superseding and fulfilment of the Mosaic law by the gospel, and to the emergence of the new Israel by faith in Jesus. When the author of *Jn. i. 14.* the fourth Gospel stated in the preface that the, Word was made flesh; that is, that the word which had formerly been written on two tables of stone had now been written in the flesh and blood of Jesus; and when he

74

also declared that whereas the law came by Moses, grace and truth came by Jesus Christ, he gave formal expression to what was everywhere implied in the earlier gospels. The four evangelists agree in setting the life and death of Jesus firmly within the context of the Old Testament scriptures; and each evangelist presumes that no other context can provide an adequate understanding of the nature of the action that God had wrought through his Son, Jesus Christ.

No modern critic can leave the matter here. All that has been so far established is that the evangelists have written their gospels with a purpose. But the four gospels are not independent literary works. Two at least of the evangelists were literary editors rather than authors. The author of the fourth Gospel certainly knew St. Mark's gospel, probably knew also St. Luke's gospel, and perhaps was familiar with all three synoptic gospels. If therefore one main purpose of the historical criticism of the New Testament is to discover the origin of this peculiar interweaving of the Old Testament with the life and death of Jesus of Nazareth, it is imperative that some attempt be made to go behind the synoptic gospels as they stand, in order if possible to lay bare the nature of the tradition concerning Jesus before it was handled by the editors and incorporated in their narratives. This involves a careful investigation of the methods of editing employed by the evangelists where these methods can be tested. The whole problem is commonly called *The Synoptic Problem.*

## NOTE

For the influence of Psalm xxii on the passion narratives in the synoptic gospels see Professor Martin Dibelius *From Tradition to Gospel*, English translation, London, 1934, Chapter VII.

## Chapter V

## The Synoptic Problem

The investigation of the literary relations between the first three gospels is not a mere exercise in literary criticism. It is a necessary prolegomenon to the reconstruction of that original and particular history which underlies the New Testament writings. All modern New Testament study rests upon the remarkable achievement of the scholars of the last generation, who discovered the solution of the synoptic problem. It had long been recognized that the first three gospels present an intricate literary puzzle. The striking similarities,

*Mk. ii. 1-12;*
*Mt. ix. 1-8;*
*Lk. v. 17-26.*

not only of wording, as for example in the Healing of the Paralytic, but also of the order of incidents, especially of the order of incidents where a particular order is of trivial importance, as for example the series of episodes recorded in Mark x. 13-34, and appearing in Matthew xix. 13—xx. 19 and Luke xviii. 15-34. Such identity of order cried out for some explanation other than that three evangelists wrote three independent narratives. In short, after a long succession of tentative solutions which were proved inadequate, certain general agreements have been reached. The authors of the first and third Gospels had the gospel of Mark before them as they wrote. What is common to all three gospels is due to the dependence of Matthew and Luke upon Mark. Matthew and Luke also made use of another document or documents, now lost, which explains the presence in their gospels of almost identical material that is absent from Mark. Lastly, each had access to further material of which the other was apparently unaware.

76

The general agreement among modern scholars that this is not only an adequate explanation, but indeed the only adequate explanation of the highly intricate and complex literary problem presented by the synoptic gospels, is a monument to the skill and patience of the scholars of the last generation. Attempts have, of course, been made to go beyond what has been called the fundamental solution, but these have secured no general agreement. Some have held that the lost document of which Matthew and Luke made use was the work referred to by a writer in the middle of the second century, named Papias, who said that the apostle Matthew arranged in order the sayings (of Jesus) in the Hebrew (?Aramaic) language. Some have attempted to reconstruct the lost document. Others have supposed that it is possible to detect the presence behind the first and third Gospels of other documents from which Matthew and Luke extracted their special material or even to discover an earlier document which Mark incorporated in his gospel. But these and many other hypotheses concern only the specialist, because they go beyond the clear evidence of the existing documents. Nothing can be built upon theories which remain wholly unproven.

The modern scholar is thus thrown back upon the fundamental solution, and with this he must work when he passes on from the literary analysis of the documents to attempt to reconstruct the original history. He has, however, no right to complain of what has been achieved by his predecessors.

In the first place, immediately it is recognized that Matthew and Luke used Mark as a literary source, it becomes obvious that they must have selected his work because they attached peculiar importance to it. Further, since both Mark and their own gospels (which incorporate Mark) are still in existence, it is possible to make a minute examination of what changes, additions, rearrangements, and omissions they made in rewriting Mark. Their 'redaction' should reveal the reasons which led them to alter what Mark had written. Where the words of a story are changed or a discourse is enlarged, where a series of parables is rearranged or an incident is omitted, there editorial tendencies may be detected and defined. The very fact, for instance, that both Luke and Matthew supplemented Mark shows that they were not satisfied that Mark was in itself complete for their purpose. Accordingly it should be possible to define quite precisely the purpose of each evangelist by noting carefully how he treated his Marcan source, which fortunately still exists.

But it is not only by comparing these two gospels with Mark that the tendencies of their authors may be detected. Now that it is agreed that much of their non-Marcan material was known in a more or less identical form to both of them, it should be possible to gain a good deal of information from a comparison of the different ways in which they handled and ordered this non-Marcan material. And finally, the manner in which each evangelist introduced his special material into his narrative should provide corroborative evidence as to their particular aims and interests.

In the second place, the critical historian, who bases his work upon the literary analysis, is not operating simply with three gospels. He has in his hands four great blocks of material, and he is also presented in addition with two editors, whose interests he can to some extent detect. The four blocks of material are the gospel of Mark; the matter common to Matthew and Luke, but absent from Mark; that which is recorded by Matthew only; and that which is recorded only by Luke. The two editors are named Matthew and Luke from the traditional titles of their books. This division of the material cannot, it is true, be altogether rigid, because at any given point what is technically, according to the literary analysis, special Matthaean or special Lucan material may originally have been a section of a lost document which they both knew, but which one or other of them omitted. Or again, what may seem to be material to which Matthew or Luke had special access may have originated in the process of editing, and may have had no previous existence. In spite, however, of these qualifications, it is possible to distinguish behind the gospels of Matthew and Luke four independent strata of tradition concerning Jesus of Nazareth, and, in addition to these strata, it is possible also to disentangle the actual editorial interests of the evangelists which presumably reflect opinions current in the primitive church, and do not spring entirely from their own independent prejudices.

It is a very strange and almost unaccountable fact that the older critics, having accomplished the literary analysis, and having with extraordinary skill achieved the solution of the main problems presented by the literary analysis, seem to have exhausted their critical faculties. For either, ignoring the further critical problems raised by it, they hastened at once to reconstruct the Jesus of history, or else, stopping short at this point, they doubted the ability of the critical method to achieve any historical reconstruction whatsoever.

Thus the critical method was suspended, as it were, in mid air. But their own critical work demanded that an even more critical procedure should follow. The critic is not free, having accomplished the literary analysis, to select this or that element in the tradition, and to pronounce it true to the original history; nor, conversely, to discard this or that element as due to the imposition upon the original history of Christian faith, or of primitive Christian superstition. Still less can literary criticism be indulged in as though it had no historical implications. Unless historical reconstruction be undertaken, the older critical method is rendered completely sterile. Nevertheless, the transition from literary analysis to historical reconstruction demands an increasingly critical procedure.

The literary analysis has clear implications for the historian. He has been provided with a means of checking the editorial interests of Matthew and Luke and the purpose which holds together the structure of the Marcan narrative. Mark gave the material a clear significance. Matthew and Luke gave to it a significance that was even clearer. If these three men adopted entirely different explanations of the ministry of Jesus, some disturbance must have complicated the course of the transmission of the story. But if they agree in the main significance of the history they record, their agreement must at least be taken seriously, even though that significance may be repugnant to modern ideas.

But this is not all. It is now possible to check the procedure, not only of the editors, but even of Mark himself. For although all three may agree in the significance they ascribe to the ministry of Jesus, modern criticism is not at their mercy. Literary analysis has disentangled, and so revealed, four blocks of primitive Christian tradition. These can be analysed separately, then in conjunction with each other, and then set over against the known aims and interests of the final editors. In this way it may be possible to check and discount any editorial bias, and to determine the sense of the tradition that lay behind the editors. If there be no discoverable unity in the various strata, and if the editors be found to be imposing their ideas upon a chaotic material; then the historian will be forced to own himself baffled, and must content himself with describing tendencies of faith and controversy in the primitive church. The Jesus of history will have escaped from his knowledge in the midst of the variegated life of the early Christians. If the editors be found to be imposing their ideas upon a recalcitrant material it may be possible to recover the Jesus of history in spite of editorial misrepresentation. But if, on the other hand, analysis should reveal a steady unity of direction: if the four great blocks of material show a general agreement, and the editors are found to be mainly engaged in exposing a significance already contained in the material that they are handling, then, however awkward the result may be, it is difficult to avoid the conclusion that this unity of direction was set in motion, not by the creative faith of the primitive church, but by the teaching and actions of Jesus of Nazareth.

There can be no advance in the interpretation of the New Testament until this work be done upon the basis of the older literary analysis. It must be also remembered that the conclusions to which this work leads have implications not only for the reconstruction of the original history, but also for a proper judgement upon the work of St. Paul and of the author of the Johannine writings. They affect, in fact, the treatment of the whole of the New Testament, and consequently of the history of Christianity in the first century. Did the Christians progressively lose touch with the actual original happening in Palestine, and was there a gulf fixed between the teaching of Jesus and the teaching of the primitive church? Or did the primitive church bear on the whole correct witness to the significance of what occurred in Palestine, and was its faith securely grounded upon that witness?[1]

The literary analysis and the fundamental solution of the synoptic problem involve therefore a further historical investigation, equally critical and equally rigorous.

[1] In theory there is a third possibility. It used to be maintained that the original Christian gospel was a Christ-myth, which was subsequently clothed with flesh and blood, so that the clear, historical figure of Jesus is the outcome and not the cause of the development of Christian thought and experience, and the incarnation of Christ is the history of the Church. This possibility cannot be considered in an historical study since on this assumption the Jesus of history would become a proper subject for historical investigation only at the Last Judgement.

## NOTE

The most accessible analysis of the synoptic gospels, bringing out the four distinct strata of the material, is to be found in Dr. Streeter's *The Four Gospels*, Chapters VII and IX. London, 1924.

## Chapter VI

## Matthew and Luke

When once the fundamental solution of the synoptic problem has been achieved, the editors, Matthew and Luke, need no longer remain names standing at the head of their respective gospels. The manner in which they treated Mark is more than a subject of mere literary analysis: it betrays the interests of the men themselves. The older critics were fully alive to the importance of the editorial changes which Matthew and Luke made in their handling of Mark. They made a valiant attempt to see in these changes the complication of an earlier and simpler tradition, a complication brought about by the introduction of precisely those elements in primitive Christianity which they judged to be foreign to the life and teaching of the Jesus of history. By this process the editors, they said, heightened the Christology, placed Jesus in a more and more supernatural setting, and, in fact, paved the way for that 'catholicizing' of the church which wholly, or almost wholly, obscured the memory of him at the beginning of the second century.

A certain uneasiness concerning this judgement upon the work of Matthew and Luke arose, it is true, in the heart of the older radical criticism itself, but now that uneasiness has ripened into what must be called a revolt. It is therefore necessary to point out what has led to this growing change of critical opinion. A detailed account of the editorial methods of Matthew and Luke is clearly outside the scope of this book. It is possible to consider only the more striking divergences from the gospel of Mark.

Certain characteristics of Matthaean and Lucan editing hardly need discussion, for they are nowhere denied. It is clear that both editors felt the Greek of Mark to be rough and his method of writing narrative to be verbose. Consequently, both improve his grammar, remove obscure or vulgar words, and generally trim his narrative, partly by grammatical alterations, partly by rewriting awkward passages, and partly by quite radical abbreviation. Most of the minor differences of words, order, and even narrative, many of their omissions also, are due to the desire to make the story of the life and death of Jesus more readable. Both, for example, incorporate the Marcan story of the Healing of the Paralytic almost as Mark had recorded it; but whereas Mark had used colloquial words for the roof through which the paralytic was lowered and for the bed on which he was carried, Luke in both cases substitutes more dignified words; and Matthew not only substitutes other words, but abbreviates the passages in which they occur. Their care for quite small details of style is shown in their treatment of Mark's redundant expression: 'At even, when the sun was set'. Luke retains only 'And when the sun was set', Matthew prefers 'At even'.

*Mk. ii. 1-12.*
*Mt. ix. 1-8.*
*Lk. v. 17-26.*

*Mk. i. 32.*
*Mt. viii. 16.*
*Lk. iv. 40.*

But these editorial alterations do not explain the main differences between the gospels of Matthew and Luke and the gospel of Mark. A very superficial comparison of the first three gospels shows that they are vastly different in general plan. The main difference, and it is surely a very remarkable difference, lies in the emphatic description of Jesus in both Matthew and Luke as a teacher. Mark frequently describes Jesus as teaching: ten times he records that he was addressed as teacher, and elsewhere he definitely states that his hearers were astounded at his teaching. But again and again, when Mark thus describes Jesus, he gives no word of what he taught. Mark records only two extended parables, but he expressly states that Jesus was accustomed to use this form of teaching. It is however only from Matthew and

*Mk. iv. 2.*
*cf. Mk. xii. 1.*

84

Luke that a comprehensive knowledge of the contents of this teaching can be gained. Mark emphasizes the fact that the parables were unintelligible to the crowd. His own disciples had to ask for an interpretation, and when one was given did even then not fully understand. Mark, it is true, records an eschatological speech, and also *Mk. xiii.* controversies with the Jewish authorities; but, on the whole, he leaves the impression that the main subject *Mk. viii. 31 f.;* of the teaching of Jesus to his disciples was that the Son *xi. 31 f.* of man must suffer. It is to Matthew and Luke that the reader must go for any comprehensive record of the *Lk. xv. 11-32;* teaching of Jesus concerning the nature of the kingdom *x. 30-35; xvi.* of God: to Luke for the parables of the Prodigal Son, the *19-31; xviii.* Good Samaritan, Dives and Lazarus, and the Pharisee *9-14.* and the Publican: to Matthew for the parables of the *xxv. 31-46; xx.* Ten Virgins, the Great Assize and the Labourers in the *1-16.* Vineyard. Only Matthew and Luke record the great *Mt. v-vii.; Lk.* discourse concerning the righteousness of the kingdom *vi. 17-49.* known as the sermon on the mount or the sermon on *Mt. vi. 9-13;* the plain, and above all the Lord's Prayer itself. *Lk. xi. 2-4.*

But this deep-seated emphasis upon Jesus as teacher is not only secured by what Matthew and Luke add to Mark; it is also evident in their actual editing of what Mark does record. Their procedure may be illustrated by the manner in which they handle the Marcan usage of the noun 'gospel'. Neither Matthew nor Luke adopts the title with which Mark heads his work—'the gospel *Mk. i. 1.* of Jesus Christ'; and whereas the noun 'gospel' appears seven times in Mark, it occurs only four times in Matthew, and not at all in Luke. Luke, indeed, uses the *e.g.* kindred verb 'to gospel' or 'to preach good tidings'; but *Lk. viii. 1;* even so, never where Mark had used the noun; instead *ix. 6.* he very carefully omits the Marcan noun, and equally *Mk. i. 14, 15.* carefully paraphrases the passages where it occurs. *Lk. iv. 14, 15.* Matthew retains Mark's noun twice, once exactly as *Mt. xxvi. 13;* Mark had it, and once with the addition of the defining *xxiv. 14.* genitive 'of the kingdom'. Elsewhere his usage of the *Mt. iv. 23; ix.* word is similarly qualified. For Matthew the gospel is *35.*

the gospel of the kingdom. These phenomena suggest that both Matthew and Luke were for some reason or other uneasy with Mark's use of the word.

Why did Mark choose to call his work 'the gospel of Jesus Christ'? Classical and contemporary Greek offers no explanation, for the word *evangelion*, especially in the singular, is a very rare word indeed, and when used means the reward given to someone who brings good news. There is some evidence that in the plural it could also mean good news itself, or a sacrifice offered when the good news was received. It is only when reference is made to the Septuagint version of the Psalms and of the Book of Isaiah that a background for Mark's usage of the word is discovered. There a Hebrew verb meaning 'to announce good tidings' had been translated by the Greek verb corresponding to the noun *evangelion*. In its context in the Psalter and in Isaiah this verb is used to express the declaration of the good news that God was fulfilling his promises, was acting, or was about to act. It is connected with the advent of the salvation of God, with his mercy, with remission of sins, with the peace of God and with the coming of his righteousness, with the acceptable year of the Lord, with the justification of the poor, with the emergence of Zion as the centre of the world where the action of God would take place. It belongs therefore to the rich vocabulary of the Old Testament expectation of salvation. This Old Testament background is clearly presumed in the title of Mark's book. 'The gospel of Jesus Christ' means either the good tidings about Jesus Christ or the good tidings which he brought. In either case, the story of Jesus is linked to the action of God, and in some sense *is* that action. Its significance, therefore, lies in the fact that it is the fulfilment of Old Testament hope.

*e.g. Is. xl. 9;*
*lii. 7-10; lx. 6;*
*lxi. 1.*
*Joel ii. 32.*
*Ps. xcvi. 2.*
*Nah. i. 15.*
*Ps. xl. 9.*

*Mk. i. 1.*
*Mk. i. 14 f.*

Mark follows up his title with a summary in which he announces and introduces the ministry of Jesus.

*Mk. i. 14 f.* 'Now after that John was put in prison, Jesus came into Galilee, heralding the gospel of God, and saying, "The time is fulfilled, and the kingdom of God is upon you;[1] repent ye, and believe in the gospel".'

All the Old Testament vocabularly of salvation is called up by the definition of the ministry of Jesus in relation to the gospel of God. In Mark's next use of the *Mk. viii. 34 f.* word, the connexion is even more pronounced.

'If any man would come after me, let him deny himself and take up his cross, and follow me. For whosoever would save his life shall lose it: and whosoever shall lose his life for my sake and the gospel's shall save it.'

Here the decision to follow Jesus involves not merely a relationship to him, but also a relationship to the promised action of God which is the good news.

When the disciples are astonished at the difficulty of *Mk. x. 26-30.* entering the kingdom of God, Peter protests, and exclaims, 'Lo, we have left all, and have followed thee.' And

'Jesus said, Verily I say unto you, There is no man that hath left house, or brethren, or sisters, or mother, or father, or children, or lands, for my sake, and for the gospel's sake, but he shall receive a hundredfold now in this time . . . and in the age to come eternal life.'

So close a connexion between Jesus and the gospel suggests that the title, 'The gospel of Jesus Christ', does not merely mean, 'The good news which Jesus Christ brought in His teaching', though this is, of course, involved. 'The gospel' is for Mark an all-embracing term which gives a peculiar significance to his narrative of Jesus of Nazareth, his teaching, his actions, and, finally, his death and resurrection. The whole ministry of Jesus, according to Mark, is the advent of precisely those things which were sighed for in the messianic hope of the Jews. It has already been seen that Jesus is represented as promising 'salvation' to those who follow him. *e.g.* He responds to the call 'son of David, have mercy upon *Mk. xiii. 13.*

[1] 'At hand', the usual translation of the Greek, is not strong enough since it lacks the suggestion of arrival.

*Mk. x. 47 f.* me'; he is shown exercising authority to remit sins, and
*Mk. ii. 10.* bringing peace to those possessed by evil spirits; he calls
*Mk. v. 15.* sinners to repentance. But with all those who are con-
*Mk. ii. 17.* vinced that they are righteous he has no concern, except
to place them under the judgement of God. He teaches
*Mk. i. 22, 27.* with authority and wields power with authority. The
gospel, therefore, is not only the gospel brought by
Jesus Christ, but the gospel of Jesus Christ: The good
tidings of the expected action of God which is, accord-
ing to Mark, the ministry, passion, and resurrection of
Jesus.

This all-embracing significance, which is attached to
the noun 'gospel', and which, because of its Old Testament background, is consequently attached to the whole
ministry of Jesus according to Mark, involves a considerable manipulation of the Old Testament passages
which contain the word 'gospel'. In fact, in the relevant
passages the noun is used neither in the Hebrew original
nor in the Greek translation, and this is because nowhere in the Old Testament is the future action of God
named 'the gospel'. It is rather the witness of men to
the action of God which is described by the verb 'to
announce good tidings'. To Mark, however, Jesus both
announces the good news and is himself the good news.
Hence Mark portrays him throughout as bearing witness
to himself, not merely in his teaching, but even, and
indeed primarily, by his actions. The interest of the
narrative is fixed upon the question whether men and
women will recognize in Jesus the gospel of God, and
will accept the witness which he bears to himself.

Mark therefore places a considerable strain upon the
word 'gospel'. In fact, the word is obscure as he uses it.
It is this obscurity which both the editors tend to remove.
They rivet the word 'gospel' to the teaching of Jesus
concerning the nature of the kingdom or rule of God,
and consequently Luke, approximating more closely to
Old Testament usage, employs throughout the verb and
not the noun, while Matthew qualifies the noun with

the addition of the genitive—'of the kingdom'. Jesus proclaims, rather than is, the gospel.

Matthew speaks three times of the gospel of the kingdom. Twice it appears in a set formula which summarizes and replaces Mark's detailed description of main episodes in the ministry of Jesus: 'And Jesus went about all Galilee, teaching in their synagogues, and preaching the gospel of the kingdom, and healing all manner of sickness and all manner of disease among the people.' Once it appears with reference to the end: 'And this gospel of the kingdom shall be preached in all the world for a witness unto all nations: and then shall the end come.' This is an emendation of the Marcan 'And the gospel must first be preached unto all the nations'. It would seem therefore, that for Matthew the gospel is before anything else 'good tidings of the kingdom'. *Mt. iv. 23, and ix. 35.* *Mt. xxiv. 14.* *Mk. xiii. 10.*

Luke uses not the noun, but the verb. Twice he speaks of 'gospelling' the kingdom of God: once when he changes the Marcan 'Let us go elsewhere into the next towns, that I may preach there also' into 'I must gospel the kingdom of God to the other cities also', and once when he gives a saying curiously paralleled in Matthew: 'The law and the prophets were until John: since that time the kingdom of God is gospelled.' In two other cases he substitutes 'gospelling' for the Marcan 'preaching' or 'teaching'. His conception of 'gospelling' seems therefore more like that of Matthew than that of Mark, since the word describes the characteristic feature of the teaching of Jesus. Consequently, he uses the word in Acts, not only for the preaching of Jesus, but also for the continuation of his teaching by his apostles and disciples. The word then describes the witness which is borne to the action of God in which Old Testament hope is fulfilled. *Mk. i. 38.* *Lk. iv. 43.* *Lk. xvi. 16. cf. Mt. xi. 12. Lk. ix. 6, and xx. 1. cf. Mk. vi. 13 and xi. 27.* *e.g. Act xiv. 7.*

Both Matthew and Luke, then, emphasize the fact that Jesus was a teacher. For this purpose both of them incorporate into the Marcan narrative massive material illustrating his teaching, and simplify the Marcan usage of the word 'gospel' making it refer only to the teaching of Jesus.

A serious problem now arises. Is it possible to describe this particular editorial process as 'heightening the Christology'? Is not the reverse nearer the truth? Would it not be possible to say that it is in the Matthaean and Lucan gospels, especially if the Marcan material be removed, that there emerges the picture of Jesus as a teacher of righteousness, as a man who disclosed to men the outline of the moral life as God wills it, and who died rather than compromise the truth as he saw it? Such a conclusion could be reinforced by the fact that on the whole Matthew and Luke do not introduce into their accounts of the ministry additional miraculous narratives. They are content to reproduce the Marcan miracles—abbreviating them radically—and to add to them, presumably because it stood in their non-Marcan *Lk. vii. 1-10.* common source, the story of the healing of the cen- *Mt. viii. 5-13.* turion's servant or son (the meaning of the word used *Lk. vii. 11-17.* by Matthew varies). The Lucan account of the raising from the dead of the young man at Nain is not an illustration of a general tendency, it is an exception, *Lk. vii. 22.* which has a peculiar explanation. Luke wishes to support the saying that he is about to record containing the statement that 'the dead are raised up'; he therefore introduces this particular episode in order to justify it.

Were Matthew and Luke justified in making these drastic changes in the Marcan narrative? In so doing, did they distort the picture of the Jesus of history, by making him more of a teacher than either the Marcan gospel or the actual history warranted? Did they subtly alter the Marcan perspective: and is their handling of the word 'gospel' a significant illustration of this subtle alteration? Can this united emphasis upon Jesus as a teacher of righteousness be justified? What kind of a teacher and what kind of righteousness are they imposing upon the Marcan narrative?

When Matthew introduced the sermon on the mount

into his gospel, he made no arbitrary interpolation. He carried out a very definite plan. The sermon ends with a formula, which reappears four times in his gospel, at the end of four great discourses. But each of these discourses is introduced at a point where the Marcan material requires some such teaching. Each of the discourses contains a certain amount of Marcan material, a greater amount of material taken from the common source, and a certain amount of special Matthaean material. All five discourses are conglomerations, but conglomerations of such high workmanship that they have both unity and clarity. And this is of importance. For it means that the reader can turn up and see clearly and at once what Jesus said about offences, or about the end of the world, or what were his directions to his disciples. Again, Matthew made these additions to the Marcan narrative because he had access to a great deal of non-Marcan tradition concerning Jesus, which contained not merely illustrations of the teaching of Jesus, but precisely those illustrations which were necessary to make sense of what Mark had written.

*Mt. vii. 28.*
*Mt. xi. 1;*
*xiii. 53; xix. 1;*
*xxvi. 1.*

Further, Matthew did not create the picture of Jesus teaching by means of connected discourses. The source which he used side by side with Mark already contained discourses. This is clear from a comparison of Matthew's sermon on the mount with Luke's sermon on the plain. The skeleton of the discourse is common to Matthew and Luke, and was therefore contained in their common source.

*Mt. v-vii;*
*Lk. vi. 17-49.*

The emphasis which Matthew lays upon Jesus as teacher is therefore in no sense arbitrary. Matthew had before him in his non-Marcan sources a mass of sayings of Jesus and the framework of a sermon. Matthew was therefore wholly justified in giving great weight to the picture of Jesus teaching. He was justified by the Marcan gospel, and he was more than justified by the non-Marcan material to which he had access, and which enabled him to supplement the inadequate illustrations of the teaching of Jesus contained in the Marcan gospel.

The purpose of Luke was identical with that of Matthew, though his method of introducing the material from the common source and from his own special material was different. He also was able to do this because his oral and written sources provided him with what he required.

Matthew and Luke were equally justified in concentrating this teaching upon the theme of the kingdom of God. Whereas Mark had used the phrase fourteen times, Luke uses it more than thirty times, and Matthew even more frequently.[1] Five of the Lucan occurrences are found to be changes of the Marcan material. Thus *Mk. x. 29.* where Mark has 'for my sake and the gospel's', Luke *Lk. xviii. 29.* has, 'for the kingdom of God's sake'; where Mark *Mk. xiii. 29.* writes, 'when ye see these things coming to pass, know ye that he is nigh, even at the doors', Luke has, *Lk. xxi. 31.* '. . . when ye see these things coming to pass, know ye that the kingdom of God is nigh'. Evidently both these changes were made for the sake of clarity. In the latter it is not quite certain who was meant by 'he':[2] in the former, 'for my sake and the gospel's' is a cumbersome expression. But they reveal a change of emphasis. Luke, like Matthew, thought of the gospel more naturally as a whole set of ideas connected with the kingdom of God, whereas Mark seems to have been occupied chiefly with the personal activity and authority of Jesus, and with the kingdom only because the rule of God was revealed in his concrete actions. Here was for Mark the sphere in which the active rule of God was bursting forth.

*Lk. iv. 43.* The other changes made by Luke show that he *(Mk. i. 38.)* thought of the activity of Jesus and of the twelve as

---

[1] Matthew nearly always paraphrases 'kingdom of God' in Semitic fashion: 'kingdom of heaven'.

[2] A.V. and R.V. Marg. translate by 'it', referring vaguely to the summer.

'preaching the kingdom of God and healing the sick', *Lk. ix. 2.*
just as Matthew was wont to summarize it as 'preaching *(Mk. vi. 7 f.)*
the gospel of the kingdom and healing all manner of *Lk. ix. 11.*
disease and all manner of sickness among the people'. *(Mk. vi. 34.)*
*Mt. ix. 35.*

But Matthew and Luke have very good ground for
emphasizing the kingdom of God as the theme of the
teaching of Jesus. Not only did it stand in Mark, it
stood also in their common source, where stood the injunction to the disciples to 'heal the sick' and to say *Mt. x. 7 f.;*
'The kingdom of heaven is upon you'. Indeed, the *Lk. x. 9.*
theme of the kingdom permeated the material which
they introduced from their non-Marcan sources.

The differences between the Matthaean and Lucan
gospels and the Marcan gospel can therefore be quite
precisely explained. They are due first of all to a knowledge of material other than the Marcan gospel. The
editors are wholly unconscious that the introduction of
this other material involved any alteration in the Marcan picture of Jesus. They expanded and supplemented
rather than corrected, since at each point they were
merely amplifying and illustrating something already
present in the Marcan gospel. Secondly, their procedure is occasioned by the fact that the Marcan gospel
is in detail and in general an obscure and difficult
document, especially for Greek readers unfamiliar with
Jewish idiom, and consequently unable to detect that
subtle background of scriptural allusion which provided the essential context of the earlier tradition about
Jesus. The changes and corrections which the editors
made and the manner in which they added their non-
Marcan material were an attempt to achieve greater
clarity and better arrangement, to simplify the material
and above all to make more obvious the allusions to the
Old Testament. In particular Matthew compiled his
material with the greatest regard for order. He presented the teaching of Jesus in five great discourses,
which clearly demonstrated the contrast between his
teaching and the teaching of the Jewish law, and

showed that the Old is superseded and fulfilled in the New. But in this process of compilation he was markedly guided by the tradition which lay behind him. The reader of his gospel is not disturbed, as the reader of Mark is, by odd little scraps of teaching or by odd isolated narratives of healing. Matthew sometimes collects, sometimes conflates—for example, he substitutes one healing of two blind men, for two separate healings of single blind men—and sometimes replaces a particular action by a generalized summary. This is not haphazard. He is concerned that his readers should have the tradition about Jesus in an accessible and ordered form, and he is even more concerned that they should understand the implications of the tradition for their own behaviour. He therefore, as in his record of the entry into Jerusalem, underlines the fulfilment of the Old Testament citation by quoting it, and even by adjusting the episode to the prophecy. But he is not introducing the Old Testament allusion, he is only making plain what in Mark would be quite unintelligible to Greek readers. At times we can almost see him struggling with a very awkward saying of Jesus, which is intelligible only when its Aramaic background is recognized. There was a saying in the common source, 'Blessed are ye poor', which when translated literally into Greek, becomes simply a crude approval of lack of money. So it stands in Luke. But Matthew knows that the Aramaic word, which underlies the Greek word translated 'poor', has other suggestions. It denotes those who are oppressed by the tyrannical power of evil and who long for the intervention of God. The poor are primarily the faithful men and women whose spirits are oppressed by the present order. Hence Matthew adds, and no doubt adds correctly, 'poor in spirit', in order to avoid misunderstanding. We may wonder whether the Greek readers did without further instruction understand the Matthaean gloss. But Matthew did his best to render into Greek a very intractable Jewish idiom.

*Mt. xx. 29-34;*
*Mk. viii. 22-26;*
*x. 46-52.*
*Mt. iv. 23;*
*Mk. i. 23-25.*

*Mt. v. 3;*
*Lk. vi. 20.*

94

Luke has a far less massive sense of orderliness than Matthew. But he also sought clarity, better arrangement, and simplification. He preferred, where there was redundance in his sources, to omit radically rather than to conflate. When he put sayings together, he was far less meticulous than Matthew about the aptness of the sequence. A single word in common was sufficient *e.g.* to attract together widely disparate material, and he *Lk. xvi. 9-13;* could conclude an episode with a series of crisp sayings, *14-8.* the precise relevance of which is extremely difficult to discover. Luke also emphasized the Old Testament background by his quite amazing power of writing Greek so that it evokes the memory of the Greek version of the Old Testament. But he displayed no such understanding of the meaning of the rough material as did Matthew. Not only did he omit crudely Hebraic passages, but it is in his, rather than in Matthew's, editing that the rough material is smoothed out so that it becomes more easily intelligible to Greek readers and also less liable to shock their sensibilities. His parables are illustrations of goodness rather than difficult stories requiring explanation. Luke does not really interpret the awkward material behind him, he simplifies it. The result is that those passages which Luke has rewritten, rather than merely edited, provide the modern reader with his best illustrations of a general humanitarianism, uncomplicated by a peculiarly awkward Jewish background. Luke, of course, did not intend to give this humanitarian impression, but he was a Greek who possessed a sense for the dramatic and for what is moving, and was capable of giving this literary form. The important critical conclusion is that this is a simplification of the tradition behind Luke. The original material is far rougher than Luke at times allows us to perceive, and it is an almost intolerable critical procedure to fix upon this editorial simplification, and to announce that there we have the Jesus of history, which modern criticism has unearthed. In fact, the simplification is secondary and Lucan, and is the product of Luke's inability to struggle, as Matthew did, with the rough Jewish material behind him. There are, however, points in the Lucan writings at which this roughness is *Lk. xviii. 1-8.* not only preserved but recognized, as, for instance, in *Act. xvii. 31;* the parable of the Importunate Widow, and in the *cf. xx. 28.* conclusion of St. Paul's speech at Athens.[1]

Orderliness, explanation, simplification, illustration, are the characteristic marks of Matthaean and Lucan editing.

The supreme question now arises. Did Matthew and Luke distort by this procedure the Marcan picture of the ministry? Did they alter the Marcan perspective and is their handling of the word 'gospel' an illustration of such alteration? In the end did they misunderstand Mark, and substitute a teacher who announced and described the imminent action of God in place of the Christ of Mark, whose life, death, and resurrection *was* the action of God, the fulfilment of prophecy, and the ground of human salvation?

These questions have only to be formulated to be answered. The editors may have simplified Mark in detail, and at times may have misunderstood the significance of this or that passage. But their emphasis upon the teaching of Jesus does not for one moment lead them to present him merely as a teacher or merely as a prophet, who like the teachers and prophets in the Old Testament announced an inevitable and imminent intervention of the living God. It is not the conception of Jesus as a teacher which leads them to represent him as one. The teaching of Jesus is for Matthew and for Luke, as for Mark, a necessary aspect of his messianic activity.

*Mt. v.* When Matthew portrays Jesus standing on the mountain, demanding with the authoritative 'But I say unto you' the immediate fulfilment of the law of God, and

---

[1] In St. Paul's speech to the heathen at Lystra (Acts xiv. 15-17) the challenge which concludes the speech at Athens is significantly omitted.

illustrating in detail precisely how it must now be fulfilled, the reader is not confronted with a teacher outlining certain new ideas or setting forth some new ideal for human life. The reader is confronted with the messiah who demands the complete fulfilment of the law of God, and who once stood in the midst of Palestine and called men to himself. Not for one moment does Matthew intend to detach the teaching of Jesus from his actions. When he summarizes his ministry he refers always to the interweaving of teaching and authoritative healing as characteristic of it. Nor is it otherwise with Luke. He most carefully introduces the ministry as the fulfilment, not of one single aspect of the hope of the prophet Isaiah, namely the announcing of good news, but of the whole panorama of God's *Lk. iv. 18.* awaited salvation. The actions and teaching of Jesus are presented as the place where the salvation of God is manifested in human life. Nor again do either of the editors suggest that the crucifixion was merely the murder of a prophet or of a teacher. Luke with great care marks the death as the culmination of the ministry, for he adds to the Marcan account of the transfiguration a note that Moses and Elijah conversed with Jesus 'of his decease which he should accomplish at Jerusalem'. *Lk. ix. 31.* In describing the events that led to the death of Jesus, Luke, like Mark, shows that the initiative lay with Jesus rather than with the Jews, as when he presses home in the narrative of the walk to Emmaus the divine neces- *Lk. xxiv. 26 f.* sity of that death, necessity, that is, according to the scriptures; when he thrusts into the story of the last supper a collection of sayings reversing natural human *Lk. xxii. 24-* conceptions of greatness and clearly directing the *30.* reader's attention to the greatness which is to be revealed in the crucifixion of the messiah; when he ends the words of Jesus with an open avowal that his death is the fulfilment of Isaiah's prophecy of the suffering servant: 'For I say unto you that this which is written *Lk. xxii. 37.* must be fulfilled in me, And he was reckoned with the transgressors'; and finally, when he places in St. Paul's mouth the well-known words to the elders of the Church

*Acts. xx. 28.* at Ephesus, commanding them to 'feed the church of the Lord, which he purchased with his own blood'. Nor is it otherwise with Matthew. He preserves the structure of the Marcan gospel with its steady movement towards the crucifixion as the climax of the ministry. Like Mark, he records the words spoken to the disciples in the upper room in which Jesus declares his death to be the foundation of the new covenant between God and man; and

*Mk. xiv. 24.* he glosses the words 'This is my blood of the covenant which is shed for many' with the explanatory addition

*Mt. xxvi. 28.* 'unto remission of sins', thus making the death of Jesus the ground of redemption.

When the teaching of Jesus is read in the whole context of their gospels it is plain that for Matthew and Luke as for Mark the kingdom of God is manifested in the whole ministry of Jesus, and that for them as for Mark it is the fulfilment of the hope of the prophets of Israel.

That they quite consciously intend this is finally proved by the fact that both editors preface their narratives by recording the miraculous birth of Jesus, and by recording it, not as an isolated miracle which compels belief simply because it is a miracle, but as the fulfilment of Old Testament prophecy. They record the birth of the messiah, and they emphasize his birth as the inauguration of the new order of salvation for men, not as the birth of a prophet or teacher. Concerning the origin of the belief in the virgin birth the critical historian can say nothing. The two editors agree only in

*Is. vii. 14.* recording the birth of Jesus as the fulfilment of a par-

*Mt. i. 23.* ticular prophecy. Otherwise their infancy narratives

*Lk. i. 26-32.* have no points of contact. This single point of agreement proves only that neither evangelist was responsible for originating the belief. Mark had no birth narrative, and the Jesus of the Marcan gospel remains to its readers an enigma. He appears suddenly bringing the salvation of God, and, more than that, he is salvation, since everything, even eternal life, depends upon whether men do or do not accept him, believe in him, surrender to him, and take up the cross and follow him. He does what in the Old Testament is attributed to God alone. But Mark does not explain why one who seems to be a mere man should act and speak with ultimate divine authority. Matthew and Luke adopt the virgin birth into their narratives in order to make the Marcan gospel less enigmatic. Whether they were historically justified in so doing no critic can say, because it is impossible to know what was the form of the tradition before Matthew and Luke edited it and expanded it, and therefore impossible to discover on what authority they introduced it into their narratives. It is possible to say, and, indeed, quite emphatically, that there is here no heightening of the picture of Jesus which already stood before them in the Marcan gospel.

The recognition that Matthew and Luke introduced the story of the virgin birth into their gospels in order to explain the authority of Jesus, may lead to a misunderstanding on the part of the reader, since, once it is presented to him, it is possible for him to concentrate attention on the miracle, isolate it, and then find in it the revelation of the power of the living God. Matthew and Luke did not here misunderstand Mark, nor for one moment did they intend their readers to see in the virgin birth the fulfilment of the hope of the prophets. The fulfilment is to be found in the ministry of Jesus, not in his miraculous birth.

There is, however, misunderstanding to be detected in the Matthaean-Lucan editing of Mark. In the Marcan gospel Jesus is isolated and wholly misunderstood, not only by the crowds and by the Jewish authorities, but also by his family or kindred, and by his chosen disciples. In Mark this is of vital importance because it is precisely in this complete humiliation and isolation that the revelation of God takes place. The salvation of men is wrought out as an *opus operatum* by Jesus in complete isolation. The gulf which separates Jesus from the Jews is hardly greater than the gulf which separates him from his disciples. Both the editors are unable to preserve this isolation with the consistent rigour of Mark. To them this terrible misunderstanding seems derogatory to the apostles, to the family of Jesus, and even to Jesus himself.

*Mk. vi. 4.* 'A prophet', records Mark, 'is not without honour, but in his own country, and among his own kin, and in his own house.' In editing this passage Matthew *Mt. xiii. 57.* writes: 'A prophet is not without honour, save in his own country, and in his own house.' And in a parallel *Lk. iv. 24.* passage Luke writes: 'No prophet is acceptable in his own country.' In neither of these cases are the 'kin' of Jesus mentioned, and it is difficult to resist the conclusion that this is an editorial omission. Mark goes on to say:

*Mk. vi. 5.* 'And he could do there no mighty work, save that he laid his hands upon a few sick folk, and healed them. And he marvelled because of their unbelief.'

Matthew changes this statement, which might suggest that Jesus' power was conditioned by the belief of his audience, substituting 'And he did not many mighty works there because of their unbelief' which leaves the initiative definitely with Jesus. In his account of the incident Luke cuts the gordian knot by altogether omitting any mention of works of healing in Nazareth and, indeed, records that the hostility of his countrymen was so fierce that Jesus was deprived of the opportunity of doing any charitable work there at all! But, in effect, like Matthew, he removes the uncomfortable suggestion of the Marcan narrative.

In neither of these cases, however, does Mark mean to suggest anything derogatory to Jesus, or to depreciate his power. Neither of these generalizations lies outside the perspective of the Marcan narrative. The first is an *a fortiori* argument. If the prophetic emissaries of God were misunderstood among their own people, an even greater misunderstanding awaits the Christ, the Beloved Son of God. This argument is paralleled in the parable of the Wicked Husbandmen. In the second passage Mark does not in fact lapse into the representation of Jesus as a mere faith-healer. The work of the messiah is to evoke faith, and the great work which results from faith and discipleship is the gift of eternal life. Throughout the Marcan narrative any instinctive movement towards Jesus, however inadequate, is rewarded by a great display of messianic power. In Nazareth, however, there is no motion of faith, and consequently no signal messianic action. The editors, misunderstanding Mark's meaning, or thinking it to be capable of misunderstanding, change the Marcan words; but the result is not to heighten the power of Jesus. The result is rather to obscure the very precise emphasis upon the nature of his power which is characteristic of Mark's narrative.

Two other illustrations of Matthew's so-called 'heightening of the Christology' are offered in most modern critical studies of the gospels. The first occurs in the Matthaean account of the baptism, where he interpolates into the Marcan narrative a conversation between the Baptist and Jesus, the purpose of which is to show that John recognized him as the sinless messiah, for whom no baptism for the remission of sins could conceivably be necessary. But Mark had not intended to suggest that Jesus was a sinner like other men, that he was purged by baptism, and received a prophetic call after his purging. He simply recorded that Jesus came to John in the midst of the crowds as the unrecognized messiah, the Son of God, the Beloved, and that with his coming the ministry of God's salvation was inaugurated amongst the people whom John had prepared to meet him. No doubt the Marcan narrative is open to misunderstanding by those who fail to catch the

*Mk. xii. 1-12; cf. Mk. x. 28-30.*

*e.g.*
*Mk. x. 46-52.*

*Mt. iii. 14 f.*

Old Testament allusions in his account; but no heightening of the Marcan picture of Jesus is really possible. Matthew has attempted to remove this possible misunderstanding, but at the cost of introducing the recognition of Jesus by John, and thus damaging his complete isolation, one of the most characteristic features of Mark's gospel.

The second illustration is provided by the Matthaean alteration of the Marcan introduction to the story of the rich man who loses eternal life by his refusal to surrender his wealth and follow Jesus. Mark wrote that *Mk. x. 17 f.* the man thus addressed him: 'Good Master, what shall I do that I may inherit eternal life?' Jesus picks out his casual use of the adjective 'good' and asks him: 'Why callest thou me good? None is good save one, even God.' *Lk. xviii. 18 f.* Luke leaves the Marcan passage almost unaltered; but *Mt. xix. 16 f.* Matthew removes, or tries to remove, any possible implication that the adjective 'good' was inapplicable to Jesus and rephrases both question and answer: 'Master, what good thing shall I do, that I may have eternal life?' and the answer runs: 'Why askest thou me concerning that which is good? One there is who is good.' Matthew is certainly struggling to remove a ground of misunderstanding. But he is not transforming an imperfect man Jesus into the sinless Christ. Can it be seriously maintained that Mark regards the epithet 'good' as inapplicable to Jesus? To do so would make complete nonsense of the Marcan gospel. Jesus, according to Mark, is the messiah in whom the righteousness of God is concretely present in the midst of Israel. The question merely tests the sincerity and intelligence of the man's address, 'Good Master', and the rest of the story shows how little his words really meant, since he refused to obey the call of Jesus, and consequently lost eternal life. Here again there can be no possible heightening of Mark's picture of Jesus of Nazareth. Matthew has only attempted to remove the possibility of a very unintelligent reading of the story, and in so doing has made it more difficult to understand the episode correctly.

What then in the end are the results of an investigation of the Matthaean-Lucan editing of Mark? The editing is occasioned by the difficulties of the Marcan narrative. The authors of the two later gospels are concerned for their Greek readers. They add, in order to make clear what Jesus demands of his disciples. They simplify, in order to avoid crude misunderstanding. They omit what appears to be trivial and unnecessary. They order and arrange the tradition, in order that it may be the more easily read in public or in private, and they improve the grammar and style, in order that their intelligent readers may not be unreasonably provoked. They attempt to answer gross attacks made by the Jews against the truths upon which the gospel of the church is grounded. They remove the pitiless Marcan insistence that the apostles to the end of the earthly life and death of Jesus hopelessly misunderstood the meaning of his words and actions; and they throw back into the period of the ministry the faith of the apostles which in fact emerged as the result of the resurrection. But in the whole of this process of editing they nowhere heighten Mark's tremendous conception of Jesus. No deifying of a prophet or of a mere preacher of righteousness can be detected. They do not introduce hellenistic superstitions or submerge in the light of later Christian faith the lineaments of Mark's picture of Jesus. They attempt to simplify Mark. He is more difficult to understand than they are. In fact, it is quite impossible to set Luke against Matthew or Matthew against Luke, or both of them against Mark. All three evangelists record the intervention of the living God in the heart of Judaism at a particular period of history in the words and actions and death of Jesus of Nazareth: all three describe this intervention in the context of Old Testament prophecy: and all three regard these happenings as one great act of God by which his rule is inaugurated on earth, and as a result of which those who believe are enabled to do the will of God, are freed from the powers of evil, are forgiven their sins, and are given a confident hope that they will share in that life which belongs to the era that is to be.

But this does not necessarily mean that the historian has discovered the Jesus of history. It only means that he is thrown back on a more thorough investigation of the Marcan document, on the material which Luke and Matthew have in common, and on those traditions, concerning Jesus, which we know only from Luke or only from Matthew. Is it possible to go behind the Marcan narrative? If not, may it not at any rate be possible to find a contradiction between Mark and the non-Marcan material to which the editors had access? After all, it may be Mark who has, under some influence or other, complicated the story of Jesus of Nazareth. If so, a comparison of Mark with the other strata of tradition ought to reveal the nature of the complication he introduced.

## NOTE

For an analysis of the meaning of the words εὐαγγελίζομαι, εὐαγγέλιον, προευαγγελίζομαι, εὐαγγελιστής, see the article in Kittel's *Theologisches Wörterbuch zum Neuen Testament*. The article is by Gerhard Friedrich, a pupil of Julius Schniewind whose immense work entitled *Euangelion* has been in course of publication since 1927. The conclusion of Dr. Friedrich's analysis of the meaning of the word εὐαγγέλιον in the synoptic gospels is as follows:

The question whether Jesus made use of the word εὐαγγέλιον or not is in the end the problem of his messiah consciousness. If he knew himself to be the Son of God who should die and rise again, then he also recognized that he was himself the subject matter of his disciples' preaching. His gospel is not a new doctrine: rather, he brings himself. His gospel is provided with content by what has been given in his person. Therefore, for his disciples, the gospel means the disclosing of the secret of the messiah.

Compare Gerhard Kittel, *Die Probleme des palsätinischen Spätjudentums und das Urchristentum*. Stuttgart, 1926, pp. 129-140.

## Chapter VII

## Mark

The author of the First Epistle General of Peter thought of Jesus in terms of the suffering servant of Isaiah's prophecy. Matthew and Luke describe him as Son of God born in miraculous fashion. These, and other similar titles, taken either from the Old Testament or from the New, conveniently sum up the several ways in which the messiahship and person of Jesus were regarded in various parts of the New Testament, and are styled 'Christologies'. Thus, by a 'Lamb of God Christology' is meant the interpretation of Jesus as victim in a supreme sacrifice, with all the Old Testament background which such language presumes; by a 'Son of David Christology' the interpretation of him as messianic king of the Davidic line. So, when the author of the fourth Gospel records that John the Baptist declared Jesus to be the Lamb of God, and subsequently *Jn. i. 29, 36;* elucidates this statement in his narrative of the passion, *xix. 33-36.* a 'Lamb of God Christology' is indicated; and when blind Bartimaeus is healed in response to the cry, 'Son *Mk. x. 46-52.* of David, have mercy upon me', the incident reflects a 'Son of David Christology'. When such distinctive Christologies appear in the various strata of tradition it may be found that they are attached loosely to it, and, consequently, are capable of isolation. In which case it may be possible even to date their emergence in the primitive church.

The result of the attempt to discover and to analyse the editorial tendencies of Matthew and Luke has been to thrust the reader back upon the Marcan gospel. And he must have been led to suspect that Mark had written his gospel with a quite definite Christological purpose, and to suspect also that his purpose may not only have coloured his gospel, but have caused him to manipulate the tradition drastically in order that it might conform to his peculiar Christology. This inevitable suspicion must now be justified or discarded, and this is possible since we are by no means at his mercy. By a comparison of Mark with the other three blocks of material—that which is common to Matthew and Luke; that which Luke alone used; and that which Matthew alone used— it should be possible to discover whether there is a Christology which is characteristically Marcan; whether, that is, the Marcan interpretation is, so far as we can judge, merely one among many primitive Christian interpretations of a simple original history.

If the impression of the Marcan gospel given in Chapter IV is justified, it is clear that Mark states his thesis in his first words: The gospel of Jesus Christ. Since, however, at great moments in his narrative the title Christ is glossed and defined by Son of God, it is evident that the gospel as a whole represents a Son of God Christology. In order to estimate editorial tendency on Mark's part, the evidence for the existence of this Christology in the rest of the synoptic material must be examined.

The other strata at least contained the title, 'Son of God'. The source common to Matthew and Luke clearly had it, since both record the temptations of Jesus as *Mt. iv. 3, 6;* temptations of the Son of God—'If thou be the Son of *Lk. iv. 3, 9.* God . . .': and both have a saying of Jesus: 'No one *Mt. xi. 27;* knoweth the Son, save the Father, neither doth any *Lk. x. 22.* know the Father, save the Son, and he to whomsoever the Son willeth to reveal him.' But the fact that the same title is used does not make it certain that the Christology attaching to that title has not been developed in a peculiar direction by Mark. The Son of God might mean one who is miraculously Son in the sense that he was conceived as a result of such a miracle as is recorded

in the Matthaean and Lucan nativity stories: or it
might mean one who recognizes the fatherhood of God
in a unique but quite human way. Mark's Christology
will have to be examined more precisely before it can
be determined what is meant by Son of God in the
Marcan gospel, and whether this meaning is corro-
borated in the other synoptic material.

It has been said that the author of the Marcan gospel
was primarily concerned to prove that Jesus is the Son
of God. But, strangely enough, the term rarely occurs
in his gospel. Apart from the doubtful variant reading
in the first verse it is, in fact, used only seven times.
Twice it occurs in declarations from heaven. At his
baptism and at his transfiguration a voice proclaims his
Sonship: 'Thou art my beloved Son; in thee I am well *Mk. i. 11.*
pleased' 'This is my beloved Son: hear ye him.' Twice *Mk. ix. 7.*
the evil spirits recognize him thus: 'Thou art the Son of *Mk. iii. 11.*
God.'—'What have I to do with thee, Jesus, thou Son *Mk. v. 7.*
of the most high God?' Finally, the narrative of the
crucifixion concludes with the centurion's confession:
'Truly this man was Son of God.' *Mk. xv. 39.*

Guarded though the use of this term is, it is nevertheless manifestly important and its guardedness deliberate. The first half of this gospel contains only supernatural witnesses to Jesus as the Son of God. Twice he
is so named by God, twice by evil spirits. Men think
of him variously throughout his ministry, as madman,
fanatic, prophet, or messiah: but only in the depth of
his humiliation does one man venture to call him Son
of God. For some reason, although Mark presumes and
indeed insists that Jesus is in fact the Son of God, and
arranges his material so as to lead men to the conception of Jesus which the title expresses, he shows, apparently deliberately, that a true understanding of his
Sonship can be reached only through recognition of his
humiliation, completed in the crucifixion, and vindi-
cated by his raising from the dead. And it is in this context of humiliation that the analogy of Father and Son

Mk. xii. 6. is used, in the parable of the Wicked Husbandmen and
Mk. xiii. 32. in the saying that 'of that day and that hour knoweth no man, no, not the angels which are in heaven, neither the Son, but the Father.'

During the course of the ministry, Mark employs another title, which Jesus himself substitutes for Peter's
Mk. viii. 29-31. confession of faith: 'Thou art the Christ. And he charged them that they should tell no man of him. And he began to teach them, that the Son of man must suffer many things. . . .' In the Marcan gospel, Jesus uses the title 'Son of man' of himself fourteen times. Of these, the
Mk. ii. 10. first two are claims to authority: 'The Son of man hath
Mk. ii. 28. power on earth to forgive sins.'—'The Son of man is Lord also of the sabbath.' The remainder are prophetic. The title 'Son of man' is used in prophecies of the rejection, of the death and resurrection of Jesus, and finally in prophecies of his future coming in glory. Three times Mark reiterates in almost identical words that

Mk. viii. 31.      'The Son of man must suffer many things, and be rejected
Mk. ix. 31.   of the elders, and of the chief priests, and scribes, and be killed,
Mk. x. 33.    and after three days rise again.'

This rejection is interpreted as the fulfilment of Old
Mk. ix. 12. Testament prophecies: 'How is it written of the Son of man, that he should suffer many things and be set at
Mk. x. 45. nought?'—'For verily the Son of man came not to be ministered unto, but to minister, and to give his life a ransom for many.' As the passion approaches, the crucifixion is shown more and more clearly to be the fulfil-
Mk. xiv. 21. ment of these prophecies: 'The Son of man goeth, even as it is written of him: but woe unto that man through
Mk. xiv. 41. whom the Son of man is betrayed!'—'Behold, the Son of man is betrayed into the hands of sinners.' But in the midst of all this emphasis upon the rejection of the Son of man there is also an insistent emphasis, first upon his
Mk. ix. 9. resurrection from the dead, and secondly upon the necessity of his coming again in glory. This coming is also grounded upon Old Testament prophecy.

In the great Marcan discourse about the end of the age, Jesus declares: 'Then shall they see the Son of man coming in the clouds with great power and glory.' And when the high priest asks him whether he is the Christ, the Son of the Blessed, Jesus replies: 'I am: and ye shall see the Son of man sitting on the right hand of power, and coming in the clouds of heaven.' These sayings are a deliberate application of the passage in the book of Daniel which describes a glorious future coming on the clouds of heaven, and also contains the phrase 'son of man'. In Mark, however, the title has two different associations. First it is applied to Jesus in humiliation: then to his future coming in glory. These associations are not merely successive but interdependent. For

*Mk. xiii. 26*

*Mk. xiv. 62.*

*Dan. vii. 13.*

'Whosover therefore shall be ashamed of me and of my words in this adulterous and sinful generation; of him also shall the Son of man be ashamed, when he cometh in the glory of his Father with the holy angels.'

*Mk. viii. 38.*

But the coming in humiliation, that is, the ministry of Jesus, has already, according to Mark, introduced the kingdom. It is not by chance that Mark records that the head of Jesus was anointed by a nameless woman and was crowned by soldiers, or that a kingly title was nailed to his cross. The kingdom of heaven is like a grain of mustard seed sown upon the earth. In fact, it is paradoxically already present and yet still to come. So the intrusion of the action of God in the humiliation of the Son of man, and that faith in Jesus which carries with it a sure hope of eternal life, completely revise the old expectation of the last things. Here again Mark represents the life and death of Jesus as the scene of the action of God. This background of divine action is just as necessary for an understanding of the title 'Son of man' as it is for a right understanding of the title 'Son of God'. For, immediately after the proclamation of divine Sonship at the transfiguration, Mark records that

*Mk. xiv. 3.*
*Mk. xv. 17.*
*Mk. xv. 26.*
*Mk. iv. 31.*

'As they came down from the mountain, he charged them

*Mk. ix. 9.*

that they should tell no man what things they had seen, till the Son of man were risen from the dead.'

And when the high priest asked Jesus,

*Mk. xiv. 61 f.*  'Art thou the Christ, the Son of the Blessed?'

Jesus said,

'I am: and ye shall see the Son of man sitting on the right hand of power, and coming in the clouds of heaven.'

But this fastening of the Son of man Christology upon a necessary humiliation of the Son of God and upon his subsequent coming in glory upon the clouds, and this use of the title Son of man to hold together these two advents of the messiah which seem so characteristically Marcan, are found not only in the gospel of Mark. Matthew and Luke, it is true, did not leave the Marcan Son of man passages unchanged. They tried to make the *Mt. xvi. 16.* meaning clearer in the account of Peter's confession, *Lk. ix. 20.* and in the trial, by stating definitely that the Christ *is* *Mt. xxvi. 63.* the Son of God. They kept the title 'Son of man', but *Lk. xxii. 70.* were evidently not at ease with it; yet, nevertheless, they were compelled to incorporate Son of man sayings into their gospels, not only because they stood in Mark, but also because they stood in their common source and in their special material. The common source contained at least six sayings about the Son of man, which fall into precisely the two divisions of the Marcan sayings. Two are prophetic of the future coming:

*Mt. xxiv. 26 f.;* 'Wherefore if they shall say unto you, Behold, he is in the *cf. Lk. xvii,* desert; go not forth: behold, he is in the secret chambers; believe *23 f.* it not. For as the lightning cometh out of the east, and shineth even unto the west; so shall also the coming of the Son of man *Mt. xxiv. 44;* be.'—'Therefore be ye also ready: for in such an hour as ye *cf. Lk. xii. 40.* think not the Son of man cometh.'

*Mt. viii. 20;* Three are connected with the rejection and humilia-
*cf. Lk. ix. 58.* tion. The Son of man has nowhere to lay his head. The
*Mt. xi. 16-19;* crowds reject the Son of man as a wine bibber, just as

they rejected John the Baptist as an ascetic. A word spoken against the Son of man is blasphemy, but blasphemy that can be forgiven. Finally, the Son of man, like Jonah, shall be a sign to this generation.[1]  *cf. Lk. vii. 31-34.*  *Mt. xii. 32; cf. Lk. xii. 10.*

The material preserved only in Matthew and only in Luke also contains Son of man passages. The special Matthaean material contains references to the sign of the Son of man appearing in heaven at the end, and also a further description of his coming in glory with his angels to sit upon his throne. It contains, moreover, the parable of the Tares, which emphasizes the identity of the man who sowed the good seed with the man who at the harvest orders his husbandmen to destroy the tares and to gather the wheat into his garners. Whether the subsequent interpretation that this man is the Son of man was originally in his source, or is the work of Matthew, the parable itself links together two successive and related actions by assigning them to the action of one person. Clearly these actions are the actions of the Christ. Moreover, since the action of sowing refers to Jesus himself, the harvesting must be his work also.  *Mt. xii. 38-44; cf. Lk. xi. 29-32.*  *Mt. xxiv. 30.*  *Mt. xxv. 31.*  *Mt. xiii. 24-30.*  *Mt. xiii. 36-43.*

The special Lucan material contains references to 'one of the days of the Son of man', that is, to one of the last days, 'which men shall long to see'; it contains also a description of the final revelation of the 'day of the Son of man', and a question whether 'at his coming he shall find faith upon earth'; and finally it refers to the earthly life of Jesus as a coming of the Son of man in a statement that 'The Son of man came to seek and to save that which was lost'.  *Lk. xvii. 22.*  *Lk. xvii. 30.*  *Lk. xviii. 8.*  *Lk. xix. 10.*

A conclusion from this comparison of Mark with the other strata of tradition is now inevitable. The very remarkable 'Son of man' Christology is not a creation

---

[1] Matthew states that by the sign of Jonah is meant the three days in which Jesus lay buried like Jonah in the belly of the whale. Luke also can hardly refer primarily to Jonah's preaching, for he uses the future '*shall be a sign*', when Jesus was already preaching.

of Mark, and is not the result of his manipulation of the tradition. The whole tradition concerning Jesus, as it is presented by a critical separation of sources, emphasizes two comings, the first in humiliation, and the second in glory. These are held together by the application of the title 'Son of man' to Jesus himself. Mark seems, it is true, to have emphasized the humiliation of the first coming deliberately. Son of God he believed Jesus to be; Son of God he was known by God to be; and as Son of God the evil spirits recognized his authority. But, throughout his ministry and passion, this must not, and indeed cannot, be disclosed in a setting of unbelief. The evil spirits are bidden to be silent and the disciples to say nothing of what they have seen. But there is not the slightest ground for supposing that Mark had no justification for concentrating so emphatically upon Jesus as the humiliated Son of man, or that he had no justification for displaying his divine Sonship through and in this humiliation.

It is now possible to estimate the significance of the 'Son of God' Christology in Mark. The Sonship did not merely consist in a recognition of God as Father. Nor did the evil spirits call him Son of God because his powerful acts could only be attributed to a supernatural figure, for there is no reason to suppose that Mark, *Mt. xii. 27;* any more than Matthew or Luke, regarded the casting *Lk. xi. 19.* out of a devil as a unique event. The spirits see through the flesh and blood figure, that is, through Jesus as Son of man, to Jesus as Son of God. Mark implies that true disciples of Jesus must possess a similar insight, and insists that they, unlike the evil spirits, must take up their cross and follow him in his humiliation. The coming in glory is the coming in his unveiled power and authority. But this second coming lies wholly in the future. The Marcan Christology clearly means that in Jesus the rule of God did break into this world from the other. The Son of man has power *on earth*. The kingdom of God *is* upon you. The bridegroom *is* present.

In spite of the fact that most of the non-Marcan synoptic material is concerned with parables and sayings, the same sequence of ideas appears there also. In the material peculiar to Matthew, Jesus demands the complete fulfilment of the old law with a self-consciousness that is tolerable only when it is recognized that the authority with which he speaks is the same authority which gave the Jewish law its form and substance. In the material peculiar to Luke, Jesus, with the same apparent egoism, declares: 'To-day hath this scripture been fulfilled in your ears.' And in the common source not only does he answer John's question about his messiahship by appealing to his actions as the fulfilment of scripture, 'And blessed is he that is not scandalized by me', but also he declares the kingdom to have 'come upon them' 'if I by the finger of God (or Spirit of God) cast out devils'. Luke quotes from his special source the saying: 'Behold, the kingdom of God is in your midst.' Jesus expounds the Mosaic law and with the same authority expels the evil spirits. It is precisely this authority which he claims when he says, according to the common source of Matthew and Luke: 'All things have been given to me by my Father.' And so in the non-Marcan as in the Marcan material the words and actions of Jesus are portrayed as the incursion of the authority of God into the affairs of men.

*Mt. v. 22, 28, 34, 39, 44.*

*Lk. iv. 21.*

*Mt. xi. 4 ff.; cf. Lk. vii. 22 f. Mt. xii. 28; cf. Lk. xi. 20. Lk. xvii. 21.*

*Mt. xi. 27. Lk. x. 22.*

Not only in Mark is Jesus depicted as the humiliated Son of man. Not only in Mark is this humiliation shot through with the glory of a future coming in visible authority and power. Not only in Mark is the power of Jesus and the kingdom which he inaugurates a breaking in of that which is beyond historical investigation. This fascinating and terrifying Christology is found imbedded in the material which lies behind the editors, Matthew and Luke. Throughout the whole synoptic material Jesus is called 'Son of God'. Neither this title, then, nor the Christology attached to it, can be attributed to a tendency of Mark. That there is a tendency based upon it in his gospel is true. He, like Matthew and Luke in other ways, makes the paradoxical material of the tradition clearer for his readers. He emphasizes by careful arrangement the necessary humiliation of the Son of God. But the Marcan arrangement and the Marcan emphasis are evoked by the material which the evangelist has received. 'I came to bring fire to the earth; and what will I if it is already kindled?[1] But I have a baptism to be baptized with; and how am I straitened till it be accomplished!' This saying, found in Luke alone, is neither more nor less than that gospel which Mark has declared in the careful structure of his narrative.

*Lk. xii. 49, 50.*

Thus the attempt to throw upon the evangelists the responsibility of having manipulated the earlier tradition in the interests of a remarkable Christology does not survive a rigidly critical examination. The interpretation put upon the actions and life and death of Jesus did not originate in the minds of the men who compiled the gospels in their present form. Their records have a clear and conscious purpose. That is obvious. But they extracted their purpose from the traditions they received: they did not impose it roughly upon a material unable to bear it. Their editing did not complicate the material, but simplified it. For the clearing away of obscurities—whether of language, of style, of meaning, or even of Christological significance—was everywhere an attempt to clarify the issues found in the tradition which lay before them.

Two conclusions, therefore, may be drawn with some confidence. In the first place, the difficult Christology which holds together the whole fabric of the tradition is not imposed by any of the evangelists, not even by Mark. The difficult Christology is lying in the various strata of material which they handled, and not only lies there, but controls it. The history of Jesus of

[1] Moffatt translates, surely rightly, 'would it were kindled already!'

Nazareth was already a highly interpreted history, interpreted through the medium of the Old Testament.
Moreover, in the material, the actual history was conditioned by the interpretation. Jesus acted as he did
act and said what he did say because he was consciously
fulfilling a necessity imposed upon him by God through
the demands of the Old Testament. He died in Jerusalem, not because the Jews hounded him thither and did
him to death, but because he was persuaded that, as
messiah, he must journey to Jerusalem in order to be
rejected and to die. This violent and voluntary death
is the *opus operatum* which inaugurates the new order.
Neither Mark, nor Luke, nor Matthew, is interpreting
a mere series of facts: still less are they imposing a
Christology upon an undefined human personality. The
interpretation is given them in the material which comes
to them from various sources, and it is the same interpretation which is being presented to them throughout.
The Christological, Old Testament interpretation is
lying in the history of Jesus of Nazareth in so far as they
know the tradition.

Secondly, so difficult is this Christology that it cannot
remain static. The evangelists find it impossible merely
to repeat it as it lies imbedded in the tradition. It requires elucidation and simplification. Mark inaugurates
this process of elucidation in the form of a gospel in
which the Christology is brought out more or less clearly.
But his gospel is still obscure, and the later evangelists
continue his work of clarification, which is completed,
as far as the New Testament is concerned, with the
writing of the fourth Gospel.

*Chapter VIII*

## Miracles, Parables, and Aphorisms

In the preceding chapter it has been shown that the various strata of tradition which are brought together in the synoptic gospels do not provide evidence of the presence in the primitive church of a number of different ideas about Jesus. The further the critic is able to dig into the tradition the more clearly is the Christology seen to be one single Christology expressed in terms of Son of man and Son of God. Jesus is the messiah who came in humiliation, and who in his humiliation inaugurated the kingdom of God and fulfilled the righteousness demanded by the law and the prophets. Jesus is also the messiah who will come in glory at the end of the present order, and will establish the final kingdom. Those who believe in the humiliated messiah, and share in his humiliation, will also share in his glory and in the eternal life of the kingdom. Not only is this Christology present in the various strata of the tradition, but the whole material is controlled by it. This last statement requires justification.

The material which composed the tradition may be separated into miracles, parables and aphoristic utterances. It must now be considered whether these elements are distinct elements, separable from and indeed actually independent of the Christology; and whether there is evidence that the Christology has been imposed upon or has been intruded into a material which existed originally in a non-Christological form. If it be found possible to separate the material from the Christology, the conclusion must almost inevitably follow that the Christology originated with the faith of the early

Christians, and not with Jesus himself. All that will have been proved is that this interpretation was imposed upon the ministry of Jesus at an earlier period in the history of Christian piety than the older critics have supposed.

## 1. Miracles

The gospels are largely occupied with the miraculous. The ministry of Jesus there consists of healing as well as teaching; his life is marvellous as well as exemplary. And therefore, however firmly the reader himself may believe or disbelieve the possibility of the events therein recorded; however predisposed he may be to see in miracles either an embroidery upon the simplicity of Jesus, or a main argument for his claims; he cannot, in obedience to some such predisposition, adopt or reject where and what he pleases. The fact that a miraculous element exists in the material must first be examined. This can be done only by estimating the significance which it bears in the material itself.

Matthew and Luke were not led to revise Mark through any craving for the miraculous. It was for the sake of clarifying and emphasizing the significance which they found attached by him to miracles that they modified his accounts. They did not create the marvellous for the sake of the marvellous. On the contrary, they show a tendency to edit or to omit stories of miraculous healing which they think unedifying or capable of misunderstanding. Neither, for instance, retained two very elaborate Marcan miracles, the healing of a deaf stammerer and the restoration of sight to a blind man. Yet these two miracles raise the whole problem of the place of the miraculous in the gospels. *Mk. vii. 31-37. Mk. viii. 22-26.*

These two miracles are recorded in such a manner as to present Jesus as a superstitious wonder-worker. He performs two cures with the use of saliva and certain manual acts. He spits upon the tongue of the stammerer, placing his fingers into his deaf ears; he spits upon the eyes of the blind man, and lays his hands upon him. Such a use of saliva was well known in antiquity. The *Tacitus, Hist. iv. 81.* Emperor Vespasian is said to have performed a cure by means of it at Alexandria. The Rabbis later denounced *Swete ad Mk. vii. 33.* the practice. Jesus is therefore represented by Mark as behaving in the common fashion of a wonder-worker. Moreover, the use of the hand or of the fingers, illustrated in these Marcan stories, appears elsewhere to be *Mk. i. 31; v.* curiously conventionalized. Three times the method of *41; ix. 27.* the cure consists in taking the sick person by the hand and raising him up. Matthew and Luke are as disturbed by this behaviour as they were by the use of saliva. In *Mk. i. 31;* the case of Peter's wife's mother, who, in the Marcan *Lk. iv. 39;* story was cured by this method, the one merely says *Mt. viii. 15.* that Jesus touched her hand, the other that he rebuked the fever. But if there is anything more than coincidence in the three Marcan instances of this form, they suggest, when coupled with the accounts of the placing of fingers into ears, and the touching of eyes, that he definitely acted as a wonder-worker and that the procedure of the editors shows their anxiety to be rid of this impression.

In the case of exorcism, the use of contemporary methods is even more pronounced. Twice Jesus, in rebuking evil, is recorded to have used an expression best *Mk. i. 25.* translated 'Be thou muzzled'. In the first case this might seem to be an injunction to silence, since the devils to whom it was spoken had been crying out that *Mk. iv. 39.* he was 'the Holy One of God'. But in the second case it is addressed to a storm. There is good evidence in contemporary documents to show that it was a common form used for binding a person by means of a spell so as to make him powerless for harm. Again, in the *Mk. v. 9.* exorcism of the demoniac of the tombs, Jesus cannot cast the devil out until he has learned his name. Knowledge of a name was commonly considered by the ancients to give power over its owner, and a formula for exorcism in the great Magical Papyrus of Paris leaves a space for the name of the devil who is to be cast out.

In spite of the relation between this picture and the behaviour of contemporary wonder-workers, Mark draws the attention of his readers, in fact, wholly elsewhere. It is clear, both from Mark and from the common source of Matthew and Luke, that in the tradition these miracles of healing and exorcism were presented as messianic miracles, that is, as miracles that fulfilled Old Testament prophecies of the messianic age. When, for instance, John inquires whether Jesus is 'he that should come', his messengers are bidden to tell him 'what they saw and heard'; and it is implied that they were seeing and hearing a number of things which clearly fulfilled the prophecies of Isaiah. A cleansed leper is sent, according to Mark, to show himself to the priest 'as a testimony to them'. Even the two Marcan miracles mentioned at the beginning of this discussion seem to be introduced into the Marcan narrative in order to point to the fulfilment of Old Testament prophecy. One is the cure of a blind man, who is taken aside privately, that is, away from the crowds: the other of a man who was deaf and stammered, and who was cured with the same privacy. The word 'stammerer' is in this case suggestive. It occurs only once in the New Testament, and only once in the Septuagint version of the Hebrew Old Testament, and there in this remarkable prophecy:

*Mt. xi. 2-6; Lk. vii. 19-23.*

*Mk. i. 44.*

*Mk. viii. 22-26.*

*Mk. vii. 31-37.*

'Be strong, ye relaxed hands and palsied knees. Comfort one another, ye faint-hearted. Be strong, fear not. Behold, our God renders judgement, and he will render it; he will come and save us. Then shall the eyes of the blind be opened, and the ears of the deaf shall hear. Then shall the lame man leap as an hart, and the tongue of the stammerer shall speak plainly.'

*Is. xxxv. 3-6.*

The similarity of these two miracles, and their congruence with this prophecy, show that the Marcan narrative depends for its understanding upon the detection of this Old Testament allusion. But it is not only these two miracles of healing which are narrated as the fulfilment of Old Testament prophecy.[1] The whole series of miraculous happenings recorded in Mark rests upon this background. For instance, the man with the *Mk. iii. 1-6.* withered hand, whose cure is related as a sign that the *Mk. ii. 3-12.* Son of man is lord also of the sabbath, and the sick of the palsy whose walking proves the reality of the forgiveness of his sins, declare the fulfilment of the same prophecy.

These last two miracles raise a further point. In both of them the physical cure is made the sign of a messianic claim: in one case a claim to be lord of the sabbath, the day of the Lord; in the other, to have power to forgive sins. In the opening chapters of Mark there is a clear alternation between actions of Jesus which manifest his authority in the physical world, and those which manifest it in the moral and spiritual sphere. This alternation *Mk. ii. 13-17.* reaches its height in the call of Levi. From the point of view of the miraculous it is an anticlimax, being merely a call to discipleship; but from the point of view of Mark's gospel it is a climax, led up to and guaranteed by the physical miracle which precedes it. The argument moves precisely as in the narrative of the man sick of the palsy: 'But, that ye may know. . . .' The physical miracles are external signs of the supreme messianic miracle, the rescue of men from the grip of the powers of evil—from sin. The supreme messianic miracle to which the miracles point is the salvation of men by the power of the living God exercised through the agency of the messiah.

So far this argument, and indeed, this whole conception, might well be the creation of Mark. But, if so, it has not only affected the narrative, but has created terse sayings of Jesus himself. For in this very context occurs

[1] Nor, of course, is prophecy of healing in the messianic age limited to Isaiah xxxv. Cf., e.g., Isaiah xxvi. 19; xxix. 18 f.; lxi. 1.

the saying, 'They that are whole have no need of a *Mk. ii. 17.*
physician, but they that are sick: I came not to call the
righteous, but sinners.' Therefore, the argument from
the physical to the spiritual miracle was either in the
tradition of the teaching which Mark received, or he
has boldly created a saying to substantiate it: in either
case it follows that the significance of the miracles cannot be examined apart from the significance of the
teaching attributed to Jesus. And this is abundantly
clear from other passages. The rebuking and muzzling
of evil which underlies the exorcisms and the restoring
of diseased men and women to their full physical health
points to a deeper healing which is more strictly messianic. All this is reinforced in a parable which stood both
in Mark and in the source common to Matthew and *Mk. iii. 22-*
Luke. When the scribes challenge the works of Jesus, *30.*
and maintain that he casts out devils by Beelzebul, the *Mt. xii. 23-31;*
prince of devils, Jesus answers by stating that a house *Lk. xi. 15-23.*
divided against itself cannot stand. He then plays with
the word Beelzebul, bringing out a meaning suggested
in Aramaic: Beelzebul—lord of the house, as, indeed,
the name is translated in Matthew x. 25. 'No man can *Mk. iii. 27.*
enter into a strong man's house, and spoil his goods,
except he will first bind the strong man; and then he
will spoil his house.' Clearly Jesus here declares himself
to be stronger than the devil, and consequently able to
deliver from his power the men and women whom he
has enslaved. But what else are the miracles of exorcism *cf.*
but a binding of the strong man of evil? And what are *Is. xlix. 24 ff.*
the miracles of restoration but a snatching away the *for the O.T.*
vessels from the strong man's house? *background.*

This conception of a world in the grip of evil into
which Jesus enters with divine and messianic authority
in order to save men and women therein enslaved, is
echoed in other parts of his teaching: 'If I by the finger *Lk. xi. 20;*
of God cast out devils, then is the kingdom of God *cf. Mt. xii. 28.*
come upon you.' So suitable is imagery of this kind,
that the ordinary human care of animals is itself a

parable of the necessity of caring for men and women
in their distress:

*Mt. xii. 11.*  'What man shall there be among you, that shall have one
sheep, and if it fall into a pit on the sabbath day, will he not
*Lk. xiv. 5.*  lay hold on it, and lift it out?'—'Which of you shall have an
ass or an ox fallen into a pit, and will not straightway pull him
out on the sabbath day?'

Why should Jesus, perhaps on more than one occasion, in giving an argument for healing summon up a
picture of seizing and raising an animal out of the hole
into which it has fallen? Can it be that there is a connexion between this argument and the thrice attested
seizing and raising of men and women fallen under the
spell of an evil disease? Further can it be that there is
also a connexion between this argument and the fre-
*e.g., atr andom,* quent pits and snares of evil in the psalms? And, whether
*Ps. xl. 2;* this is so or not, does the intimate contact of his hand,
*xxxv. 7;* his fingers, his spittle, point to something more than
*xxxi. 4; xxx. 3.* contemporary superstition? Is not this contact the
effective representation of the true messianic salvation
which is the lifting up of men through contact with the
messiah? Physically this salvation is manifested in the
working of miracles, but its final reality consists in that
discipleship which is demanded of Levi who is both
publican and sinner, of the man with great possessions,
and, in fact, of all those men and women whom he
called to himself. The representation is effective, because, like the alternation in the first chapters of Mark,
it displays in the sphere of physical disease the reality
of the spiritual and invisible power of God, and also
because physical healing is itself a real liberation from
the bondage of evil. But this alternation, like the alternation of storm and madness, is rooted in the Old
*Ps. cxlvii. 3.* Testament: '(The Lord) healeth the broken in heart,
and bindeth up their sorrows.' The very use of the hand
seems intended to fulfil the common metaphor there
*Ps. xxxvii. 24.* employed of the intervention of God: 'Though he fall,

he shall not be utterly cast down: for the Lord up-
holdeth him with his hand.' On such a background the
phrase so often quoted 'If I by the finger of God' becomes very suggestive. For it now appears that the
miracles, beyond any intrinsic value that they may
possess as wonders, have everywhere that double significance which has been found throughout the tradition
and the various editions of it. The primary importance
of the miracles is to portray the nature of Jesus and to
make manifest the long-awaited salvation of God.[1]

So far, this discussion has for the most part been concerned with what are usually called 'miracles of healing'. But the same significance underlies the great signs
which Jesus is supposed to have worked in the natural
as opposed to the human world, and which are usually
called 'nature miracles'. It has been seen that the
Stilling of the Storm supplies, in terms of Old Testa- *Mk. iv. 35-41.*
ment prophecy, an answer to the question, 'Who is this,
that the wind and the sea obey him?' and that this
question also introduces the transition, again present in
Old Testament metaphor, to the storms of the heart.
'Who stilleth the roaring of the seas, the roaring of their *Ps. lxv. 7.*
waves, and the tumult of the people.' Similarly, the
Walking on the Sea may have reference to the God who
alone, 'treadeth upon the high places (waves) of the *Job ix. 8; cf.*
sea'. The Feeding of the Five Thousand and of the *xxxviii. 16.*
Four Thousand, carefully set in each case 'in a desert *Mk. vi. 34-44;*
place', recall, first the miraculous feeding of the Israel- *viii. 1-9.*
ites in the desert, and then the constant expectation,
probably originally based upon it, of a great feast in the

[1] The same remarkable sequence of thought may be seen in
the relation between the collect and gospel for the third Sun-
day in Lent, where the words of the gospel 'If I with the finger
of God cast out devils, no doubt the kingdom of God is come
upon you' are applied in the collect: 'Stretch forth the right
hand of thy Majesty to be our defence.' The English reproduces
the Latin 'ad defensionem nostram dexteram tuae Majestatis
extende', the reformers expanding it with the addition 'against
all our enemies', perhaps under the influence of Ps. cxxxviii. 7.

messianic age, when all should be filled, and when 'the meek should eat and be satisfied'.

But the problem of nature miracles, and indeed, of all miracles, is presented in peculiarly acute form in the

*Mk. xi. 12-33.* story of the cursing of the fig tree. In its present setting, by which it is closely related to the Cleansing of the Temple, this story clearly declares the rejection of Israel because it had failed to bear the fruit which the messiah expected to find. In Mark and Matthew it takes the form of a very dramatic miracle. But Luke omits it, having elsewhere in his gospel a parable of a fig tree with precisely the same meaning.

*Lk. xiii. 6-9.* 'He spake also this parable; A certain man had a fig tree planted in his vineyard; and he came and sought fruit thereon, and found none. Then said he unto the dresser of his vineyard, Behold, these three years I come seeking fruit on this fig tree, and find none: cut it down; why cumbereth it the ground?'

The existence of this Parable makes it possible that the account of any given miracle as we have it in the gospels may be a dramatization of what had before been merely a story. But, if so, the change only served to emphasize the significance of the story. The point is that whatever conclusion be reached concerning the relation between teaching and miracle, the Christology is present in both and is not dependent upon the precise historicity of this or that miraculous narrative which is recorded in the gospels as they stand. Who is this who has authority to reject Israel? Who is this who has authority to forgive sin? Who is this who is stronger than Beelzebul and deprives him of his retinue of human slaves? Even if it be supposed that Jesus never worked a miracle at all, and that everywhere miracles are transformed parables, nevertheless these messianic claims still remain. And therefore this discussion of miracles may be said to have laid bare a problem which cannot have originated in them: their primary significance is the effective messianic declaration of the salvation of

God. Is this primary in the parables and sayings also?

To sum up, then: the Marcan miracle narratives which at first sight seem to record conventional actions of a wonder-worker, are found upon closer investigation to have a wholly different significance. The Marcan miracles are signs that the Christ is present in the midst of Judaism, signs warranted by Old Testament prophecy. Moreover, they are not only signs of his presence, they are signs of the nature of his power, since they point, as the Old Testament prophecies had already pointed, away from mere physical healing to freedom from sin and to the recognition of the power of the living God. They bear witness to the advent of his kingdom. It is the Christology which underlies the miracles and apparently conditions the details of the behaviour of Jesus. Nor is this merely Marcan. In the common *Mt. xi. 2 f;* source of Matthew and Luke not only are miracles of *Lk. vii. 20.* healing presumed. They have there precisely the same *Mt. xii. 28.* significance. They are not merely miracles. They are *Lk. xi. 20.* signs of the presence of him who should come and who *Compare* is the victor in the contest with evil, signs also of the *special Luke:* advent of the kingdom of God. *Lk. xiii. 32.*

It is, then, not in the least surprising that the editors Matthew and Luke should remove phrases in the Marcan narrative which might suggest to the careless reader that Jesus was a conventional wonder-worker, and should draw out more clearly the Old Testament background of his miracles. Thus Matthew applies *Mt. viii. 17.* Isaiah's prophecy of the suffering servant to the whole *Is. liii. 4.* healing activity of Jesus: 'Himself took our infirmities and bare our diseases'; and Luke introduces his narrative of the ministry with the quotation:

'The Spirit of the Lord is upon me,     *Lk. iv. 18 f.*
Because he anointed me to preach good tidings to the poor: *Is. lxi. 1.*
He hath sent me to proclaim release to the captives,
And recovering of sight to the blind,
To set at liberty them that are bruised,
To proclaim the acceptable year of the Lord.'

It is clear, however, that with all their interest in Old Testament prophecy, neither Matthew nor Luke is able fully to detect the whole wealth of Old Testament allusion contained in the Marcan miraculous narratives. Again, the greater complication lies not in the work of the editors, but in the material behind them.

## 2. Parables

At two definite points in the investigation of the significance of the miracle narratives, a close relation between miracles and parables has been detected. The *Lk. xiii. 6-9.* Lucan parable of the Fig tree throws clear light upon *Mk. xi. 13, 14,* the significance of the cursing and withering away of *20-22.* the fig tree in the Marcan narrative; both express the judgement pronounced by Jesus the messiah upon Israel; both are meaningless apart from his claim to utter such judgement with sovereign and effectual authority; both are also meaningless apart from a conception of Jesus as the messiah who demands repentance and righteousness, and who pronounces judgement where these are not at once forthcoming. Similarly, the *Mk. iii. 27;* parable of the Binding of the Strong Man, which is in- *Mt. xii. 29;* cluded both in Mark and in Matthew and Luke's com- *Lk. xi. 21 f.* mon source, emphasizes the same themes as the stories of miraculous healing. Both emphasize a contest between Jesus and the powers of evil, both declare him to be their master and that his actions involve the advent of the kingdom of God, and both rest upon great passages in the book of Isaiah for their understanding. That is to say, both the actions and the parable presume the presence of the messiah and declare the nature of the power of God operative in his ministry.

A clear problem therefore arises in the interpretation of the parables as a whole. Are these two parables peculiar in being so closely related to the actions and claims of Jesus? and is it in these two cases only that parables must be interpreted in the light of the Christo-

logy or not interpreted at all? Are the parables in general a method of illustrating in easily intelligible form
simple moral and spiritual truths; or is it that a peculiar
Christological claim and the course of a very particular
history everywhere condition and control their form
and content?

There are two distinct methods of proved value for
giving forcible expression to certain truths or ideas:
metaphor and simile. Metaphor, in order to give force
to a statement, couches it in terms of a different series
of ideas. It is metaphor to say 'Thou art my house of
defence and my castle'. The reader understands very
well that God is represented in this way because the
writer wishes to express his guardianship and constant
protection of men. The writer could have said so in as
many words. He chose to use metaphor instead. Simile,
on the other hand, uses a different range of terms to
express a conception which could not otherwise be made
so explicit. 'My soul gaspeth unto thee as a thirsty
land.' The writer demonstrates the peculiar intensity of
his longing after God, by calling to the reader's mind
a parched countryside stricken for want of rain. Only
this simile could express his feelings: it could not be
paraphrased without losing force.

Both metaphor and simile form the basis of distinct
methods of story-telling. If a story is told in a series of
metaphors, it is called 'allegory'; if it is told in a continued simile, it is called 'similitude'. Allegory expresses
the relation between certain persons and things by substituting a whole range of persons or things from an
entirely different sphere of experience. The relation of
man to material goods may be told in a story in which
a fox is substituted for man, and grapes for the object
of his desires. But, not only could the story be told without this ruse, it could be told in many other fabulous
ways: a child sighing for the moon or a dog longing for
a bone. And, although actually told in disguise, the
relation between the man and the goods is not changed:

there is no suspicion of simile. No fox ever jumped after a bunch of grapes and proceeded to revile them when he found them unattainable. But in similitude a relationship, which normally exists in the sphere of the story, is chosen to express a relationship in another sphere, which the writer cannot otherwise make clear. Because there is a particular relationship between a parched land and the rain which it needs and desires, that relationship is chosen to demonstrate the longing of the psalmist for God.

This distinction is of importance because the very various interpretations of parables ultimately depend on decisions to see in them either allegories or similitudes, and to explain them as such. The tradition of the church for many centuries was to see the parables as allegories. It was accordingly thought possible to interpret them by substituting nouns in the theological or ecclesiastical sphere for the nouns which formed their subject, just as the fable of the Fox and the Grapes is interpreted by substituting man for fox and riches for grapes. So the two pence in the parable of the Good Samaritan were interpreted as the sacraments of penance and of the altar, and the sellers of oil in the parable of the Virgins were interpreted as the ministers of religion. But more modern commentators, dissatisfied with this treatment, have regarded the parables rather as similitudes. The oil sellers accordingly are only a detail in a simile illustrating the need for patient watching and praying: the two pence only a detail denoting the extreme care with which neighbours are to be loved.

Nice as is the distinction between allegory and similitude, it normally exists only in theory. In practice most allegories contain simile, and most similitudes are tinged with metaphor. These very different interpretations of the parables of the New Testament have suggested that they are no exception to this rule. Although modern critics are still inclined to explain away most of the allegorical element as the embroidery of a later date, there are now few who would judge it to have been altogether absent from the stories in their earliest form. And, indeed, if interpretation is to avoid becoming completely arbitrary and prejudiced, it must attempt to explain the existence of both these elements in the material as it stands.

In the interpretation of the parable of the Sower *Mk. iv. 13-20.* given in Mark the parable is treated as an allegory. The seed by the wayside is shown to represent those from whom Satan takes the word; the seed on stony ground, those who have no root in themselves; the seed among thorns, those who are troubled by the cares of the age and the beguilement of riches. But, whereas this is all sufficiently obvious, and it is difficult to see how it could have been missed by the disciples, the main points of the parable are not touched by the interpretation. What was the word? And when was the great harvest of such exceeding and exceptional abundance? It seems as though this parable is not really explained, even by the interpretation given by the evangelist. Were the parables ordinary allegories?

On the other hand, sayings that form the main argument for the interpretation of parables as similitudes are equally difficult.

'Is the lamp brought to be put under the bushel, or under the *Mk. iv. 21 f.* bed, and not to be put on the stand? For there is nothing hid, save that it should be manifested; neither was anything made secret, but that it should come to light.'

If this is interpreted as a similitude, the meaning appears to be that just as the proper place for a lamp is on a stand, in order that it may light the room, so it is proper that the gospel shall be revealed. But is it possible to stop there? Surely it calls for the addition 'in order that it may light the world'. And if so, was the choice of the simile made not for any purely intrinsic aptitude, but because Jesus thought of the gospel, and of the disciples who possessed the gospel, as the light of the world? And was this choice conditioned by the Old Testament conception of the kingdom of David as a lamp?

*2 Sam. xxii. 29.* 'For thou art my lamp, O Lord: and the Lord will lighten my darkness.'

*Ps. cxix. 105.* 'Thy word is a lamp unto my feet, and a light unto my path.'

*Ps. cxxxii. 17.* 'There will I make the horn of David to bud: I have ordained a lamp for mine anointed.'

*2 Kings viii. 19; cf. 1 Kings xi. 36; xv. 4; 2 Ch. xxi. 7.* 'Howbeit, the Lord would not destroy Judah for David his servant's sake, as he promised him to give unto him a lamp for his children alway.'

'Is the lamp brought to be put under the bushel?' But why, indeed, was there need at all for this simile? Surely it should have been obvious that the gospel was to be proclaimed? Why have the disciples to be assured that it is not to be placed under a bushel or under a bed —unless at the moment it is hidden? Can it be that we have here neither a simile nor an allegory? Must not the parable, for its proper understanding, be set firmly in the historical situation in which Jesus was endeavouring to assure his disciples that his coming was not always to be in humiliation and rejection, but that the time was coming when the light should be clearly set forth? 'How am I straitened till that come to pass!'

The parable of the Sower is not the only story told in terms of sowing and reaping. There is a parable of a *Mk. iv. 26-29.* Seed that grows by itself; another of a Mustard Seed *Mk. iv. 30-32.* which becomes a tree larger than all others, though *Mt. xiii. 24-* smaller than any other seed. In Matthew there is a *30.* parable of wheat which grows mixed with tares until the harvest. But Hosea pictures the final establishment *Hosea ii. 19.f.* of Israel, not only as a betrothal, but as a sowing:

*Hosea ii. 21-23.* 'And it shall come to pass in that day, I will answer, saith the Lord, I will answer the heavens and they shall answer the earth; and the earth shall answer the corn and the wine and the oil; and they shall answer, Whom God soweth. And I will sow her unto me in the earth; and I will have mercy upon her that had not obtained mercy: and I will say to them which were not my people, Thou art my people; and they shall say, Thou art my God.'

Jeremiah, too, uses the same figure:

> 'Behold, the days come, saith the Lord, that I will sow the *Jer. xxxi. 27f.*
> house of Israel and the house of Judah with the seed of man,
> and with the seed of beast. And it shall come to pass, that like
> as I have watched over them, to pluck up, and to break down,
> and to throw down, and to destroy, and to afflict; so will I
> watch over them, to build, and to plant, saith the Lord.'

Another prophet likens the word of God coming *Is. lv. 10 f.*
down from heaven to the rain which 'giveth seed to the
sower and bread to the eater . . . it shall not return to
me void.' We may compare:

> 'Upon the land of my people shall come up thorns and briers; *Is. xxxii. 13 ff.*
> yea, upon all the houses of joy in the joyous city: for the palace
> shall be forsaken, the populous city shall be deserted; the hill
> and the watch-tower shall be for dens for ever, a joy of wild
> asses, a pasture of flocks; *until the spirit be poured upon us from on
> high*, and the wilderness become a fruitful field. . . .'

These passages show that the metaphor of sowing in
the Old Testament almost demanded a messianic application. So did the metaphor of harvesting.

> 'For thus saith the Lord of hosts, the God of Israel: The *Jer. li. 33.*
> daughter of Babylon is like a threshing-floor, it is time to thresh
> her; yet a little while, and the time of harvest shall come.'

> 'Let the heathen be wakened, and come up to the valley of *Joel iii. 12 f.*
> Jehoshaphat: for there will I sit to judge all the heathen round
> about. Put ye in the sickle, for the harvest is ripe: come, get
> you down, for the press is full, the fats overflow; for their
> wickedness is great.'

> 'Also, O Judah, there is an harvest appointed for thee, when *Hosea vi. 11.*
> I bring again the captivity of my people.'

So far the harvest is of wrath and judgement. In a
psalm which voices the longing for deliverance from
captivity its significance is one of joy and happiness:

> 'They that sow in tears shall reap in joy. He that goeth forth *Ps. cxxvi. 5 f.*
> and weepeth, bearing precious seed, shall doubtless come again
> with rejoicing, bringing his sheaves with him.'

This last verse alone might have suggested the parable
of the Sower. For it is clear that just the same antithesis

is present in it. The sower sows, and, in spite of all adversity and waste, a huge harvest is produced. The mustard seed, the smallest of all seeds, produces a tree greater than all the trees, and putteth out great branches; so that the birds of heaven can lodge 'under the shadow thereof'. There is no need, in this case, for the parable to be declared a likening of the kingdom of God, for the figure of the birds lodging in the branches *Ezek. xxxi. 6 ff.* of a great tree is an Old Testament figure for a great *Dan. iv. 20 ff.* kingdom. The seed growing by itself similarly empha-*cf. Judges ix.* sizes the magnitude and inevitability of the harvest.
*15.*

The point must not be laboured. But the Old Testament background and the sequence in thought of these parables of sowing and harvesting warrant the suggestion that they are neither similitudes nor allegories, in the usual sense, but are authoritative and theological expositions of particular occurrences, expositions already formulated and anticipated in the Old Testament, so that the events are set forth as the fulfilment of the hope of Israel. Other parables betray the same careful choice of simile and metaphor. More than once Isaiah had referred to Israel as God's vineyard. The parables of wedding feasts and of the waiting of the Virgins for the bridegroom are foreshadowed in the betrothing of Israel to God and in the great feast of the coming age typified by the manna in the wilderness. The likening of him who keeps the words of Jesus to the wise man who builds on rock is suggestive of the tried *Is. xxviii. 16 f.* stone laid in Zion, which will stand though 'the hail shall sweep away the refuge of lies, and the waters shall overflow the hiding place'.

The matter of the parables of Jesus is taken from the ordinary common life of Palestine and at times from incidents that had occurred either in the experience of a particular family or in the wider political life of the country as a whole, but the parables cannot for this reason be explained as mere illustrations of this or that moral truth, seen with the eyes of a poet and clothed in a poet's perfection of language. The selection of themes is in the main an Old Testament selection, the poetry is the poetry of Old Testament prophecy, and, more than this, the themes had already been endowed with a peculiar significance. They look forward to a divine event. Everywhere in the parables of Jesus this peculiar significance is presumed. No doubt Jesus spoke the meaning of what he saw and heard, but he saw and heard as one created by the prophets of Israel. Yet in his eyes and on his lips the themes are no longer prophetic, but messianic. They declare the divine event to be now taking place and the destiny of men to be dependent upon their acceptance or rejection of this event.

This Christological penetration of the parables renders them everywhere less illustrations of moral or spiritual truths which are easy of understanding than an integral element in the revelation of God that is taking place in Palestine with the advent of the messiah in his humiliation. Their understanding therefore depends upon the recognition of Jesus as the messiah and upon the recognition of the kingdom of God which is breaking forth in his words and actions. As a result of this particular historical situation, the Greek word *parabole* escapes from its Greek context, escapes also from the meaning which the Rabbis attached to its Hebrew equivalent, *mashal*, and acquires the meaning which *mashal*, translated by *parabole*, possessed in certain important Old Testament passages. There the word was used to denote Israel as a surprise or a byword, a scandal or an enigma to the nations, because the chosen people composed the concrete sphere of God's revelation to the world. In their captivity they revealed His judgement upon disobedience:

'I will even give them up to be tossed to and fro among all *Jer. xxiv. 9.* the kingdoms of the earth for evil; to be a reproach and a proverb (*mashal-parabole*), a taunt and a curse, in all places whither I shall drive them';

in their possession of the law they displayed the righteousness which he demanded:

*Deut. xxviii. 37.* 'And thou (Israel) shalt become an astonishment, a proverb (*mashal-parabole*), and a byword, among all the peoples whither the Lord shall lead thee away.'

It is therefore not in the least surprising to find Mark recording that the parables of Jesus were the means by *Mk. iv. 11.* which he presented to his disciples 'the mystery of the kingdom', and that he expected his disciples to perceive this meaning. To the crowds who had no personal relation with him his parables must remain unintelligible. Moreover, this whole conception of parables as mysteries of the kingdom of God is not a Marcan interpretation of them, or at least Mark does not give this impression, for he records a saying of Jesus which assigns to them *Mk. iv. 11.* this significance: 'Unto you is given the mystery of the kingdom of God: but unto them that are without, all things are done in parables.' It is therefore impossible to remain satisfied with the meaning which the Greek lexicographers Liddell and Scott give to the word *parabole* in the New Testament: 'a fictitious story by which some religious or moral lesson is conveyed'.

The parables, then, are shot through with the same Christological significance as the miracle narratives; with the same emphasis on something hidden now which is to be revealed openly in the future; with the same emphasis upon the necessity of recognizing what is now hidden, if men are to share in the glory which is to be; with the same confidence that this very hiddenness is not an intentional covering up of truth but its necessary manifestation in humiliation; and finally, with the same concentration upon the single historical figure of Jesus of Nazareth, so that the movement of Old Testament simile and metaphor comes to rest in this particular history. And yet the parables are everywhere driving home an urgent moral demand. They therefore bring into prominence those moral aphorisms of Jesus which are not expressed in parables. Consequently, the last stage of the investigation of the synoptic material must deal with these aphorisms, for here at last it may be possible to get behind this peculiar Christology and lay bare a teacher of morals, a reformer of Judaism, who claimed no more than the true insight of a prophet.

## 3. Aphorisms

The attempt on the part of Christian scholars to discover in the teaching of Jesus some new teaching about ethics or morals has completely, or almost completely, broken down. Those modern Jewish scholars who have busied themselves with a comparison between the ethical teaching of Jesus and the ethical teaching of the rabbis have given this judgement, that there is no single moral aphorism recorded as spoken by Jesus which cannot be paralleled, and often verbally paralleled, in rabbinic literature. With this conclusion Christian scholars working in the field of rabbinics are showing more and more agreement. For example, there can be no doubt that such a saying as 'The sabbath was made *Mk. ii. 27.* for man, and not man for the sabbath' would have been regarded as a self-evident truism by the best of the rabbis. Similarly, the constant insistence by Jesus that the righteousness which God demands is a righteousness of the heart could not have been strange or new teaching. And, indeed, this is definitely stated by Jesus in the Matthaean gospel, 'the scribes and the Pharisees *Mt. xxiii. 2 f.* sit in Moses' seat: all therefore whatsoever they bid you observe, that observe and do'. Even the Golden Rule *Mt. vii. 12.* has its parallel in rabbinic teaching. Moreover, the similarity between the ethical teaching of Jesus and the ethical teaching of the rabbis is evident not only in the substance of the teaching, but also in its form. When Jesus utters a series of Beatitudes, 'Blessed are the *Lk. vi. 20.* poor. . . . Blessed are those that hunger. . . .' he is casting his teaching in a familiar mould. Parables were commonly used by the rabbis to illustrate their discourses. Jesus adopted their custom. Such set introductory formulae as 'To what shall we liken . . .?' and the use of rhythmic parallelism,

*Lk. vi. 27, 28.*

Love your enemies,
  Do good to them which hate you,
Bless them that curse you,
  And pray for them which despitefully use you.

*Lk. vi. 44.*

Of thorns men do not gather figs,
  Nor of a bramble bush gather they grapes,

were also characteristically rabbinic.

There is, it is true, considerable difficulty in dating with precise accuracy the emergence into a pregnant saying of this or of that fragment of rabbinic moral teaching, but no competent scholar would deduce from this uncertainty dependence on the part of the rabbis upon the teaching of Jesus. It is also true that there is much in the moral teaching of the rabbis which goes beyond his recorded teaching. His teaching is selective, and the selection is no doubt significant. Yet, in view of this very modern agreement between Jewish and Christian scholars, it is tempting to conclude that after all Jesus must be placed in the succession of Jewish moral teachers, and that the address 'Rabbi' does at least set him in the correct historical context.

It is impossible, however, to read much of the surviving rabbinic literature without recognizing the gulf which separates the gospels from this Jewish literature. This difference penetrates even the aphorisms of Jesus. It is not sufficient merely to draw up a list of parallels between his teaching and that of the rabbis. What requires explanation is the authority with which he spoke, the urgency which accompanied his moral demands, and the evident judgement of God which he declared would inevitably follow any refusal to obey him. And why should the Jewish religious authorities have demanded his death, if he had merely taught what many of them were accustomed to teach, and differed from them only in that his teaching was more carefully selected and was shrewdly protected against the accusation of sedition?

The moral utterances of Jesus are frequently introduced with the words, 'But I say unto you . . .' There are examples of this introduction in all four strata of the material, and accordingly it seems to have been frequently on the lips of Jesus. But it is difficult to suppose that it was no more than an habitual didactic form, or the mere mannerism of a teacher; for it serves at times to draw attention to an antithesis, and, in several cases to an antithesis not merely between the teaching of Jesus and contemporary ethical opinion, but between his demands and statements in the Mosaic law. In the Sermon on the Mount, Matthew sets forth teach- *Mt. v.* ing upon a series of subjects, introducing each of them by such words as 'Ye have heard that it was said . . .' 'Ye have heard that it was said to them of old time . . .' and immediately quoting such sayings as 'Thou shalt not kill . . .'—'Thou shalt not commit adultery . . .' taken from the heart of the law laid down in Exodus, Leviticus, and Deuteronomy as the verbal commands of God himself. The citation is made not merely in order to evoke, here and now, a fulfilment of the letter of the command, not merely to secure recognition of its spirit, but also to insist that its full implications must take control of every fragment of human life. For instance:

'Ye have heard that it was said, Thou shalt not commit *Mt. v. 27 f.* adultery: but I say unto you, that every one that looketh on a woman to lust after her hath committed adultery with her already in his heart. . . . And if thy right eye causeth thee to stumble, pluck it out. . . .'

This means, not the pressure of the moral demand into the sphere of the heart, but the pressure of the righteousness of the heart outwards into quite concrete physical action.

The precise and pregnant sayings, in which Jesus formulated his ethical teaching, are everywhere expositions of the revealed law of God. The righteousness which Jesus demanded is lacking in originality, not because it was similarly formulated by the rabbis, but because it was the demand of God revealed to the Hebrew people. Jesus was able to summarize this demand by taking two passages from the law and quoting them verbally.

*Mk. xii. 29-31. cf. Deut. vi. 4, 5, and Lev. xix. 18.*

This apprehension of the demand of God involves the setting aside of whole elements in the Mosaic law, because they were concessions to the weakness of men authorized by Moses himself. Some Pharisees, for instance, question Jesus on the subject of divorce. He asks them what Moses taught, and, when told his teaching, declares that it was written only for the hardness of their hearts; and, in order to reveal the true law of God, appeals from the Mosaic law to the opening chapter of the book of Genesis. Mark, who records this incident, shows in other parts of his gospel that Jesus was ready to set aside, not only the tradition of the elders, or scribes, not only, in fact, Judaistic conceptions of the law, but even, if necessary, the Mosaic code, which was credited with, and indeed claimed to have, divine origin. For instance, his justification of the fact that his disciples were not keeping a fast which Jewish custom demanded, and his justification of their plucking corn on the sabbath day with an argument turning upon David's overriding of the law, show that he regarded certain of its commandments as no longer binding on those who have obeyed the call to follow him. But he demanded an immediate and complete obedience to the will of the living God, and described his work not as patching an old garment with new cloth, but, it must be inferred, as making a new garment of new cloth; not as pouring new wine into old bottles, but as pouring it into new bottles created for the new wine. Such an attitude explains Mark's comment that the people were

*Mk. x. 2-9.*

*Mk. vii. 1-23.*

*Mk. ii. 18-22.*
*Mk. ii. 23-28.*

*Mk. ii. 21 ff.*

*Mk. i. 22.*

astonished at his teaching, saying that he taught as one having authority, and not as the scribes.

The impression given by Mark is borne out in the other strata of the material. And this in spite of the apparent contradiction of such a saying, recorded by Matthew, but probably taken from the source used also by Luke:

'Till heaven and earth pass, one jot or one tittle shall in no wise pass from the law, till all be fulfilled.'

*Mt. v. 18.*
*Lk. xvi. 17.*

The saying which precedes it, and which was probably derived from Matthew's special material, explains the apparent contradiction. 'I am not come to destroy the law or the prophets, but to fulfil.' Jesus demands that the law of God must be fulfilled to the uttermost. This demand alone fully explains the condemnation of 'this adulterous and sinful generation', that culminates in the Woes to the scribes and Pharisees found in the common source:

*Mt. v. 17.*

*Mk. viii. 38.*

'Woe unto you also, ye lawyers! for ye lade men with burdens grievous to be borne, and ye yourselves touch not the burdens with one of your fingers.'
'Woe unto you! for ye build the sepulchres of the prophets, and your fathers killed them.'
'Woe unto you lawyers! for ye have taken away the key of knowledge: ye entered not in yourselves, and them that were entering in ye hindered.'
'Therefore also said the wisdom of God, I will send unto them prophets and apostles, and some of them they shall slay and persecute; that the blood of all the prophets, which was shed from the foundation of the world, may be required of this generation; from the blood of Abel to the blood of Zacharias which perished between the altar and the temple: verily I say unto you, It shall be required of this generation.'

*Lk. xi. 46.*
*cf. Mt. xxiii. 4.*
*Lk. xi. 47. cf. Mt. xxiii. 29.*
*Lk. xi. 52. cf. Mt. xxiii. 13.*
*Lk. xi. 49-51. cf. Mt. xxiii. 34-36.*

Here is no ethical idealism, but an urgent moral realism. It is not, however, upon this authoritative exposition of the law of God that the emphasis mainly lies. The emphasis lies not merely upon the urgency of the present demand, but upon its cause. The urgency is occasioned by the presence of Jesus in their midst, by the imminence of his removal, and by his call that men should follow him. It is his presence that makes necessary the immediate fulfilment of the demand of God revealed in the law and occasions his exposition of the precise nature of that demand.

*Lk. xvi. 16.*  'The law and the prophets were until John: since that time
*cf. Mt. xi. 13.*  the kingdom of God is preached.
*Mt. xiii. 16.*  'Blessed are your eyes, for they see; and your ears, for they
*cf. Lk. x. 23.*  hear.'
*Mt. viii. 22.*  'Follow me; and let the dead bury their dead.'
*cf. Lk. ix. 60.*

Consequently, it is upon those who have left all and followed him that the whole weight of the law of God falls, with the confident hope that they can bear it and undertake a greater purification:

*Mt. v. 13.*  'Ye are the salt of the earth.'
*Mt. v. 14.*  'Ye are the light of the world.'
*Mt. v. 20.*  'For I say unto you, that except your righteousness shall exceed the righteousness of the scribes and Pharisees, ye shall in no case enter into the kingdom of heaven.'
*Mt. v. 48.*  'Be ye therefore perfect, even as your Father which is in
*cf. Mt. xix. 21.*  heaven is perfect.'

This does not mean that God does not demand obedience from the crowds, but that the obedience demanded is confidently awaited in those who have obeyed the call of Jesus and persist in discipleship.

*Lk. ix. 62.*  'No man, having put his hand to the plough, and looking back, is fit for the kingdom of God.'

Jesus, then, cannot be fitted into contemporary Judaism; he goes behind it to the law and the prophets and definitely states that now is the time of their fulfilment.

*Mt. v. 17.*  'I am not come to destroy, but to fulfil.'
*Mk. ii. 21.*  'No man also seweth a piece of new cloth on an old garment.'
*Mk. ii. 22.*  'And no man putteth new wine into old bottles.'

The sequence of ideas may be made clear by drawing

attention to the Matthaean collection of sayings concerning divorce, and to the teaching concerning money, which is scattered about the gospels. Matthew adds to the Marcan account of the teaching of Jesus on the incompatibility of divorce with the law of God, a very human question asked by the disciples:

'If the case of the man be so with his wife, it is not good to *Mt. xix. 10-12.* marry. But he said unto them, All men cannot receive this saying, save they to whom it is given. For there are some eunuchs, which were so born from their mother's womb: and there are some eunuchs which were made eunuchs of men: and there be eunuchs, which have made themselves eunuchs for the kingdom of heaven's sake. He that is able to receive it, let him receive it.'

This clearly implies that the advent of the kingdom may require a complete separation from ordinary human life, and fits exactly into the more comprehensive teaching on family ties elsewhere laid down for the disciples. Discipleship may entail separation from father, mother, brethren, sisters, even, perhaps, from wife as well. But it is a discipleship in which human life is reformed in a new dimension. The

'hundredfold now in this time, houses, and brethren, and sis- *Mk. x. 30.* ters, and mothers, and children, and lands, with persecutions'

which a man shall receive who has left

'house, or brethren, or sisters, or father, or mother, or wife, or *Mk. x. 29.* children, or lands, for my sake, and the gospel's'

is made understandable by the parallel saying,

'Whosoever shall do the will of God, the same is my brother, *Mk. iii. 35.* and my sister, and mother.'

The sequence is, therefore, the revelation of the law of God, the mission of Jesus, the acceptance of his call, the advent of the kingdom of God, and the consequent requirement of obedience to the law of God. This is the background of the sayings, 'Be ye perfect, as your Father in heaven is perfect'—'Ye are the salt of the earth.'

The same sequence appears in the Marcan narrative

of the rich man, and here the series of ideas reaches its
*Mk. x. 17-22.* inevitable climax. A man comes running to Jesus. 'Good
Master, what shall I do that I may inherit eternal life?'
He has kept the commandments from his youth up.
Jesus looks at him and loves him, and says: 'One thing
thou lackest: go, sell whatsoever thou hast, and give to
the poor, and thou shalt have treasure in heaven: and
come, follow me.' The man goes away, refusing not only
to provide for the poor, but also to follow Jesus. Jesus
comments, 'How hardly shall they that have riches enter
into the kingdom of God!' The disciples are amazed,
and are told that it is impossible with men, though not
with God. 'It is easier for a camel to go through a
needle's eye, than for a rich man to enter into the kingdom of God!' The salvation of a rich man is possible
only by an act of God. Peter says: 'Lo, we have left all,
and have followed thee.' Jesus then solemnly promises
to those who have left all, for his sake and the gospel's,
eternal life in the age to come. This teaching is echoed
in the special Lucan story of Zacchaeus, who, when he
*Lk. xix. 8 f.* declares that he will make fourfold restitution to those
he has defrauded, and will give half his possessions to
the poor, is told that salvation has come to his house.
That this salvation of God occurs in the context of
obedience to the call of Jesus and not merely as a result
of the surrender of wealth is made clear in a passage
from the same source, addressed to the disciples. Following the description of God's care for the birds and
*Lk. xii. 28-33.* of his clothing of the grass of the field, Luke proceeds:

'How much more will he clothe you, O ye of little faith? And
seek not ye what ye shall eat, or what ye shall drink, neither be
ye of doubtful mind. For all these things do the nations of the
world seek after: and your Father knoweth that ye have need
of these things. But rather seek ye the kingdom of God; and all
these things shall be added unto you. Fear not, little flock; for
it is your Father's good pleasure to give you the kingdom. Sell
that ye have, and give alms; provide yourselves bags which
wax not old, a treasure in the heavens that faileth not, where
no thief approacheth, neither moth corrupteth.'

In this teaching about riches the same series of ideas is found as in the Matthaean teaching concerning divorce. The complete fulfilment of the law of God is effected in and by acceptance of the call of Jesus. This is the salvation of the living God, and bestows his supreme treasure, which is eternal life in his kingdom.

There is, however, a further emphasis in the aphorisms of Jesus. He insists upon a present humiliation contrasted with a future glory. The disciples must share in his humiliation.

'Foxes have holes, and the birds of the air have nests, but the Son of man hath not where to lay his head.' *Mt. viii. 20. Lk. ix. 58.*

'And he that taketh not his cross and followeth after me, is not worthy of me.' *Mt. x. 38. cf. Mk. viii. 34;*

The new family is a persecuted family: 'with persecutions'. In this context must be placed the following passage, in which the humiliation of the disciples is linked to his own humiliation: *Lk. xiv. 27; Lk. ix. 23; Mk. x. 30.*

'Ye know that they which are accounted to rule over the Gentiles exercise lordship over them; and their great ones exercise authority upon them. But so shall it not be among you: but whosoever will be great among you, shall be your minister: and whosoever of you will be the chiefest, shall be servant of all. For even the Son of man came not to be ministered unto, but to minister, and to give his life a ransom for many.' *Mk. x. 42-45.*

Similarly, when James and John desire to sit with him in glory, he accepts their readiness to drink the cup that he drinks, and to be baptized with the baptism with which he is baptized and answers:

'Ye shall indeed drink of the cup that I drink of; and with the baptism that I am baptized withal shall ye be baptized: but to sit on my right hand and on my left hand is not mine to give; but it shall be given to them for whom it hath been prepared.' *Mk. x. 39 f.*

Both these last sayings, however, do more than link the humiliation of the disciples with his own. They contrast future glory with present humiliation, and future openness with present secrecy, as is insisted upon elsewhere:

*Mt. x. 23.*    'Ye shall not have gone over the cities of Israel, till the Son of man be come.'

*Mt. x. 26 f.*    'Fear them not therefore: for there is nothing covered, that shall not be revealed; and hid, that shall not be known. What I tell you in darkness, that speak ye in light: and what ye hear in the ear, that preach ye upon the housetops.'

*Mt. xxiv. 27 f.*    'For as the lightning cometh out of the east, and shineth even
*cf. Lk. xvii.*    unto the west; so shall also the coming of the Son of man be. For
*24, 37.*    wheresoever the carcase is, there will the eagles be gathered together.'

*Lk. xii. 50.*    'I have a baptism to be baptized with; and how am I straitened till it be accomplished!'

Finally, the humiliation is not a mere means of entry into glory on the part of Jesus and his followers; it is a victory over the powers of evil, already begun:

*Lk. x. 17-20.*    'And the seventy returned again with joy, saying, Lord, even the devils are subject unto us through thy name. And he said unto them, I beheld Satan as lightning fall from heaven. Behold I give unto you power to tread on serpents and scorpions, and over all the power of the enemy: and nothing shall by any means hurt you. Notwithstanding in this rejoice not, that the spirits are subject unto you; but rather rejoice, because your names are written in heaven.'[1]

The conclusion which follows from an investigation of the aphorisms found in all strata of the synoptic material is that they are utterances of the messiah who is inaugurating the kingdom of God in which the law of God revealed to the Hebrew people is fulfilled. Further, the kingdom is inaugurated in humiliation, in the midst of persecution and misunderstanding; and this humiliation is not merely the necessary prelude to the final kingdom, it is the condition of entry into it.

The aphorisms of Jesus, then, cannot be detached from this messianic background, and they cannot be

[1] The passage is addressed to the disciples, though the framework containing the number seventy is probably a piece of Lucan editing.

detached from particular events in Palestine. They are not merely general ethical aphorisms: they declared the presence of the kingdom of God, and are rooted in a peculiar messianic history. Thus the aphorisms have to be placed with the miracles and the parables. The peculiar Christology penetrates the aphoristic teaching of Jesus as it penetrates the record of his miracles and of his parables. The Christology lies behind the aphorisms, not ahead of them; this means that at no point is the literary or historical critic able to detect in any stratum of the synoptic material evidence that a Christological interpretation has been imposed upon an un-Christological history. This does not of course mean that the framework in which the evangelists have set the miracles, parables and aphorisms of Jesus is necessarily historical. Nor does it mean even that the miracles, parables and aphorisms themselves, when isolated from the framework, are straight historical records. What it does mean is that both the framework and the miracles, parables and aphorisms set in it, emerge from, lie upon, and rightly interpret, the general matter of the tradition. Rightly, as far as we are able to judge, since the analysis of the gospels does not anywhere show the grain of the tradition running in a contrary direction. The material is everywhere Christological, although it remains, none the less, fragmentary and episodic. The three evangelists have done little more than arrange the tradition.

## NOTE

Professor C. H. Dodd has recently written a very valuable book on the parables, *The Parables of the Kingdom*, London, 1935. For the picture they provide of contemporary life compare his *The Authority of the Bible*, London, 1928, pp. 148-152.

For the method of form criticism that has analysed the material on the assumption that it is separable into isolated episodes or fragments, see particularly Professor Rudolf Bultmann, *Geschichte der synoptischen Tradition*, second edition, 1931.

Dr. B. T. D. Smith's *The Parables of the Synoptic Gospels*, published in 1937, is indispensable for the English student.

## Chapter IX

The Theologians: St. Paul, the author of the
Johannine Writings, and the author of The
Epistle to the Hebrews

It has been commonly held that, when the synoptic
gospels have been critically examined, the whole
material strictly relevant to the history of Jesus of
Nazareth will have been exhausted, and that, whereas
the older evangelists and editors of the tradition may be
found to be competent historians, no such competence
can be credited to the theologians of the New Testament. For theologians are commonly supposed to be
moving in a world of their own notions and ideas un-
controlled by any regard for strict historical truth. But,
since the theologians of the New Testament vigorously
protest against so brutal a dismissal, and since one of
them has set his theology in the framework of a clear
historical narrative, their claim to be bearing witness to
an historical event cannot be wholly disregarded.

The material of the synoptic gospels raised the question whether extraneous theological notions may have
moulded the tradition and whether its present form is
the result of this theological penetration. The remainder
of the New Testament presents an opposite problem. In
the synoptic gospels the history seemed at first sight to
have preceded the theological interpretation it was
found to contain. In the rest of the New Testament it
seems at first sight that the theological interpretation
not only precedes the history, but almost renders it
unnecessary.

Even though it is difficult to suppose that the history
recorded by the evangelists was at any time free from
Christological significance; even though the simplest

146

actions and words of Jesus appear upon investigation pregnant with messianic content; yet the evangelists write as historians and not as theologians. The form of the tradition may have been moulded by some theological purpose; the original history may even have been conditioned by it; but nevertheless the evangelists attempt only to recount events as they took place. They describe the life, actions and death of a man, at a certain date, in a certain part of the world. Behind this man, inextricably connected with his words and with his actions, with his very person, is God. But the man sleeps, suffers, prays and dies. Whatever else he may be, he is a man.

But can the same be said of the Jesus of the Johannine Writing, of the Epistles of St. Paul, or of the Epistle to the Hebrews? These three groups of writings assume the divine sonship of him they call Jesus Christ. The authors of the Johannine writings and of the Epistle to the Hebrews insist upon this unique relationship to God in their opening words, explaining it by a statement of his pre-existence with God. St. Paul, too, is no less ready to assume it, and explicitly concurs, in various parts of his writings, in the same doctrine. Neither St. Paul nor the writer to the Hebrews, however, sets out to retail the events which had taken place in Palestine; and, moreover, their writings are singularly lacking even in references to those events. If, when St. Paul was writing, stories of Jesus were being carefully treasured and passed on from mouth to mouth, it seems strange that only in one or two places does he definitely quote them. It seems strange also that, while he devotes large portions of nearly all his letters to an ethic so identical with that taught by Jesus in the first three gospels that that alone would stamp him Christian, yet he scarcely ever uses the same terminology to express it. Again, can it be supposed that the author of Hebrews derived his ideas from the Jesus who taught in Palestine? No doubt he knew something of his life and death. But is he not merely grafting upon the tradition an Alexandrian, semi-Platonic philosophy of the Jewish sacrificial system, which is to his mind of far greater importance?

The author of the fourth Gospel apparently set out to write a gospel, a story of the life, death and resurrection of Jesus. How is it that no living scholar can confidently claim any part of it, as it stands, to be definitely historical? Why is it so obviously distinct from its three predecessors? Like them, it is a narrative of words and doings which testify that Jesus was the Son of God. But it is almost impossible to avoid the critical conclusion that, although the fourth evangelist depends upon and has made use of records of the words and actions of Jesus known to us from the synoptic gospels, and also of a wider circle of tradition or information presumably of a similar character, he has refashioned everything that he has chosen to record in a consistent, literary form. Far from being composed, for instance, like the synoptic gospels, of short sayings and incidents, the fourth Gospel takes the form of an almost continuous argument, which passes quite imperceptibly from narration to explanation, so that it is impossible, at times, to be sure whether the author is recording words of Jesus or commenting upon them. But this results in a new picture of Christ's ministry. Where are the short epigrammatic sayings, the semi-poetic aphorisms, the parables suddenly thrown out after the manner of the rabbis? With the exception of Matthew's conflated discourses, and of the great eschatological compilation of Mark (itself almost certainly editorial, in its present form), the synoptists nowhere suggest that Jesus was wont to preach at great length. Yet the fourth Gospel is mainly composed of long discourses. And, quite apart from their length, they have a highly distinctive spiral form of argument, which sets out from a great saying, comments upon it, winds round and round again enlarging on it, and all the time preserves an admirable sequence, so that it is possible to analyse the whole gospel in paragraphs or chapters, each with divisions and subdivisions, yet all contributing to the one single purpose of the author. Moreover, the great miracles are included in this spiral argumentation and serve to draw out more clearly this purpose and design.

Another, and perhaps even more individual feature of the Johannine writings is the use of abstract terms to describe God: 'God is spirit', 'God is love'; or to define *1 Jn. iv. 8, 16.* the mission of Jesus: 'I am the way, the truth, and the *Jn. xiv. 6.* life.' 'In him (The Word) was life, and the life was the *Jn. i. 4.* light of men.'—These are metaphorical descriptions which have no parallel in the synoptic gospels. They are usually explained as originating either in an hellenic method of thought, or in the experience of the primitive church, or possibly, since the primitive church comprehended Greeks, in both. Thus Jesus reveals, as the author had already shown in the first chapter of his gospel, the will and purpose of God, and so is named 'the truth'. To give another example, he has striven so hard to give precision to his understanding of God's work for men, that, mighty as is that work, it is finally expressed sufficiently in one word, itself completely redefined in the process—love. This whole procedure has given rise to the assumption that the author of the fourth Gospel had been fitted for theologizing by a schooling in Greek ways of thought.

On the other hand, there is a statement in the gospel itself which is frequently taken to provide the key to his writings: 'Howbeit, when he, the spirit of truth, is come, he shall guide you into all the truth.' He is *Jn. xvi. 13.* accordingly represented as thinker and mystic; a man whose life had been controlled by spiritual communion with God; who knew Jesus Christ first of all in the working of the Paraclete, that other comforter who comes to all 'who believe on his name' and have thereby become 'sons of God, born of the will of the Father'. Quite *Jn. i. 12 f.* secondary to his knowledge of this Spirit of Christ, it is supposed, were the stories and traditions handed down to him by those who had known Jesus of Nazareth. His mysticism, then, explains both his abstraction, and his use of history. In fact, it is said, it is impossible to understand the Johannine writings except on the basis of the spiritual experience of their author. Where he seems to write history, he is interpreting his experience in terms of history. Though details may appear in some cases to argue his presence at the events he describes, the events are, in fact, entirely subservient to his spiritual motive, and his presence is a spiritual presence, the result of his sense of union with the risen Christ and of communion with the Spirit of the living God.

If the starting-point for the understanding of the Johannine writings is said to be the Paraclete, the starting-point for the understanding of St. Paul is similarly said to be his 'Christ-mysticism'. St. Paul constantly employed an expression which may mean either 'in Christ' or 'by Christ'. This expression is said to explain the intense theological wrestling of his mind as revealed in his letters, a wrestling which proceeds from an overwhelming experience of redemption, justification and sanctification through mystical union with the Spirit of God, whom he names the Christ. He meets with this experience not only in his own heart, but in the hearts of other Christians. His letters are therefore to be explained, not on the supposition that he had constructed a theological system, or that he was developing a philosophical or theological system in which he had been brought up, but that he was struggling to express a mystical experience, and to answer the needs of the early church in terms of it.

In the Epistle to the Hebrews also, an obsession with allegory, learnt from his environment, may have led some Greek-speaking Jew, conscious that he had encountered the supernatural in his spiritual experience, to explain it in terms of Old Testament sacrificial conceptions based upon the idea of a Priest-Messiah, and fastened quite superficially to the Jesus of history.

If these impressions of the Pauline and Johannine writings and of the Epistle to the Hebrews are justified to any extent, in each case the actual history becomes secondary, so that these documents apparently present a problem which is just the reverse of that of the synoptic material. They imply that the historical figure of Jesus, the life which he lived in the flesh, is of little importance in comparison with the experience of the 'Christ-Spirit' possessed by primitive Christians. In the fourth Gospel, the history of Jesus of Nazareth is simply symbolic of the new spiritual life in Christ; in St. Paul, and in the Epistle to the Hebrews, historical allusions are so few and far between that they appear unnatural. In short, in all three groups of writings, any references to Jesus who lived and died in Palestine are perhaps best accounted for as a lapse into that older traditional gospel which, although of little value to men who knew Christ through his Spirit, could not have been entirely unknown to them, and which, accordingly, they occasionally, and perhaps quite unintentionally, preserved. Consequently, it has become almost habitual in modern treatment of the New Testament to regard these writings as evidence for the spiritual life of the primitive church, but to deny expressly or by implication their value for the reconstruction of the history of Jesus of Nazareth. This is the logical implication of much recent criticism, although it is not usual to describe it so rigorously, or to draw out so relentlessly what it involves.

When once the centre and authority of religion is found, not in the action or revelation of God in the person of the man Jesus, but in the spiritual experience of those who claim to know Christ in their hearts, the historical life of Jesus is relegated to a secondary place, and ceases to be a necessary dynamic part of religion, so that it is merely retained as the myth in which the spiritual experience of the church is, as it were, focused. The story of a life, of a voluntary death, of a resurrection, merely provides a terminology sufficient for the rationalization of spiritual experience. The assurance of the validity of that experience, which might have been looked for in the historical events, is the spiritual experience itself. It is no longer necessary to be sure that Jesus Christ was a real man, and suffered and died as a real man may suffer and die: the story of his passion and resurrection has value only in that it serves to define the way of salvation and enables the much more real spiritual experience of 'crucifixion of the flesh' and of 'new life in the Spirit' to be analysed and explained. An apparent death and resurrection would have been from this point of view equally valuable. Indeed, a pure fable, arising, it may be, from dramatization of the cycle of seed-time and harvest, would have taught as much. What importance could a description of trivial actions performed in Palestine have for Greeks bubbling over with a personal and spiritual knowledge of God?

This conception of the relation of history to spiritual experience is exactly that of the contemporary religions of the Greco-Roman world. These, the mystery religions, although highly diverse in detail, agreed in attaching themselves to some story of a hero god or gods. They made no pretence to show the validity of the story as history. They were not for a moment concerned to do so. But they held out the prospect of a salvation which could be attained by means of certain rites and dramatizations of the story of their god, by means of initiation into their 'mysteries' and of communion with their divinity in ecstasy, leading to a knowledge of supernatural things, and, ultimately, to a state of perfection guaranteeing immortality.

The resemblance of these religions to the description of Christianity which has just been outlined, justifies, superficially at least, the assertion of some modern scholars that primitive Christianity, and, in particular, the Christianity which was the result of the work of St. Paul, was neither more nor less than a mystery religion. Not only does this assumption explain the absence in many of the New Testament writings of quotations from the words or actions of Jesus as set forth in the synoptic gospels; not only does it explain the presence in them of the conceptions of salvation, wisdom and knowledge; it provides an adequate explanation of apostolic insistence upon the ceremonies of baptism and communion, and also of the conspicuous success of Christianity in proselytizing the pagan world.

The problem, then, is to discover whether such passages as St. Paul's description of the Second Adam, the Johannine assertion that 'the Word became flesh', and the description in the Epistle to the Hebrews of Christ's sufferings in the days of his flesh, are merely lapses into history on the part of men normally moving in pure hellenic mystery religion, in which case the great theologians of primitive Christianity are valueless for the reconstruction of the history of Jesus of Nazareth: or whether these passages express the very foundation of their theology, in which case these writings may provide important evidence of the nature of that history. *Rom. v. 12-21. Jn. i. 14. Heb. v. 5-10.*

What significance did St. Paul attach to the coming of Christ in the flesh? That it was the basis of the traditional gospel which he himself had received is clear.

'For I delivered unto you first of all', *1 Cor. xv. 3 ff.*

he writes to the Corinthians,

that which I also received, how that Christ died for our sins according to the scriptures; and that he was buried, and that he rose again the third day according to the scriptures: and that he was seen of Cephas. . . .'

This summary, in which certain modern scholars have recognized the earliest form of the preaching of the gospel in apostolic times, suggests that the death of Christ in the flesh had already, when received by St.

Paul, a supreme significance attached to it. The many references to the death scattered throughout his epistles show that he had no wish to disturb the tradition he had received. For instance, he speaks of Jesus Christ:

*Rom. iii. 25.* 'Whom God set forth to be a propitiation, through faith, by his blood.'

*Rom. v. 6.* 'While we were yet weak, in due season Christ died for the ungodly.'

*Rom. v. 10.* 'We were reconciled to God through the death of his Son.'

*Rom. viii. 32.* 'God . . . delivered up . . . his own Son for us all.'

*1 Cor. vii. 23.* 'Ye were bought with a price.'

*2 Cor. v. 15.* 'He died for all.'

*Eph. ii. 13.* 'Ye that once were far off are made nigh in the blood of Christ.'

*Col. ii. 13.* 'And you, being dead through your trespasses, and the uncircumcision of your flesh, you, I say, did he (God) quicken together with him (Christ).'

Side by side with this continual insistence upon the need for the price that had been paid, upon the need for a death that had done away with the enmity between God and men, there is a continual insistence upon the *1 Cor. xv. 14.* resurrection: 'If Christ hath not been raised, then is our preaching vain, your faith also is vain.' Earlier in the *1 Cor. xv. 3-9.* same chapter St. Paul enumerates the resurrection appearances which guarantee his faith. Indeed, so certain is he of the power of the death, resurrection and ascension of Jesus, that he writes to the Ephesians:

*Eph. ii. 4 ff.* 'But God . . . even when we were dead through our trespasses quickened us together with Christ (by grace have ye been saved), and raised us up with him, and made us to sit with him in the heavenly places, in Christ Jesus.'

So far it is clear that St. Paul conceived the death and resurrection of Jesus, which took place once and for all in Palestine, to have supreme significance for men and women. It is thus that Jesus has given them life. But here another and associated conception appears. The life is not merely life given to men who are physically dying; it is life given to men who spiritually are already dead. This resurrection is to be appropriated by them by dying to the sinful flesh with Christ and by living with him:

'If we be dead with Christ, we believe that we shall also live with him.' *Rom. vi. 8.*

And more, even the manner of Christ's death is used to describe the spiritual experience of dying with him. St. Paul can speak of being crucified to the world with Jesus, of dying and being buried with him, not only at baptism, but also day by day. And just as the death is moral, so is the resurrection. How can he use the history of Christ to illustrate the spiritual experience of himself and of his fellow Christians? Because that death and resurrection has for him the significance of victory in the moral sphere. The death of Jesus was the triumph of righteousness over the sinful world: of a righteousness which, because it could not and would not submit to the world, died to the world. His resurrection was the action of God by which this righteousness and this victory were ratified.

The death of Christ, then, was an *opus operatum*: something done once and for all to effect a purpose. It is not merely symbolic of spiritual and moral experience, nor yet a formal act of reconciliation performed by the Son of God which may be described as a sacrifice. It is both, and more than both. The reconciliation was achieved by the moral perfection of Jesus, the moral perfection of one who might have sinned. The redemption was wrought out in the isolated figure of Jesus. This was the foundation of the theology of St. Paul.

To St. Paul, then, Christ is not merely the pre-existent Son of God, but the perfect man. His righteousness and his obedience, just because they were a human righteousness and a human obedience, were the dynamic factors in the atoning act of God:

'So then as through one trespass the judgement came unto all men to condemnation; even so through one act of righteous- *Rom. v. 18, 19.*

ness the free gift came unto all men to justification of life. For as through the one man's disobedience the many were made sinners, even so through the obedience of the one shall the many be made righteous.'

This is no mere lapse into the language of synoptic tradition. It is the basis of St. Paul's whole teaching. Whenever he mentions the death of Christ, he has in mind the death of one who took the form of a servant and humbled himself during the whole of a life which culminated in his death. The death, indeed, just because it is the culmination of the life, is used to summarize it. *Gal. iii. 1.* That is why St. Paul can describe his gospelling of the Galatians as placarding Christ crucified before their *Gal. v. 11.* eyes. That is why the stumbling-block of the cross is the essential basis of his teaching.

If this be a truer estimate of St. Paul's attitude to the coming in the flesh than that which led to the 'mystery religion hypothesis', the fact that his writings have been misunderstood must be explained. In part misunderstanding has been due to a failure to see that he everywhere mingles two complementary though distinct points of view. On the one hand St. Paul sees the Christians, the members of the Church, over against the Christ. From this point of view, Christ is the revelation *Eph. v. 22-33.* of God, pre-existent with God, and come into the world for the salvation of men, the bridegroom who left his Father to cleave to his bride that he might become one with her: his death is in this sense an historical fact making redemption possible. But, just because the bridegroom has become one with his bride, the church, there is another point of view. Christ is the first-born of the new creation, the corner-stone upon which his temple the church is built, the head of his body the church, the first Christian. In this sense his death is an action which must be partaken in, imitated, continued *1 Cor. xi. 1.* by his followers. Hence St. Paul is an imitator of Christ. *Eph. v. 1 f.* Hence the Ephesians are to be imitators of God, as beloved children, walking in love even as Christ loved them. Hence St. Paul's renunciation of those things which had been gain to him was in order that he might

'gain Christ, and be found in him, not having a righteousness of mine own, even that which is of the law, but that which is through faith in Christ, the righteousness which is of God by faith: that I may know him, and the power of his resurrection, and the fellowship of his sufferings, becoming conformed unto his death; if by any means I may attain unto the resurrection from the dead'. *Phil. iii. 8 ff.*

Here knowledge of the risen Christ is definitely regarded as dependent upon and subsequent to the imitation of his life in this world. And later in the same argument this becomes clearer still.

'Our citizenship is in heaven; from whence also we wait for a Saviour, the Lord Jesus Christ: who shall fashion anew the body of our humiliation, that it may be conformed to the body of his glory, according to the working whereby he is able even to subject all things unto himself.' *Phil. iii. 20 f.*

This conception, indeed, is best explained by St. Paul's own drawing out of an analogy between the Christian life in this world, and that of the Israelites in the desert. Just as the Israelites had passed through the Red Sea, so have the Christians been baptized. In baptism they have left the house of bondage, the servitude of the flesh of sin, and have been brought into intimate contact with God, being fed with manna from his hand, and drinking the water from the rock, Christ. The Christians live by the Spirit. But they are not yet removed from the sphere of temptation. They are still in the flesh, although they have died to its sinful lusts, and they may still be overcome by it. That was exactly, for St. Paul, the position of Christ humiliated in this world. It is through their own humiliation, accordingly, inevitable in the life of the sons of God in a fleshly world, that they hope to be finally conformed to his sufferings, and to attain to his resurrection. And so this intolerable position, which must cause suffering in this age, can be *1 Cor. x. 1-13.*

*Col. i. 24.* described by St. Paul as the filling up on his part of that which is 'lacking in the afflictions of Christ in my flesh for his body's sake, which is the church'. This does not mean that there was something lacking in Christ's suffering, but that there was something lacking in St. Paul's. He desires that his body may be, as it were, the arena where the obedience to God may be as wholly displayed as it had been in the passion of Jesus Christ.

St. Paul, then, regards the life and death of Christ from two points of view. His metaphor of a building is twisted unnaturally by his insistence that Christ is not only the foundation but the architect, and his whole thought is twisted by his oscillation between these two points of view. For instance, it is a commonplace to say that justification by faith is a fundamental tenet of St. Paul. But by whose faith? The expression which he frequently uses means, literally: 'on the basis of faith of Christ Jesus'. In many cases this is clearly objective, and is rightly translated, 'on the basis of faith *in* Christ Jesus'. But in others it has a subjective force 'on the basis of Christ Jesus' faith'. Such a conception, for instance, provides the most natural translation of the otherwise difficult passage in the Epistle to the Ephe- *Eph. iii. 11. f.* sians: 'according to the eternal purpose which he purposed in Christ Jesus our Lord: in whom we have boldness and access in confidence *through his faith*'. It is straining the Greek to translate, as do the English versions, 'through our faith in him'. St. Paul's 'by faith' therefore meant the faith of Christians in Christ and through him in God, a faith at once typified and created by Jesus' own faith, who was faithful unto death.

But, although it is possible for us to analyse St. Paul's conceptions in this way, it must never be supposed that he himself consciously did so. To him faith was one, just as the death of Christ in the flesh and of Christians through his Spirit to the flesh was one. Above all, his conception of Christ's own person was one. It is as wrong to suppose that he ever thought of Jesus merely as a manifestation of the 'image of God', a mere revelation of that redeeming and reconciling Spirit of whose operation his heart had been assured, as it would be to suppose that he could ever think of him simply as a man who was subsequently raised by an act of God to God's right hand. Such analysis belongs to later theologizing. The Christ of St. Paul is one person, so intimately bound up with God that he can be spoken of as the revelation of the unseen God, as pre-existing with God, as having the truth of God; so intimately bound up with God's action that his life and death are the action of God; so intimately bound up with the new creation that results from that action, that the church of God can be called the church of Christ, and that life 'in Christ' can be spoken of as 'life in God'; but, with all this, so really human that his life is the type of perfect Christian life and the summary of all Christian life; that his faith, his obedience, and his knowledge of God are the first-fruits and foundation of Christian faith, Christian obedience, and Christian knowledge. Call him 'Son of man', and that is a description of the God who loves; call him 'Son of God', and that is a description of his perfect obedience. Such is St. Paul's Christology. It has no parallel in the mysteries of Greece.

The judgement which represents the Christology of St. Paul as an innovation rests upon a misunderstanding of the whole occasion of his writings. They were evoked, not by any desire to popularize a theory of his own, but by the need of dealing with bodies of Christians already in conscious existence. As he writes he has before him a church consisting of men who know that they have been brought, by the Gospel of Jesus, into contact with the Spirit of God. He names them saints, as men who have been touched by the action of God. His conception of their new life 'in Christ' cannot be founded merely upon an exceptional spiritual experience of his own. It must have been, even though unanalysed, a commonplace of conversion. But it was just this consciousness of the energy of the Spirit operative in himself and in others which could, as he very well knew, lead to an emotional mysticism, if it were not controlled continuously by the actual history in which this outburst of spiritual power had originated. St. Paul is therefore everywhere concerned to force the Christians back upon the foundation of their salvation, to hold them to the history of Jesus, and, extracting the significance from the history, to present it to the intelligence and will of his readers. It is true that it is a spiritual insight which enables him to extract the significance from the history. He knows Christ no longer in a fleshly manner, that is, *2 Cor. v. 16.* as a Jewish reformer, as a revolutionary fanatic, or as a destroyer of the law who had been rightly put to death. Thus had he thought of him when he persecuted the church before his conversion. But now he knows him spiritually. Jesus is not a man who has advanced to union with God; he is lord and saviour. But this spiritual knowledge is a knowledge of Jesus, who was born of the seed of David, and is directed towards him crucified. He claims to know him as he *was and is*. And as he had known men once as Jews or Greeks, slaves or freemen, now he knows them so no more. He knows them in spiritual fashion to be sinners in need of salvation, and either to be passing to corruption in unbelief or to be heirs of the kingdom of God because they have believed in Jesus. But this spiritual knowledge is a knowledge of living men, of men of flesh and blood. The difference between a carnal and a spiritual knowledge consists in a difference of judgement. So the change from a carnal to a spiritual knowledge of Christ does not mean that the object of his knowledge has changed from the Jesus of history to the Spirit-Christ. To suppose this would be to make nonsense of his epistles. As he says, his gospel was the placarding of Christ crucified before the very eyes of his hearers, and his determination was to know nothing but Jesus Christ and him crucified. His description of the Christians as 'in Christ' can be explained only on the supposition that conversion, if it is to be fruitful, must bring with it a comprehension of the earthly life of Jesus in the flesh and an actual sharing in his obedience to the will of God.

The author of the Johannine writings, like St. Paul, is faced by a riot of disordered religious romanticism. Because the church is evidently controlled by the obedience of Jesus, St. Paul has only to appeal to this obedience for the Christians to understand at once what he means and to find in the church the escape from the anarchy of pagan mysticism; the author of the fourth Gospel, on the other hand, writing at a later date, has to prove that the church is subject to this historical *1 Jn. i. 1-4.* control. When he writes, spiritual romanticism has entered the church, and is there confidently declared to be the essence of the Christian religion. He is therefore less concerned with spiritual romanticism in the world than he is with its appearance in the church; and he is compelled to put forth his whole pastoral and literary energy in order to recover the control of the church by the life and death of Jesus.

In the opening verses of the First Epistle he sets the fellowship of the church upon the foundation of the witness of those who saw and handled the Word of life; and in the chapters which follow he returns again and again to this historical event. He shows that the life and death of Jesus was not a mere visual or sensual manifestation of something from the supernatural sphere, but, in its very form, a manifestation by which certain unprecedented results were achieved:

'Ye know that he was manifested to take away sins.' *1 Jn. iii. 5.*
'To this end was the Son of God manifested, that he might *1 Jn. iii. 8.* destroy the works of the devil.'

*1 Jn. iv. 9.* 'Herein was the love of God manifested in us, that God hath sent his only begotten Son into the world, that we might live through him.'

*1 Jn. v. 20.* 'We know that the Son of God is come, and hath given us an understanding.'

This historical event must condition Christian behaviour:

*1 Jn. iv. 10, 11.* 'Herein is love, not that we loved God, but that he loved us, and sent his Son to be the propitiation for our sins. Beloved, if God so loved us, we ought also to love one another.'

*1 Jn. iii. 1.* 'For this cause the world knoweth us not, because it knew him not.'

*1 Jn. iii. 5 f.* 'Ye know that he was manifested to take away sins; and in him is no sin. Whosoever abideth in him sinneth not: whosoever sinneth hath not seen him, neither knoweth him.'

*1 Jn. iii. 16-18.* 'Hereby know we love, because he laid down his life for us: and we ought to lay down our lives for the brethren. But whoso hath the world's goods, and beholdeth his brother in need, and shutteth up his compassion from him, how doth the love of God abide in him? My little children, let us not love in word, neither with the tongue; but in deed and truth.'

Not only is the newly begotten fellowship of sons of God directly created by the coming of Jesus; not only does its continued existence depend upon imitation of his life: but the recognition that he has come in the flesh provides the test of spiritual experience:

*1 Jn. iv. 2 f.* 'Hereby know ye the Spirit of God: every spirit which confesseth that Jesus Christ is come in the flesh is of God: and every spirit that confesseth not that Jesus is come in the flesh is not of God: and this is that spirit of antichrist, whereof ye have heard that it should come; and even now already is it in the world.'

The church is thus shown to rest not upon spiritual experience, but upon the life and death of Jesus. The Epistle was evidently provoked by the immediate need of refuting inside the church itself a spiritual speculation which denied the necessity of believing that Jesus Christ had really come in the flesh. That such opinions were current at the time when the Epistle was written is clear from the almost contemporary writings of St. Ignatius, bishop of Antioch.

The same controversial purpose is evident in the fourth Gospel. The fact that the author presented theology in the form of a gospel is a declaration that Christianity rests upon the words and actions and death of Jesus. The prologue, which, like the opening verses of the Epistle, places in a cosmological setting the coming of Jesus Christ and the consequent appearance of the fellowship of men newly begotten in him, begins by showing the effect of his entry into the world. He came in order to give to as many as received him the authority

'to become the sons of God, even to them that believe on his name: which were born, not of blood, nor of the will of the flesh, nor of the will of man, but of God'. *Jn. i. 12, 13.*

And the climax of the prologue is the declaration that this coming took the form, not merely of becoming man, for that might occasion a false interpretation, but of becoming *flesh*: 'the Word was made flesh, and dwelt among us'. The glory from the Father had been seen and handled by men. So, before the actual narration of the life and death and resurrection is begun, the concrete reality of the coming is insisted upon, together with its necessity for the new creation of sons of God. *Jn. i. 14.*

The author is, however, not content with his own witness. His gospel is so constructed as to throw into strong relief the witness which was borne to Jesus and by him in the course of the ministry itself. At the beginning of the gospel the Baptist declares him to be 'The Lamb of God, which taketh away the sin of the world.' At the end the beloved disciple, who at the moment of the death saw him give up the spirit, and saw blood and water flow forth from his side, witnesses: 'And he that hath seen hath borne witness, and his witness is true: and he knoweth that he saith true, that ye also may believe.' *Jn. i. 29; cf. 36. Jn. xix. 35.*

Between these two testimonies, which enclose the

163

record of the life and death of Jesus, the author inserts a whole series of testimonies which combine to rivet salvation to the particular history. The disciples bear witness. The Samaritan woman bears witness. The works of Jesus bear witness. The scriptures bear witness. Jesus bears witness to himself; and his witness is the witness of the Father, for he and the Father are one. So the Father who has sent him bears witness to him. Finally, the work of the Spirit is to bear witness also.

*Jn. iii. 11;*
*iv. 39;*
*v. 36, 39;*
*viii. 12 ff.;*
*xiv. 11 ff.;*
*xviii. 37;*
*v.37; xv. 26 f.*

And so the work of Jesus, his whole life and death, is not the fortuitous operation of a man, however high his calling, but the working of God:

*Jn. v. 17.*
*Jn. iii. 35 f.*

'My Father worketh even until now, and I work.'
'The Father loveth the Son, and hath given all things into his hand. He that believeth on the Son hath eternal life; but he that believeth not the Son shall not see life, but the wrath of God abideth on him.'

Throughout the narrative run two contrasted movements. Jesus consistently declares his creative significance for the world: the Jews hear him and as consistently reject him. The whole story is bound together by a series of statements in which the significance of the history is laid bare. Thus 'I am the bread of life' explains the feeding of the five thousand, and 'I am the light of the world', 'I am the way and the truth and the life' expose the significance of the healing of the blind man and of the raising of Lazarus. But the immediate result is rejection by the hearers. They take up stones to cast at him, and many even of his disciples go back and walk no more with him. In rejecting him they stand condemned. Refusing to see the light, they remain in utter darkness:

*Jn. xii. 47, 48.*

'And if any man hear my words, and believe not, I judge him not: for I came not to judge the world, but to save the world. He that rejecteth me, and receiveth not my words, hath one that judgeth him: the word that I have spoken, the same shall judge him in the last day.'

The words and teaching of Jesus, then, are of infinite and critical importance for those who hear them. Yet they lead on inevitably to the supremely important event—his death. This event, which in the narrative has been foreshadowed throughout the ministry, is solemnly shown to be its completion by the words 'It is finished'; and the author at once writes: 'He bowed his head, and gave up the spirit.' The death of Jesus is presented as a dynamic action, and elsewhere the author declares the blood, the water and the Spirit which proceed from him to be the necessary foundation of the church. With the resurrection is inaugurated the new creation, for, as at the first creation God breathed into the nostrils of men the breath of life, so the author writes that Jesus, on the first day of the week came and stood in the midst of his disciples and said unto them: *Jn. xix. 30.*

*1 Jn. v. 6, 7.*

'Peace be unto you: as my Father hath sent me, even so send I you. And when he had said this, he breathed on them, and saith unto them, Receive ye the Holy Ghost.' *Jn. xx. 21 f.*

Thus the foundation of the church is shown to be the actual words, actions, death and resurrection of Jesus who came in the flesh. And it is from him that the Spirit proceeds. The coming of the Spirit, indeed, is the final witness which not only testifies that Jesus has come in the flesh, but *1 Jn. iv. 2.*

'will reprove the world of sin, and of righteousness, and of judgement; of sin, because they believe not on me; of righteousness, because I go to my Father, and ye see me no more; of judgement, because the prince of this world is judged.' *Jn. xvi. 8 ff.*

Moreover,

'He shall receive of mine, and shall shew it unto you.' *Jn. xvi. 14.*

This is the Johannine gospel, written to defend the Christian religion on the one hand against the Jews who denied that the Christ had come, and on the other hand against those Christians who, in the interests of a free development of life in the Spirit, denied the control of the Jesus of history.

Its author claims to be extracting from the history of Jesus of Nazareth its true significance. No doubt the form of the Christology, of the discourses, and even of the narratives, has been wholly recast; recast to such an extent that at no point can we be certain that he gives us any new historical incident or any new saying of Jesus. But what has he extracted and laid bare? He insists upon a victory over the powers of evil actually achieved in the obedience of Jesus, the Son of God, to the will of the Father who sent him; he insists that this achievement was the creative fulfilment in the flesh of the law and of the Old Testament scriptures; he insists that the death of Jesus was a voluntary death in which this fulfiment was finally achieved; and he insists that the *opus operatum* of the life and death of Jesus requires imitation, and that as a result of it men can in very truth overcome the world. When all has been said about the method which the author employed in bringing out this significance, is what he says so different from what Mark had said or from what is involved in the whole material which composed the earlier tradition?

Nor is it otherwise with the other great theologian of the New Testament, the author of the Epistle to the Hebrews. Amidst continual emphasizing of the pre-existence of Jesus, his work contains more clear references to the story of Jesus of Nazareth as it was set forth in the synoptic tradition, than all the epistles of St. Paul together. Were there no other primitive Christian literature in existence, it would be possible to learn from *Heb. vii. 14;* this epistle that Jesus 'sprang out of Judah', that he *i. 2; iv. 2.* preached, and that his words had been handed down by those who had heard him. The author regards this teaching as of so great importance that he is afraid lest a later generation may drift away from it, and the great *Heb. ii. 1-3.* salvation be neglected. He refers quite naturally to Jesus

as enduring the contradiction of sinners, and states that *Heb. xii. 3.*
his prayers, supplications, strong crying, tears and godly *Heb. v. 7-9.*
fear achieved his triumph. He asserts that he died on a *Heb. xiii. 12.*
*Heb. xii. 2.*
cross, in despite of shame, outside the gate; and that *Heb. xiii. 20.*
God brought him again from the dead to the right hand *Heb. i. 2 f.;*
of his majesty on high; and, finally, he says quite simply: *viii. 1.*
'Unto them that look for him shall he appear the second *Heb. ix. 28.*
time without sin unto salvation.'

Yet, though such references show a thorough knowledge of the tradition, and a thorough sense of its importance, they do not in themselves determine what is
the foundation of the writer's thought. He, of course, like
nearly all the New Testament writers, is trying to meet
and to remedy a specific and critical situation. In his
opinion, those to whom he is writing have become dull
of hearing and need to be retaught the 'rudiments of the *Heb. v. 11 f.*
first principles of the oracles of God'. The first principles
are the assurance that God has prepared for men a
heavenly country or city, to which the Christians may
attain by faith, by boldness, and by resistance of temptation. This salvation is assured because Jesus, variously
described as the priest after the order of Melchizedek
(in order to show the eternity of his priesthood, and
therefore of their salvation), or as the great high priest
(in order to show the sufficiency of his one shedding of
blood), has already penetrated beyond the veil of the
sanctuary, into the holy of holies of God. But—and here
is the crux of the whole argument—Jesus was himself of
the same stuff as those whom the writer claims have
been saved by him. His penetration into the holy of
holies would have been without effect and without relevance had he not been one with them. The author carefully lays this down before he can proceed at all:

'Since then the children are sharers in flesh and blood, he *Heb. ii. 14.*
also himself in like manner partook of the same.'
'Wherefore it behoved him in all things to be made like unto *Heb. ii. 17.*
his brethren, that he might be a merciful and faithful high priest
in things pertaining to God, to make propitiation for the sins

of the people. For in that he himself hath suffered being tempted, he is able to succour them that are tempted.'

To this solid foundation he returns again and again in the elaboration of his argument, because upon it depends the possibility of imitation:

*Heb. ix. 14.*   'Who through the eternal Spirit offered himself without blemish unto God.'

*Heb. v. 7-9.*   'Who, in the days of his flesh, having offered up prayers and supplications with strong crying and tears unto him that was able to save him from death, and having been heard for his godly fear, though he was a Son, yet learned obedience by the things which he suffered; and having been made perfect. . . .'

*Heb. iv. 15.*   'We have not a high priest that cannot be touched with the feeling of our infirmities; but one that hath been in all points tempted like as we are, yet without sin.'

*Heb. iii. 2.*   'He was faithful to him that appointed him.'

Moreover he reinforces the appeal to his clear picture of Jesus by the appeal to Old Testament scripture in *Heb. x. 5-7.* order to show that Jesus came to do the will of God. Jesus, then, was of the sensuous and mortal nature of man. Like man, he was tempted. Like man he prayed, and lived in a state in which faith and obedience and self-oblation were a matter of choice. His triumphant priesthood is due to the fact that he was tempted without sin, was faithful unto death, obedient unto death, and that he made a complete oblation of himself to do the will of God. Precisely in this obedience lay the fulment of the Old Testament scriptures.

This, then, is the same conception of an *opus operatum* by a man Jesus in the flesh, once and for all, sufficient for the salvation of all men. But, as in St. Paul, men's appropriation of its results depends upon their imitation of, and identification with, his life, and upon their possession of the Spirit by which he lived. Jesus is the *Heb. xii. 2.* author and perfecter of faith, that is, of the faith of Christians.

*Heb. iii. 14.*   'We are become partakers of Christ, if we hold fast the beginning of our confidence firm unto the end.'

It is unnecessary to follow the author in the elaboration of his argument. It is necessary only to point out that he is everywhere making use of a clearly defined picture of the Jesus of history, and that his arguments have no force or relevance apart from their reference to that history. And what was that history to the author? It was a life lived in complete obedience to the will of God, lived unto death in the same obedience. Here is not only the conquest of sin and the assurance of eternal life, but that which makes sense of the Old Testament because it is its fulfilment.

The theologians of the New Testament, then, are not moving in a world of their own ideas. They are moving upon the background of a very particular history, which is itself shot through and through with theological significance. No doubt it is their own spiritual and moral experience which enables them to appreciate the significance of the history and to lay it bare; no doubt also considerable theological development results from their endeavour to extract its meaning; but neither their experience nor their theologizing has created the history which they are handling, and, consequently, the witness which they bear to it must be taken seriously in any historical reconstruction.

## NOTE

Since this chapter was originally written, very considerable arguments have been advanced for concluding that the Fourth Gospel and the First Epistle of John are not from the same hand. These arguments were set out fully by Professor C. H. Dodd in the Bulletin of the John Rylands Library, Vol. 21; and again in his commentary, *The Johannine Epistles*, in the Moffat New Testament commentary. It has not, however, seemed necessary to revise this chapter. Even if the two documents bear unmistakable marks of different authorship, they are none the less so clearly related to each other that to study them side by side is not only justifiable but necessary.

## Chapter X

## Jesus

The delicate threads which hold together the New Testament documents have been shown to be converging upon one single point. Evangelists, editors, theologians; narratives of miracles, records of parables, collections of sayings; argumentation, discourses, controversies; difficult problems in textual criticism, subtle changes in the meanings of words; all this varied material concentrates upon and has its origin in one single, isolated, historical event.

The final task of the historian is to gather up the evidence and to describe that event in such a manner that it is shown to lie within the structure of human life and to be intelligible in that context. Further, it must be described in such a manner that the emergence of the primitive church is also intelligible on the basis of the life and death of Jesus of Nazareth. For any historical reconstruction which leaves an unbridgeable gulf between the faith of the primitive church and the historical Jesus must be both inadequate and uncritical: inadequate, because it leaves the origin of the church unexplained; and uncritical, because a critical sifting of the evidence of the New Testament points towards the life and death of Jesus as the ground of primitive Christian faith, and points in no other direction.

The critical historian is not concerned with the ultimate truth of what Jesus taught, but only with the actual substance of his teaching. It is not for him to judge whether the significance which he assigned to his actions and to his person was in the end true, but only to make clear what significance he did in fact give to his work. The historian of primitive Christianity is a mere hewer of wood and drawer of water; it is his function to act as the slave of the theologian or of the philosopher, as the slave also of the simple believer or of the equally simple unbeliever. After all, it is as important for the believer to know what he disbelieves *unb* as it is for the believer to know what he believes; and the philosopher as well as the theologian must be able to form a clear notion of what he is handling when he comes to deal with the mainspring of the Christian religion. The historian has therefore to make clear and accessible the material which has shown such remarkable ability to galvanize thought and faith and unbelief. The historian, then, is neither an apologist for the Christian religion nor an apostle of irreligion; still less is he an interpreter of the New Testament in terms of modern thought. He does, however, claim the right to present, to the best of his ability, a distinct and concrete historical figure on the basis of a critical method of historical investigation; nor can he be dissuaded from doing this, even should the result prove inconvenient.

What, then, does in fact emerge? First, a clear negative conclusion. A biography of Jesus cannot be provided. Further, no single incident in his life or fragment of his teaching, if it be isolated from its context and detached, can be rendered intelligible, even if it be judged to be historical. From a mere collection of fragments, selected from the whole tradition and arbitrarily declared authentic, no outline of the concrete figure of Jesus can be drawn which for one moment carries conviction. If such a selective method be adopted, we might picture a religious personality who taught the 'brotherhood of men' and the 'fatherhood of God'; or we might roughly sketch an ethical system on the basis of a few aphorisms, and suppose that Jesus was a teacher of ethical principles; or we might sketch the career of a reformer of Jewish piety; or we might discover a religious mystic, or disclose a man possessed of intense spiritual insight depending upon a peculiar religious experience; or indeed, by piecing together a different selection of fragments, we might equally well describe the epiphany of a divine person who at no point touched human life as we know it. But these would be, not historical reconstructions, but simply selections of what seems to us convenient, or edifying, or useful, or monstrous.

An historical reconstruction is possible only when the uniform nature of the whole material at our disposal is perceived, so that each fragment is seen not only to be part of the whole, but to contain the whole; or, to put it differently, so that each fragment of it not only rests upon a common background, but expresses it. To lay bare this uniform nature, this background, is to discover the Jesus of history.

No single strand in the evidence deprives Jesus of the conscious sense that he was bringing into being a new order and working out a purpose—in complete isolation. Nowhere in the New Testament are the writers imposing an interpretation upon a history. The history contains the purpose, and is indeed controlled by it. That is to say, the historian is dealing in the end with an historical figure fully conscious of a task which had to be done, and fully conscious also that the only future which mattered for men and women depended upon the completion of his task. The future order, which it was the purpose of Jesus to bring into being, depended upon what he said and did, and finally upon his death. This conscious purpose gave a clear unity to his words and actions, so that the actions interpret the words and the words the actions. The same purpose, which caused the whole material in the tradition to move inexorably towards the crucifixion, forced the theologians to concentrate upon his death in their endeavour to expose the meaning of his life. Nor is this purpose, which binds together the life and the death, in the least degree un-intelligible as it is presented in the New Testament. The purpose of Jesus was to work out in a single human life complete obedience to the will of God—to the uttermost, that is, to death. The three great New Testament the-ologians saw this and expressed it quite clearly; indeed, this purpose alone makes sense of the tradition preserved in the synoptic gospels:

'Then said I, Lo I am come                          *Heb. x. 7.*
(In the roll of the book it is written of me)
To do thy will, O God.'
'Being found in fashion as a man,                   *Phil. ii. 8.*
He humbled himself,
Becoming obedient even unto death,
Yea, the death of the cross.'
'I can of myself do nothing:                        *Jn. v 30.*
As I hear, I judge:
And my judgement is righteous;
Because I seek not mine own will,
But the will of him that sent me.'

The recognition of this obedience of Jesus must not, however, be used to simplify the event. It cannot be concluded that much of the New Testament is filled with unnecessary complication which serves only to obscure the simplicity of a human consciousness of obedience to the supposed will of God. For, as we are reminded by the parenthesis in the passage quoted above from the Epistle to the Hebrews, it would be wrong to regard Jesus as a man mystically conscious of the need of obedience. The whole tradition agrees in depicting his obedience to the will of God as entirely unique, isolated, and creative: he consciously wrought out in flesh and blood the obedience demanded by the Old Testament scriptures and foretold by the prophets. His obedience springs from no mere attempt to range himself amongst the prophets of Israel, or amongst the righteous men of old, or amongst the best of his con-temporaries, but from the consciousness that, according to the will of God, the whole weight of the law and the prophets had come to rest upon him, and upon him only. This underlies the whole tradition about him. Consequently, if we are to be true to the evidence, the recognition of the necessity of this unique and creative obedience must be thrown back upon Jesus himself.

The author of the fourth Gospel summarizes this *Jn. i. 14.* when he writes: 'The Word became flesh.' That is to say, the Word of God ceased to be expressed in a literature or in a prophecy, and became embodied in human flesh, and there the Old Testament was fulfilled. The whole record concentrates, then, neither upon a righteousness of the heart nor yet upon a righteousness of the spirit of man, but upon a spiritual righteousness of the heart passing outwards into concrete speech and action, and finally into the bloody scene of the crucifixion. In this particular history, in this scene of flesh and blood, the creative obedience to the will of God was wrought out. The uniqueness of the obedience of Jesus in the midst of opposition and of complete misunderstanding, dictated by a creative and penetrating insight into the meaning of the Old Testament scriptures, is not an invention of the theologians or of the evangelists. This was the conscious purpose which lay behind and conditioned his words and actions.

But the obedience of Jesus was also a conscious conflict. It was a contest with the prince of evil for the freedom and salvation of men and women. Upon the outcome of this contest depended human freedom from sin.

*Is. xlix. 24, 25.*
'Shall the prey be taken from the mighty?
Or the captives of the terrible be delivered?
But thus saith the Lord,
Even the captives of the mighty shall be taken away,
And the prey of the terrible shall be delivered:
For I will contend with him that contendeth with thee,
And I will save thy children.'

Thus Jesus wrestled with the terrible and mighty power

of evil in order that it might be compelled to disgorge its prey. In his power over possessed men and women he saw the prey being actually disgorged. The whole New Testament rings with the sense of freedom from sin. But this freedom rests neither upon a spiritual experience nor upon a myth, but upon a particular history which lies in the immediate past and to which the original disciples had borne witness. The freedom of the Christians was known to rest upon a victory won in the life and death of Jesus. Here again, this primitive Christian confidence is not a piece of theologizing; it runs back to the meaning which Jesus assigned to his own actions, which is reflected in the temptation narrative, in the Beelzebul speech, in certain sayings, and in the whole detailed description of the confident manner in which he handled physical disease.

Thus far it might be argued that the evidence points to a strange human act of will by which Jesus determined to obey the will of God as he had extracted the knowledge of it from a persistent study of the Old Testament scriptures, and by which he also determined to conceive of his life as a personal conflict with the prince of evil. It might also be argued that he supposed that the carrying out of his determination to the point of a voluntary death would be fraught with immense consequences for men and women; that he would, in fact, by an act of utter obedience, bring in the new order, or, as it were, wrench it from the hands of God himself. This would make the New Testament in the end anthropocentric, for it would revolve round a human act. But this is not the truth. No New Testament writer could think of Jesus as the Greeks thought of Prometheus. We must therefore conclude that Jesus himself did not think of his life and death as a human achievement at all. Language descriptive of human heroism is entirely foreign to the New Testament. The event of the life and death of Jesus was not thought of as a human act, but as an act of God wrought out in human flesh and blood, which is a very different matter. The event was conceived of as a descending act of God, not as the ascending career of a man who was successful in the sphere of religion. No New Testament writer could think of Jesus in Pelagian[1] terms. The concrete event, which was Jesus of Nazareth, was for them the sphere in which God had effected a mighty action for the salvation of men. Again, this was no mere piece of theologizing, but the very way in which Jesus himself regarded his ministry. Human flesh and blood, words and actions, were, as it were, caught up, controlled, energized by the Spirit of God, by the Son of God, so that St. Paul could speak of *Col. ii. 9.* Christ Jesus as him in whom 'dwelleth all the fulness of the Godhead bodily', just as the author of the fourth Gospel could write of the Word becoming flesh. This emphatic assertion that Jesus is the sphere of the action of God presumes the theocentric atmosphere in which Jesus lived and died. His obedience was surrender to the unique and active operation of the living God. This was expressed by him by the relation of the Father to the beloved or only begotten Son.

The final paradox can now be stated. The action of the living God, which took place in a single human life, carried with it no spectacular display of supernatural power. For in the end, and here the New Testament authors speak with united voice, the action of God took place in complete humiliation and in what appeared to be remarkable weakness. The salvation of God occurred not in one who possessed plenary power or lived in the light of an open vision of his glory; it occurred in human faith and temptation and in a single, isolated figure. Yet the knowledge of God and his righteousness became available for men through the display of his power in the weakness of a single concrete life and death. The stone which the builders rejected became the head of the corner, and St. Paul could write:

[1] The doctrine that the human will is of itself capable of good.

'We preach Christ crucified,
Unto Jews a stumbling-block,
And unto Gentiles foolishness;
But unto them that are called, both Jews and Greeks,
Christ the power of God,
And the wisdom of God.
Because the foolishness of God is wiser than men;
And the weakness of God is stronger than men.'

*1 Cor. i. 23-25.*

In this Pauline passage is expressed with penetrating insight the conscious background of the life and death of the Jesus of history. He acted and spoke and died as the slave of God, confident that his slavery would bring into being the new people of God. Primitive christianity came into being because the Christians believed what he had said and done to have been the truth. The whole spiritual and moral power of the primitive church rested ultimately, not upon a mystical experience, but upon its belief that what Jesus had asserted to have been the purpose of his life and death was in very truth the purpose of God. Further than this the historian dare not and cannot go. On the basis of a purely critical examination of the New Testament documents he can reconstruct a clear historical figure, which is an intelligible figure; and he can, as a result of this reconstruction, show that the emergence of the primitive church is also intelligible.

The resurrection belongs properly outside the sphere of the historian, because the truth of what Jesus claimed is beyond his judgement, and because the Omega as well *Rev. i. 8.* as the Alpha, the Ending as well as the Beginning, belongs only to God. The historian must, of course, insist that St. Peter and St. Paul and others were convinced that they had seen him risen. But the resurrection itself belongs to Christian faith since it is never described as the survival of a human personality, but as the ratification by God of the obedience of Jesus and of his righteousness. The resurrection is therefore meaningless and ultimately trivial apart from the belief in the active power of the living God and in the ultimate truth of what Jesus said and did. It is also meaningless apart from the recognition that a particular historical life and death can have universal and ultimate significance.

# Conclusion

This book ends, as it must end, in an unresolved tension between confidence and helplessness. It ends confidently because the historical problem has been solved. The authors cannot pretend to regard their conclusion merely as a tentative guess at a solution. They have been swept on, at times against their will, by what seems to them quite overwhelming pressure, since the evidence, when treated critically, seems almost to rush to a conclusion. The New Testament documents do, in fact, yield to the modern critical method; and yet the solution of the historical problem does nothing either to compel faith or to encourage unbelief. There are here no 'assured results' of New Testament criticism. The historian can help to clarify the issue, but no more. He is unable to decide between faith and unbelief, or between faith and agnosticism. This is surely as it should be. The New Testament critic has far too often constituted himself the arbiter of faith and claimed a peculiar ability to deal out to the modern world what it may believe and what it may not. This is, however, wholly unjustifiable. The historian can outline the historical figure of Jesus of Nazareth. He can, moreover, demonstrate that his life and death did become the occasion of a quite remarkable outburst of faith in the power of the living God. But he can also demonstrate that it occasioned an almost equally passionate hatred and scorn. Upon the ultimate question of truth and falsehood he is unable, as an historian, to decide. And even if he had authority to make such decisions, his own results forbid him to detach portions of the New Testament as good and true, and to discard the rest as of little or of no value. The critical method has itself revealed most clearly the living unity of the documents. To praise this element and to blame that would be to destroy this very delicate unity. Indeed, it is the practice of selecting this or that element and of judging its value in isolation which has damaged much otherwise excellent critical work in the recent past. Critics have wished their work to be immediately fruitful, and have desired to present assured results which they think may be acceptable to the modern world, or may relieve the tension between the church and modern thought. The moment the critic surrenders to such a desire, he ceases to be a historian.

Yet it is none the less the historian's duty to hand over certain definite conclusions to those who are now concerned with his results. In the first place, therefore, it must be quite definitely affirmed that neither the Jesus of history nor the primitive church fits into the characteristic nexus of modern popular humanitarian or humanistic ideas. This is not merely because they belong to another age, of which the thought moved in an entirely unmodern idiom, but because their idiom was entirely foreign to that of any age, including their own. The gospel was as much a scandal to the first century as it is to the twentieth. This does not mean, however, that the gospel is in any sense anti-humanitarian. The antithesis between it and modern idealism arises, not because Jesus and primitive Christianity were less human than humanitarianism, but because they were infinitely more so. The primitive Christians found the revelation of God in an historical figure so desperately human that there emerged within the early Church a faith in men and women so deeply rooted as to make modern humanitarianism seem doctrinaire and trivial. The New Testament does not present a complex chaos of conceptions about God and man from which one or another may be picked out and proclaimed as ultimate and true because it satisfies the highest idealism of this or of all ages; it presents a concrete and definite solution of the problems of life and death, of right and wrong, of happiness and misery in a form which constitutes a challenge to all thought and to all ethical idealism. The New Testament presents the solution in a unique event, in a particular history of human flesh and blood. The New Testament is therefore neither a collection of thoughtful essays nor an attempt to construct a system of ethics. It bears witness to a unique history, and it discovers the truth in the history. The historian is compelled to state that both the unity and the uniqueness of this claim are historical facts. And, secondly, he must state quite explicitly what is here involved. The challenge presented to human thought by the New Testament is not created by the accidental emergence of a new way of thinking about these problems, which appeared first in one man, and then in the organized body of his followers. The challenge lies in the history and not in the thought detached from the history, since the history is an integral element in the new method of thought, and in fact constitutes its surprise and its scandal. The question, 'What manner of man is this?' which is so obvious throughout the synoptic gospels, is no mere literary trick of their editors. It is put, quite as provocatively, everywhere in the New Testament. The fourth Gospel persuades and entices the reader to venture a judgement upon the history. St. Paul placards before the eyes of the world, and with the most provocative intention, Christ crucified. And precisely the same compelling provocation is found throughout that material in which it has seemed possible to see the Jesus of history himself. The historian, then, must state that the New Testament demands what he, as an historian, may not give, a judgement of the highest possible urgency for all men and women.

Finally, then, the New Testament contains 'everywhere a concrete and exclusive claim to provide the revelation which solves the deepest problems of human life; it contains also everywhere a concrete and exclusive claim that a decision concerning this revelation is urgent. These claims and this demand rest, however, not upon the speculations of men as to the meaning of a myth; not upon the gradual imposition of a conglomeration of heterogeneous and exotic conceptions upon an ethic, in which the historical circumstances of its emergence were unimportant, but upon a history that was consciously conditioned by the claim that it was the very act of God. The New Testament therefore cannot be left merely to the philosopher or to the poet as though it were a contribution to speculation or to culture; it records historical facts which demand the consideration and judgement of every man and woman.

Here, then, the historian is driven to lay down his pen, not because he is defeated; not because his material has proved incapable of historical treatment, but because, at this point, he is faced by the problem of theology, just as, at this same point, the unbeliever is faced by the problem of faith.

## Appendix A

# Problems of Authorship and Dating

It is natural for those who are interested in the findings of New Testament criticism to desire as definite information as possible concerning the origin of the New Testament documents. If a document can, with certainty, be ascribed to a writer about whom something is known, if its composition can with confidence be assigned to such and such a date, its trustworthiness must clearly be affected.

The New Testament writers, however, were almost wholly unconcerned with such matters. No single document is dated; and the historical books, as opposed to the letters, are anonymous.

### THE SYNOPTIC GOSPELS AND THE ACTS OF THE APOSTLES

It was, however, not long before venerable names were attached to the anonymous books. By the end of the second century all four gospels were attributed directly or indirectly to apostolic authors, and were, at least relatively, dated. St. Matthew wrote the first Gospel, and this was the earliest of the four. St. Mark was the next to write a gospel, and it was not his gospel at all, but St. Peter's. St. Luke was the author of the third Gospel and of the Acts of the Apostles; and, since he was the companion of St. Paul, his gospel was, in fact, St. Paul's. Finally, St. John, the disciple of the Lord, published his gospel at Ephesus; and this was the last authentic gospel to be written. Thus the church at the end of the second century was confident that it possessed in the four gospels four apostolic accounts of the Lord's life, death and resurrection.

This tradition appears in the writings of several of the early fathers, and it is clear that it was known and accepted in different parts of the Church. Irenaeus of Lyons (about A.D. 140 to about A.D. 211), Clement of Alexandria (about A.D. 150 to about A.D. 215), Origen of Alexandria and Caesarea (A.D. 185-254), and the unknown author of the Muratorian Fragment (perhapf written at Rome about A.D. 200), agree in generals though not in detail, in thus reconstructing the origin o, the gospels. So do what are called the Anti-Marcionite Gospel Prologues—Prologues to Mark, Luke and John, which have been known for many years but only recently recognized as having certainly been written between A.D. 160 and A.D. 180.

The chief passages are as follows:

*'Against the Heresies', III, 1, 1; quoted by Eusebius of Caesarea (about A.D. 265 to about 340) in his 'Ecclesiastical History', V, 8, 2-4.* IRENAEUS. 'Matthew published his gospel among the Hebrews in their own language, while Peter and Paul were preaching the gospel and founding the church in Rome. After their departure (? death) Mark, the disciple and interpreter of Peter, also transmitted to us in writing those things which Peter was wont to proclaim. And Luke, the attendant of Paul, recorded in a book the gospel which Paul had declared. Afterwards John, the disciple of the Lord, who also reclined on his bosom, published the gospel, while residing at Ephesus in Asia.'

THE MURATORIAN CANON (The meaning of the words in italics is uncertain).

'. . . *But at some he* (? St. Mark) was present, and he set them down thus.

'The third book of the gospel, that according to Luke, Luke, the well-known physician, wrote in his own name in order, after the ascension of Christ, when Paul had associated him with himself as one *studious of right*. Yet neither did he himself see the Lord in the flesh; and he, according as he was able to accomplish it, began his narrative with the nativity of John.

'The fourth gospel is that of John, one of the disciples.' (Here follows an account of the occasion of his writing this gospel.)

The Muratorian Fragment was published by the

Italian scholar Muratori in 1740. It is now in the Ambrosian Library at Milan. It is written in barbarous Latin.

CLEMENT OF ALEXANDRIA. 'Again, in the same books, Clement gives the tradition of the earliest presbyters, as to the order of the gospels, in the following manner: The gospels containing the genealogies, he says, were written first. The gospel according to Mark came into being in this manner: When Peter had preached the Word publicly at Rome, and declared the gospel by the Spirit, many who were present requested that Mark, who had followed him for a long time and remembered his sayings, should write them out. And having composed the gospel he gave it to those who had requested it. When Peter learned of this, he neither directly forbade nor encouraged it. But, last of all, John, perceiving that the external facts had been made plain in the gospels, being urged by his friends, and inspired by the Spirit, composed a spiritual gospel. This is the account of Clement.' *Quoted by Eusebius, E.H. VI, 14, 5-7, from the lost 'Hypotyposeis' (sketches).*

ORIGEN. 'In his first book on Matthew's gospel, maintaining the canon of the church, he testifies that he knows only four gospels, writing somewhat as follows: *Quoted by Eusebius, E.H., VI, 25, 3-6, from Origen's commentary upon St. Matthew's gospel.*

'Among the four gospels, which are the only indisputable ones in the church of God under heaven, I have learned by tradition that the first to be written was that by Matthew, who was once a publican, but afterwards an apostle of Jesus Christ, and it was prepared for the converts from Judaism, and published in the Hebrew language. The second is by Mark, who composed it according to the instructions of Peter, who in his Catholic Epistle acknowledges him as a son, saying, "The church that is at Babylon elected together with you, saluteth you, and so does Mark, my son." And the third by Luke, the gospel commended by Paul, and composed for gentile converts. Last of all that by John.'

THE MARCAN PROLOGUE. '. . . [So] Mark asserted, who is called the "stumpy-fingered", because his fingers were too small in comparison with the rest of his body. He was Peter's interpreter [?expounder], [and], after Peter himself had departed [?died] he wrote this same gospel down, in the parts of Italy.'

THE LUCAN PROLOGUE. 'Luke was a Syrian of Antioch and a doctor by profession. He became a disciple of the Apostles and finally a close companion of Paul until his martyrdom. Having served the Lord without ceasing he died unmarried and childless, in Boeotia, at the age of eighty-four, full of the Holy Ghost.

'Although there were already Gospels in existence—that according to Matthew written in Judaea, and that according to Mark in Italy—Luke was moved by the Holy Spirit to compile the whole of this Gospel, in the country round Achaia. He pointed out in his prologue that others had been written before this one, but that it was essential to set forth an accurate record for the faithful among the gentiles to prevent their being led astray by Jewish legends or deceived by heretical and empty opinions, and so come wide of the truth. . . .'

We are fortunately able to track the tradition concerning Matthew and Mark further back. Eusebius possessed a book, now lost, which had been written by Papias, Bishop of Hierapolis, shortly before A.D. 150. The book was entitled *Explanations of the Sayings of the Lord*, and was divided into five parts. From this book Eusebius quoted the following passages:

*Eusebius, E.H., III, 39, 15 f.*

'and thus the Presbyter used to say: "Mark, having become the translator (? interpreter) of Peter, wrote down accurately, though not however in order, whatever he remembered of the things said or done by the Lord. For he neither heard the Lord nor followed him, but afterwards, as I said, he followed Peter, who adjusted his teaching to the needs of his hearers, but gave no connected account of the sayings of the Lord. Mark therefore made no mistake in thus writing down some things as he remembered them. For he was especially careful not to omit any of the things he heard nor to make any false statement." These things are recorded by Papias concerning Mark. But concerning Matthew he says: "So, then, Matthew did arrange in order the sayings in the Hebrew (? Aramaic) language, and each man translated (? interpreted) them as he was able." '

Here then is the origin of the tradition of the church concerning Matthew and Mark, for it seems certain that the early fathers depend upon Papias, and that they had no independent knowledge. The variations in the tradition are due simply to different expansions and interpretations of what Papias had said. Everything then depends upon the accuracy of Papias. What Papias means in general seems perfectly clear. Mark is to be trusted absolutely. He was not an original disciple of the Lord, and therefore possessed no personal memories.

But he was accustomed to translate Peter's teaching, and was his disciple. Consequently everything that Mark wrote was really Peter's; and the very disorderliness of Mark's gospel reflects the practice of Peter; for Peter's teaching consisted in fragmentary memories gathered together to encourage the faith of his hearers and meet their needs. Matthew's gospel, however, was quite different. It was written by an apostle; it was written in Hebrew or Aramaic; and there was originally no authorized translation of it. Those who wished to use it had to make the best translation they could.

It seems impossible to think that Papias meant his readers to understand anything else. And if so, he meant his readers to understand that the first Gospel, now familiar to Christians in its Greek form, had been originally written by the apostle Matthew in Hebrew or in Aramaic. At first, however, there existed no adequate translation of this apostolic work. But Papias carefully stated that the tradition was not his, but the elder's. That is to say, it goes back behind Papias into the first century, and is attached to the authoritative figure of the elder John. How much of the tradition was the elder's and how much was due to Papias' retelling of it, we cannot tell.

What then happens to this tradition when it is set side by side with the results of a critical analysis of the gospels themselves? We cannot escape from the conclusion that the synoptic gospels stand in a literary relationship to one another. According to the tradition, however, they emanated independently, each from an apostle. The first is claimed to be the direct work of St. Matthew; the second to be St. Mark's reproduction of St. Peter's teaching; the third to be St. Luke's presentation of the preaching of St. Paul. Tradition made no claim to date these three gospels, beyond asserting that St. Matthew was the first to write and supposing that Mark wrote either while St. Peter was still alive, or soon after his death. Luke's writing is nowhere dated. It is, then, quite clear that the tradition is not, as it stands, compatible with what is demanded by the literary analysis of the gospels themselves. Since Matthew is dependent upon Mark, it must have been subsequent to Mark; and since its author corrected Mark's Greek, it must have been written originally in Greek and in no other language. In the light of the literary analysis of the gospels, the problem of date and authorship has to be approached from a different angle. Luke and Matthew are the result of careful editing of Mark and of another source; and each also contains special material, which may be named 'special Matthew' and 'special Luke'. The making of Matthew and Luke has therefore a somewhat complicated history behind it, which is roughly demonstrated in the following diagram.

The dotted lines represent relations which the authors of this book do not accept as proven, but which have some weight of evidence to substantiate them.

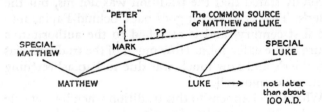

The gospels of Matthew and Luke can hardly have been written later than the end of the first century. Otherwise it is almost impossible to explain the apparent citations of Matthew in the apostolic fathers in the first half of the second century, or the attitude of Marcion to the Lucan writings in the middle of the second century, or the procedure of Tatian, who became a Christian in Rome about 160, and who combined not only the first three gospels but also the fourth into one continuous narrative or harmony, called the Diatessaron.

It will be seen then that a considerable literary activity must have taken place in the Church behind the

making of Matthew and Luke. Three questions therefore arise:

(1) Do the results of literary criticism entirely destroy
the evidence of tradition? Or does some of that evidence
throw light upon the intricate literary relations of the
synoptic gospels? In particular, does the statement of
Papias, that Matthew composed the sayings in the
Hebrew language, and that each one interpreted them
as he could, throw any light upon the curious fact that
Matthew's name came to be attached to the first gospel?

(2) Does the internal evidence of Mark conflict with
or confirm the tradition that he reproduced the teaching of St. Peter?

(3) Does the internal evidence of Luke confirm or
disturb the tradition that 'Luke the Physician' wrote
Luke-Acts?

## MATTHEW

The evidence of Papias concerning Matthew is singularly difficult to handle because of the uncertainty of
the meaning of the Greek. In the short sentence—'So,
then, Matthew *did arrange in order the sayings* in the
Hebrew language, and each *translated* them as he was
able'—each of the words in italics is a not quite certain
rendering of the Greek, especially if the passage be
taken as independent of what Papias had written of
Mark.

(*a*) *Did arrange in order:* The Greek might mean
simply 'composed' in the broad sense of 'wrote'.

(*b*) *Sayings:* The Greek might mean merely 'words'
or 'brief' utterances'. In classical usage it sometimes
meant *divine oracles*, as, e.g. 'the Sibylline Oracles'. It
was similarly used in the Old Testament with the special
significance of 'the utterances of God'. Josephus used it
for the 'prophecies of God' in the Old Testament, and
Philo, for the 'Ten Commandments'. In the New Testa-

ment it was similarly used for 'oracles of God', but in various ways. In Acts vii. 38 and in Romans iii. 2 it is used of the oracles delivered by God in the Old Testament. In Hebrews v. 12 and in 1 Peter iv. 11 it is used of the substance of the Christian religion and for the utterances of God through Christian teachers. The first Epistle of Clement to the Corinthians contains a similar use. But Polycarp uses it of the precepts of Christ, and the interpolator of the Epistle of Ignatius to the Smyrneans uses it of the New Testament scriptures.

(c) *Interpreted:* as in English, this might mean either *translated* (into Greek) or *expounded*, for homiletic purposes.

Owing to this elasticity in meaning of at least three words in this short statement of Papias it has been possible to offer very various interpretations of its evidence with some degree of confidence. It is necessary to mention here only those which find some justification in the results of synoptic criticism.

When it was discovered that Matthew and Luke had used a common source, and that this common source was largely composed of sayings, it was tempting to conjecture that the account of Papias justified the supposition that St. Matthew had collected, perhaps into some sort of order, short sayings of Jesus. This collection was at first translated into Greek 'as best they could' by the Christian missionaries. But subsequently a translation was in general circulation and this the authors of the first and third gospels used, because of its known apostolic origin, to supplement the narrative of Mark. This is a particularly tempting conclusion, not only because it gives the fragments from the common source the prestige of an eyewitness, but because it explains the procedure of Matthew and Luke by giving a name to their otherwise anonymous source. But it is no more than an hypothesis, and it is not a very easy hypothesis to accept. Papias was almost certainly writing of the origin of our gospel of Matthew. If, therefore, the passage correctly reproduces the elder's words, it has to be supposed that Papias misunderstood them, and that he misunderstood them because Matthew meant to him our Matthew and all knowledge that the apostle had written something else had been lost, or at least Papias had never heard of it. It is all very difficult. How did the work of the apostle disappear without Papias or his contemporaries being aware even of its previous existence?

An entirely different interpretation has therefore been put forward. It has been argued that, since the first missionary activity was among Jews, or at least among proselytes, who knew the Old Testament scriptures, the early missionaries must have relied largely upon the quotation of 'proof-texts', passages from the Old Testament, in order to show that the ministry and death of Jesus were the fulfilment of Old Testament prophecy. The Papias tradition might therefore imply that Matthew drew up a collection of such proof-texts which each *expounded*, or fitted into the Lord's life, to the best of his ability. This again is a very difficult explanation. It is certainly not what Papias understood. He contrasted Matthew with Mark; both wrote, not Old Testament prophecies, but narratives of the Lord's life; the one was an orderly account, the other was not. If Papias misunderstood the elder, he misunderstood him because he had no knowledge of any literary activity of Matthew except the first Gospel. Not only was Matthew's original writing lost; but all memory of it was also lost.

There are other solutions. But these two suffice to show how very pliable the evidence is. The point is that, though we may say that the procedure of Luke and Matthew is more easy to understand if they used in addition to Mark another document which had been originally written by the apostle Matthew, containing mainly sayings of Jesus arranged in orderly fashion, and that the name Matthew slipped from this second source to denote the first Gospel, this must remain only an hypothesis. It cannot be taken as an assured result of modern criticism. Still less can we assume that the apostle Matthew drew up a list of Old Testament messianic texts, and that the author of our first Gospel used this older document, extracting from it his Old Testament citations, and that this explains the survival of the name Matthew.

It must therefore be concluded that the evidence of Papias does not enable a scholarly judgement to be made either upon the authorship of the first Gospel, or upon the origin and authorship o the common source of Matthew and Luke.

## MARK

Do we find firmer ground when we consider the traditional origin of Mark? Although, as is shown by a comparison of the passages quoted from the fathers of the second and third centuries, there are certain additions to the Papias tradition, it would be hazardous to make any of these discrepancies the ground for supposing that they were not all originally elaborations of the tradition which he presented. The passage of Papias, then, is, as in the case of the first Gospel, the crux of the external evidence for the authorship of the second. This passage is less ambiguous than the passage about Matthew. But it is not absolutely certain that Papias thought that St. Mark translated into Greek St. Peter's oral Aramaic teaching, and that he then, because he was a practised interpreter, proceeded to give it written form. The word *interpreter* is capable of a less precise meaning. This ambiguity, however, is not strictly relevant to the main question, which is simply whether the internal evidence of the second Gospel substantiates this very early tradition that it emanated from St. Peter, and that it represented his disordered method of teaching.

Quite recently the late Professor C. H. Turner made a very interesting research into the gospel of Mark, which had to some extent been anticipated at an earlier period in Germany. He brought forward considerable evidence for supposing that large parts of the narrative framework, although in the third person, show signs of having been originally in the first person. The frequent phrases, 'Jesus and his disciples', 'and they come', and such introductions to incidents as 'And while they were in the way', suggest that the author, unlike Matthew and Luke, pictured the ministry as the movements of a group, Jesus and his disciples. Professor Turner held that this would be explained if Mark had heard these stories recounted as reminiscences: 'And when we drew nigh . . .'—'And while we were in the way. . . .' It may also be held to be significant that the introductory incidents before the call of Peter are recorded more summarily than the rest. The internal evidence may be said to admit of the supposition that the author of the second Gospel received the greater part of his information from an eyewitness. But it cannot be proven. More serious is the recognition that the whole book is a carefully constructed literary unity. The gospel of Mark is misunderstood if it be treated merely as a compilation of reminiscences or as a compilation of disordered Petrine teaching. And yet, this is what the Papias tradition declares the second Gospel to be. The gospel may be resting upon Petrine teaching, but the author has constructed from such teaching, whether Petrine or more general oral tradition, a carefully ordered narrative. The Petrine background of the Marcan gospel is then not *demanded* by the gospel itself.

Was the author John Mark? The answer to this question depends upon the certainty with which the contents of the gospel can be taken back to St. Peter. According to the Acts, St. Peter's immediate destination after his *Acts xii. 12.* miraculous release from prison was the house of Mary the mother of John Mark. The first Epistle of Peter also *1 Pet. v. 13.*

rather significantly couples Mark with Peter, for it ends with this salutation: 'She that is in Babylon, elect together with you, saluteth you; and so doth Mark my son.' There is New Testament evidence, then, for supposing that Mark was closely associated with St. Peter. But Acts also records that John Mark was the companion of St. Paul on his first missionary journey. If this was so, may there not have been a Pauline influence upon the second Gospel? The whole question bristles with difficulties. If Mark wrote the second Gospel, is he depending solely on Petrine teaching? Or is he setting down general oral tradition in which Petrine teaching played a large part? We do not know.

*Acts xii. 25, etc. cf. 2 Tim. iv. 11.*

LUKE—ACTS

It is well known that Dr. Harnack reacted suddenly to a belief that 'Luke the Physician', that is, the Luke mentioned in the Epistles of St. Paul to the Colossians and to Philemon, and in the second Epistle to Timothy, was the author of the third Gospel and of the Acts of the Apostles. The third Gospel and the Acts of the Apostles had, at least from the time of the Muratorian Canon, been attributed to the same author. Their style is similar; the one starts where the other leaves off; each is begun with a formal preface addressed to 'Theophilus'. They also show a similarity of doctrinal tendency which makes it almost impossible to doubt that Acts was the work of the author of the third Gospel. Now Acts contains a number of passages marked by the use of the first person plural. These are the celebrated 'We Passages'. It is difficult, if not impossible, to distinguish the style of these passages from Luke-Acts as a whole. Hence it is assumed by many critics that Luke-Acts was written

*Col. iv. 14; Philem. 24; 2 Tim. iv. 11.*

*Acts xvi. 10-17; xx. 5-15; xxi. 1-18; xxviii. 10-16.[1]*

[1] In codex Bezae and in a small number of Latin manuscripts supported by Augustine, Acts xi. 28 is also a 'We Passage'.

by a companion of St. Paul. And since tradition gives us the name Luke, why not trust the tradition? All that we are here concerned to point out is that the attribution to Luke is a critical deduction, it is not a certainty.

Far more important, and far more doubtful, is the further deduction that is made from this ascription of Luke-Acts to St. Luke, the companion of St. Paul. It is often supposed that, since he was at Caesarea[1] with St. Paul, St. Luke must have had admirable opportunities of collecting information concerning Jesus at first hand, and that therefore 'special Luke', that is that part of Luke which is not dependent upon Mark or upon the source common to him and to Matthew, is to be accepted as containing very reliable information.

But it is troublesome and disturbing to find that, though the author of Acts seems quite well enough informed about the actual movements of St. Paul to have been his companion, his reports of St. Paul's speeches fail to give a convincing indication of his teaching. We should have no conception of what St. Paul taught if we had to depend for our information upon Acts alone. There are echoes in Acts of the teaching in the epistles, but they are not more than echoes. The impression gained from a study of Luke-Acts is that the author was an artist and a literary man, and that he was concerned, in part to write an apology for the Christian religion, and in part to present Christian history to intelligent Greek readers. This seems to be the reason why in the gospel he omits material which he supposes to be intelligible only to Jews, and why in Acts he glosses over, for example, the situation caused in Jerusalem by the conversion of the Gentiles as a result of the mission of St. Paul and Barnabas, and replaces it by a council which is extremely difficult to reconcile with the tension of the Pauline epistles. This does not mean that Luke was a bad historian, or that his evidence for the history of Jesus and of the early church is worthless. But it does

[1] Acts xxi. 8 is a 'We Passage'.

mean that he was capable of smoothing out the roughness of the history and simplifying the difficult elements
in the tradition and in the teaching of St. Paul. The
author writes as a Christian of the second generation.
He may well have been conversant with eyewitnesses;
he may have been one of St. Paul's companions; but he
wrote in a definitely sub-apostolic atmosphere. The
schism aroused by the Judaizing 'troublers' of the
Galatians was past history. The consciousness of election
which had isolated the early church was beginning,
perhaps unconsciously, to be distilled in the atmosphere
of reasoning apologetic. The apostles were beginning
to be regarded as men whose unheroic lapses ought not
to be fully recorded. The eyes of the church were turning to the Roman Empire; and it was hoped that
Christianity might be understood and respected, if it
could be presented without undue harshness. For these
reasons, even if the author be Luke, the medical friend
of St. Paul, the historian has to treat him with great
care. In the end, what Luke gives us is not to be accepted because Luke recorded it, but rather because it
may be found to be running back to a tradition which
agrees with that which is known to us from elsewhere.
Where Luke goes apart from the other strata, it is not
in Luke that we can place our confidence.

*　　*　　*

If it has been found difficult, in spite of a certain
amount of evidence, to give names to the authors of the
synoptic gospels, it is much more difficult to assign their
writing to definite dates. Here there is no clear evidence
at all; and accurate dating is simply impossible. The
*terminus ad quem* must be somewhere about A.D. 100.
Since Luke and Matthew used Mark, and apparently
used him independently, Mark must have been written
some time before the other two gospels. Luke's editing
*Lk. xxi. 20-24.* of the eschatological speech in Mark xiii seems to

betray a knowledge of the siege and fall of Jerusalem in A.D. 70. If it could be proved that he had read and misunderstood the *Antiquities* of Josephus, which were published A.D. 93 (? 94), we should have an important piece of evidence. But the relation between Luke and Josephus is completely unproven. Matthew contains nothing which enables any definite date to be assigned to it. Mark xiii looks at first as though the author knew of the destruction of Jerusalem; but when carefully examined it is uncertain whether the language implies more than a prophecy of great tribulation. Otherwise Mark provides no opportunity for accurate dating. Nor is it possible to make any definite statement about the date of the non-Marcan common source of Matthew and Luke. Its date and authorship remain as elusive as the authorship and dates of the synoptic gospels themselves.

All this is very unsatisfactory, and there seems to be no reason to expect that it will remain otherwise than very unsatisfactory. The truth is that the synoptic gospels were written as anonymous and undated documents. They emerged from the primitive church, and they were thought of as representing the oral tradition of the Church in a more or less orderly form. They are therefore best handled as they were intended to be handled and read. We have no right to think of them as originally guaranteed by some prominent name.

## THE FOURTH GOSPEL

With the question of the authorship of the fourth Gospel we tread on very delicate ground. Those who are convinced that a reconstruction of the Jesus of history is possible on the basis of a critical study of the synoptic gospels, and that he can be adequately described within the framework of modern humanitarian and ethical idealism, are frankly shocked by the fourth Gospel. The whole situation is eased if the fourth Gospel can be removed from all contact with the memory of Jesus. The denial of apostolic authorship, and even of a relation to apostolic reminiscence, is felt to be essential. For those, on the other hand, who are dissatisfied with this reconstruction, the authorship of the fourth Gospel has provided the supreme battleground. So much seemed to hang upon it. If it could be proved that the author was an original disciple of Jesus, or even if it could be proved that he was in close contact with an original disciple, the whole humanitarian reconstruction would be severely shaken. For these reasons liberal and conservative scholars have been on edge whenever the question of the authorship of the fourth Gospel has been raised.

One of the main aims of this book has been to show that the battleground lies elsewhere. We are free therefore to treat the question of authorship and date on purely critical grounds. The evidence is wholly elusive. The gospel contains no definite statement that the author was named John. It is an anonymous book. But unlike the synoptic gospels, it suggests that its author was one of the original disciples, suggests also that the author was the beloved disciple, if *these things* in xxi. 24 means *this book*. But if the reader is intended to understand that the beloved disciple wrote the book, more than this is, in fact, suggested. It is suggested that the beloved disciple was the apostle John. Indeed, it may be said that the phrase *whom Jesus loved* echoes the meaning of the name *Johannes*. But who is the beloved disciple? He appears in the gospel as the ideal disciple, and pre-eminently as the great witness, whose witness is comparable only to the witness of John the Baptist. He is presented to the reader as a more intimate disciple of Jesus even than Peter. He lies on the bosom of Jesus, and Peter asks him to question the Lord; he it is, assuming the 'other disciple' to be identical with the

*Jn.*
*xiii. 23-26;*
*xviii. 15, 16;*
*xix. 25-27;*
*xx. 2-8; xxi.*
*20-24.*

beloved disciple, who enables Peter to enter the house of the high priest; he alone of the male disciples stands under the cross; to him the Lord entrusts his mother; he, not Peter, is the first disciple to declare his belief that Jesus is risen though he had not seen him; and finally, he is pictured naturally *following* the Lord, whilst Peter has to be commanded to *follow* him. Yes, but why then should he not be named? Who is the beloved disciple? It is all very puzzling. It appears as though the author wishes his readers to judge that the beloved disciple was the apostle John, but that he does not dare to say this clearly. Many explanations of this strange situation have been offered. It has been said that the author was John the apostle, but that modesty prevented his naming himself. But is modesty characteristic of these descriptions of the beloved disciple, if indeed he wrote these things of himself? It has been said that the author was a disciple of the apostle. Perhaps he was. It has been said that there was another John, also a disciple, but a young disciple, and that he wrote the book, or that a disciple of his wrote it. It has been said that the book was written by an unknown Christian, and that the beloved disciple simply represents the ideal Christian, and that the author throws his gospel guardedly upon the apostle John, and expects his readers to know what he is doing. In other words, no one knows who wrote the Johannine writings: and it is better to read the fourth Gospel and the Johannine Epistles, and to discuss the meaning of what is there set down, than to pretend to a knowledge which we do not possess.

The Johannine writings do, however, tell us something about their author. He knew the geography of Palestine; he wrote in Greek, but he thought in Semitic idiom; he knew the Jews and the Jewish religion; he was completely at home with the Old Testament scriptures and his allusions to the Old Testament are, if that were possible, more subtle than those in the synoptic gospels. But primarily he was a Christian. This had made him what he is, and he has a piercing insight into the meaning of the earlier tradition about Jesus. He worked upon that tradition as it has been set forth in St. Mark's gospel; perhaps he knew St. Luke's gospel, perhaps also St. Matthew's gospel. No doubt he knew more than this. But whether he was working upon his own reminiscences or upon those of some particular eye-witness, or upon additional oral tradition, we cannot tell. In any case, he has mastered the tradition. But he has mastered it as a Christian theologian; and it is as a theologian that he wrote, and as a theologian that he must be judged.

Nor is it possible to assign a definite date to the Johannine writings. The author knew St. Mark's gospel, and his gospel is unintelligible if he did not presume that his readers also knew the substance of Mark. But that does not help us to date his gospel accurately. If it could be proved that he presumed a knowledge of all three synoptic gospels we should have roughly A.D. 90-100 as a *terminus a quo*. The external evidence to the gospel is rather puzzling. The apostolic fathers at times use phrases which we know from the fourth Gospel. But it is difficult to pronounce them to be certainly citations from the fourth Gospel. They may be due to a common background of Christian language. The first certain quotation occurs in Justin Martyr (about A.D. 140). Origen's commentary presumes that the fourth Gospel had long been known and accepted in the Church. The discovery and publication of the *Fragments of an Unknown Gospel* (ed. by H. Idris Bell and T. C. Skeat, London, 1935), which, after Professor Dodd's analysis published in the *Bulletin of the John Ryland's Library*, January 1936, seems, in spite of the editor's judgement, to be dependent upon the fourth Gospel, and the discovery and publication of the tiny fragment of a papyrus codex of the fourth Gospel (*An Unpublished Fragment of the Fourth Gospel*, ed. by C. H. Roberts,

Manchester, 1935), suggest, if indeed they do not prove, not only that the fourth Gospel was circulating in Egypt during the first half of the second century, but that it was capable of providing the basis for further development of gospel material. Apparently it gained its position slowly. If so, it cannot be dated later than the beginning of the second century. This seems also to fit the occasion of the Johannine writings as a whole. The author is dealing with a situation similar to that which Ignatius had to face some few years later. Greek Christians were uneasy concerning the necessity of maintaining the relation between the Church and the Jesus of history. They thought that the possession of the Spirit rid them of the necessity of the control of Jesus *in flesh*, that is, of the original history. The author wrote in order to show that everything depended not only upon the original history, but upon the understanding of it. In fact, he makes it clear that the Spirit is given primarily in order that men may understand the meaning of the history of the life and death and teaching of Jesus. He rivets the church to the control of that particular history and to the apostolic understanding of it.

The fourth Gospel, then, like the first three, remains in respect of authorship an enigma and of precise date uncertain. But it may be doubted whether this uncertainty detracts anything from the significance and importance of its contents, when they are treated critically, and when they are set in the context of the New Testament as a whole.

## THE PAULINE EPISTLES, THE EPISTLE TO THE HEBREWS, AND THE FIRST EPISTLE OF PETER

Questions of date and authorship hardly arise in connexion with the other New Testament documents referred to in this book. The Pauline epistles fall into more or less distinct groups:

1 Thessalonians.
2 Thessalonians.

Galatians.
1 Corinthians.
2 Corinthians.
Romans.

Philippians.

Colossians.
Philemon.
Ephesians.

1 Timothy.
2 Timothy.
Titus.

This grouping does not refer to date, but to similarities of expression, occasion, and subject-matter. With the exception of the Epistle to the Ephesians and of the last group, known as the Pastoral epistles, all may be quite confidently pronounced to have been written either by St. Paul himself or at his dictation. A question has been raised concerning 2 Thessalonians, but there is no sufficient reason to doubt its authenticity. Ephesians has a less clear and precise historical situation than any of the other Pauline epistles and may be a sub-Pauline compendium of his teaching. But it is so subtly linked to Colossians, and the interpretation of the one is so much more easy when read side by side with the other, that it is probably better to take Ephesians as definitely Pauline, than to suppose that it was written by someone else on the basis of the Colossian epistle. The Pastoral epistles are much more doubtful. They are difficult to fit into the known framework of St. Paul's life, though this may be due to our ignorance of the circumstances of his death. More serious is the vocabulary. The Pastoral epistles are filled with words which occur nowhere else in the Pauline epistles. No modern critic is quite happy in treating these letters as Pauline in their present form.

With regard to dating, the certainly genuine epistles fall quite naturally into the Lucan story of St. Paul's journeys, and may be dated somewhere between A.D. 44 and A.D. 66. They are therefore the earliest surviving Christian documents. If Galatians be written to the Christians whose conversion is described in Acts xiii and xiv, immediately after their conversion, Galatians is the earliest Pauline epistle in spite of the overlapping of its subject-matter with Romans and 1 and 2 Corinthians.

The Epistle to the Hebrews and the First Epistle of Peter bring us back again to anonymous documents. Hebrews is, as it stands, anonymous. The readers must, however, presumably have known who wrote it, since xiii. 22-5 is a personal note. But we do not know who he was. Nor do we know when it was written, or precisely why it was written. Everywhere there are references to the Temple ritual; and it would be natural to suppose that the Temple was still standing. But this does not seem to be a necessary conclusion, since the author is arguing less upon existing sacrificial practice than upon the sacrificial system as set forth in the Old Testament scriptures. Nor is it certain to whom the Epistle was written. The author may have been writing to Jewish Christians who were contemplating a return to Judaism, or he may have been writing to Christians, whether Jewish or Gentile, who were in danger of lapsing under the threat of persecution.

There are great difficulties in accepting the first Epistle of Peter as the work of the apostle. It is probably a pseudonymous general letter composed towards the end of the first century. And yet, when this is said, the mention of Silvanus in v. 12 as the actual writer of the Epistle, may mean, not that he wrote at the apostle's dictation, but that he composed the Epistle as a disciple of the apostle. Silas and Judas are named in Acts xv. 22-29, as the bearers of the letter from the apostles and elders at Jerusalem to the church at Antioch. It is possible therefore that there is a genuine Petrine background to 1 Peter, though its direct literary affinities are with the Pauline epistles.

The purpose of this very inadequate appendix is to show how delicate and difficult are all these questions of date and authorship. There are here no assured results, nor indeed can there be. The evidence is far too slender. The modern critic is thus thrown back upon the documents themselves. The question for him is not primarily who wrote these documents or when precisely they were written or where they were written. The question is whether these documents do more than bear witness to the life of the primitive church. Do they also bear witness to Jesus of Nazareth? This book has been written to show that they do bear unmistakable witness to him, and that they are otherwise in the end unintelligible. We have, consequently, touched upon matters of date and authorship only in an appendix, in order that the real problem of the New Testament may be displayed without the disturbance of problems which are ultimately irrelevant.

## Appendix B

## A Bibliography

Since the purpose of this book has been to show the impossibility of cataloguing the 'assured results' of New Testament criticism, we are unable to provide the reader with a short and selected list of books where he may find such conclusions set forth in compact and handy form. A somewhat extensive bibliography may, however, be found useful, as at least indicating the energy which is being put forth in the attempt to perfect the critical method.

In each section which follows the books are named roughly in order of advancing elaboration of treatment and, where necessary, are grouped in subjects. Only books written in English or translated into English have been included in this list. The date of the first edition or translation into English is given and, in cases where a book has subsequently been revised, details of the last revision.

### 1. ENCYCLOPAEDIAS AND GENERAL DICTIONARIES

Hastings, J. *Dictionary of Christ and the Gospels*. Edinburgh. 1906-8.

Hastings, J. *Dictionary of the Bible*. Edinburgh. 1898-1904.

Hastings, J. *Encyclopaedia of Religion and Ethics*. Edinburgh. 1908-21.

*The Encyclopaedia Biblica*. London. 1899-1903.

*The Encyclopaedia Britannica*. 13th or 14th Editions.

# APPENDIX B

## II. GENERAL INTRODUCTIONS TO
## THE STUDY OF THE NEW TESTAMENT

Strong, J. *The Exhaustive Concordance of the Bible*. London, 1894. ───────

Smith, Sir G. A. *Historical Geography of the Holy Land*. London, 1894; 25th ed. 1931.
Sanday, W. *Sacred Sites of the Gospels*. Oxford. 1903.
Dalman, G. H. *Sacred Sites and Ways*. London. 1935.

───────

Goudge, H. L., *The Methods of Theology*. London. 1923.
*What is the Gospel?* London. 1926.
Nairne, A. *The Faith of the New Testament*. London. 1920.
Gore, Charles. *Belief in Christ*. London. 1922.

───────

Milligan, G. *The New Testament Documents*. London. 1913.
Wade, G. W. *New Testament History*. London. 1922.

───────

Salmon, G. *A Historical Introduction to the Study of the Books of the New Testament*. London. 1885. 7th ed. 1894.
Godet, F. *Introduction to the New Testament*. London. 1899.
Bacon, B. W. *An Introduction to the New Testament*. New York and London. 1900.
*The Making of the New Testament*. London. 1912.
Sanday, W., and Others. *Criticism of the New Testament*. London. 1902.
Jülicher, A. *Introduction to the New Testament*. London. 1904.
Peake, A. S. *A Critical Introduction to the New Testament*. Duckworth, 1909.
Moffatt, J. *Introduction to the Literature of the New Testament*. Edinburgh. 1911; 3rd ed. 1918.
*The Approach to the New Testament*. London. 1921.

Jones, Maurice. *The New Testament in the Twentieth Century*. London. 1914; 3rd ed. 1934.

Harnack, A. *The Origin of the New Testament*. London. 1925.

Goodspeed, E. J. *New Chapters in New Testament Study*. New York. 1937.

Clogg, F. B. *An Introduction to the New Testament*. London. 1937.

Lake, K. and S. *Introduction to the New Testament*. London. 1938.

McNeile, A. H. *Introduction to the Study of the New Testament*. Oxford. 1927.

Scott, E. F. *The Literature of the New Testament*. New York. 1932.

Dibelius, M. *A Fresh Approach to the New Testament and Early Christian Literature*. London. 1936.

## III. THE LANGUAGE OF THE NEW TESTAMENT

Souter, A. *A Pocket Lexicon to the Greek New Testament*. Oxford. 1917.

Nunn, H. P. V. *Elements of New Testament Greek*. Cambridge. 1919; 4th ed. 1926.
*Syntax of New Testament Greek*. Cambridge. 1912.

Deissmann, G. A. *Light from the Ancient East*. London. 1910; new ed. 1927.

Abbott-Smith, G. *Manual Greek Lexicon of the New Testament*. Edinburgh. 1922; 2nd ed. 1923.

Grimm-Thayer. *Greek-English Lexicon of the New Testament*. Edinburgh. 1901.

Moulton-Geden. *Concordance to the Greek Testament*. Edinburgh. 1897.

Hatch and Redpath. *Concordance to the Septuagint*. Two vols. and supplement. Oxford. 1897-1906.

Moulton and Milligan. *Vocabulary of the Greek Testament*. Edinburgh. 1914-29.

Moulton, J. H. *Grammar of New Testament Greek*. Vol. I.
'Prolegomena.' Edinburgh. 1906; 3rd ed. 1908.

Moulton, J. H. and Howard, W. F. *Grammar of New
Testament Greek*. Vol. II. 'Accidence and Word-
Formation.' Edinburgh. 1929.

Blass, F. *Grammar of New Testament Greek*. London.
1898; 2nd ed. 1905.

Robertson, A. T. *Grammar of the Greek New Testament
in the Light of Historical Research*. London. 1914; 4th
ed. New York. 1923.

Hatch, E. *Essays in Biblical Greek*. Oxford. 1889.

Dalman, G. H. *The Words of Jesus*. Edinburgh. 1902.

Cremer, H. *Biblico-Theological Lexicon of New Testament
Greek*. Edinburgh. 1872; 4th ed. 1895.

## IV. TEXTUAL CRITICISM

Turner, C. H., in *A New Commentary in Holy Scripture*
(see p. 218).

Souter, A. *Text and Canon of the New Testament*. Oxford.
1913.

Robertson, A. T. *Introduction to the Textual Criticism of
the New Testament*. London. 1925.

Kenyon, Sir F. G. *Handbook of the Textual Criticism of the
New Testament*. London. 1901; 2nd ed. 1912.
*Recent Developments in the Textual Criticism of the Greek
Bible*. London. 1933.

Lake, Kirsopp. *Text of the New Testament*. London. 1900;
6th ed. rev. by Silva New 1928.

Vaganay, L. *Introduction to the Textual Criticism of the New
Testament*. London. 1937.

Streeter, B. H. *The Four Gospels* (Chs. I-VI). London.
1924.

Kenyon, Sir F. G. *The Chester Beatty Biblical Papyri.
Introduction to the Gospels and Acts, Fasciculus II*.
London. 1933.

*The Western Text in the Gospels and Acts*. London. 1939.

Lake, K. and S. *Family 13 (The Ferrar Group): The Text according to Mark*. London. 1941.

*The Harvard Theological Review*, October 1928. 'The Caesarean Text of the Gospel of Mark.'

## V. THE HELLENISTIC BACKGROUND

Bevan, E. R. *Hellenism and Christianity*. London. 1921.
*Stoics and Sceptics*. Oxford. 1913.

Angus, S. *The Mystery Religions*. London. 1925.
*The Environment of Early Christianity*. London. 1914.
*The Religious Quests of the Graeco-Roman World*. London. 1929.

Murray, Gilbert. *Five Stages of Greek Religion*. Oxford. 1925.

Bury, J. B. and Others. *The Hellenistic Age*. Cambridge. 1923.

Temple, W. *Plato and Christianity*. London. 1916.

Fairweather, W. *Jesus and the Greeks*. Edinburgh. 1924.

Dodd, C. H. *The Bible and the Greeks*. London. 1935.

Macgregor, G. H. C., and Purdy, A. C. *Jew and Greek: Tutors unto Christ*. London. 1936.

Knox, W. L. *Some Hellenistic Elements in Pauline Christianity*. Oxford. 1944.

Halliday, W. R. *The Pagan Background of Early Christianity*. Liverpool. 1925.

Tarn, W. W. *The Hellenistic Civilization*. London. 1927.

Adam, J. *Religious Teachers of Greece*. Edinburgh. 1908.

Caird, E. *Evolution of Theology in the Greek Philosophers*. Glasgow. 1904.

Dill, S. *Roman Society from Nero to Marcus Aurelius*. London. 1904.

Zeller, E. *Outlines of the History of Greek Philosophy*. London. 1886.

Scott, W. *Hermetica*. Four vols. Oxford. 1924-36.

Nock, A. *Conversion: The Old and the New in Religion from Alexander the Great to Augustine of Hippo.* Oxford. 1933.

## VI. THE JEWISH BACKGROUND

The Revised Version of the Apocrypha.

Bevan, E. R. *Jerusalem under the High Priests.* London. 1904.

Charles, R. H. *Between the Old and New Testaments.* London. 1914.

Jones, A. H. M. *The Herods of Judaea.* Oxford. 1938.

Parkes, J. *Jesus, Paul and the Jews.* London. 1936.

Cohen, A. and Others. *Judaism and the Beginnings of Christianity.* London. 1923.

Oesterley, W. O. E. *Introduction to the Books of the Apocrypha.* London. 1935.
*The Gospel Parables in the Light of their Jewish Background.* London. 1936.
*The Jews and Judaism during the Greek Period.* London. 1941.

Oesterley, W. O. E. and Box, G. H. *The Religion and Worship of the Synagogue.* London. 1911.

Oesterley, W. O. E. (Editor). *Judaism and Christianity.* Vol. I. *The Age of Transition.* London. 1937.

Loewe, H. (Editor). *Judaism and Christianity.* Vol. II. *The Contact of Pharisaism with other Cultures.* London. 1937.

Rosenthal, E. I. J. (Editor). *Judaism and Christianity.* Vol. III. *Law and Religion.* London. 1938.

Fairweather, W. *The Background of the Gospels.* Edinburgh. 1908.
*The Background of the Epistles.* Edinburgh. 1935.

Edersheim, A. *Jewish Social Life in the Days of Christ.* New Ed. London. 1908.

Herford, R. T. *The Pharisees.* London. 1924.
*Judaism in the New Testament Period.* London. 1928.
*Talmud and Apocrypha.* London. 1933.

Finkelstein, L. *The Pharisees*. Two vols. Philadelphia. 1938.

Riggs, J. S. *History of the Jewish People*. London. 1900.

Büchler, A. *Types of Jewish-Palestinian Piety*. Oxford. 1922.

Abrahams, I. *Studies in Pharisaism and the Gospels*. 2 vols. Oxford. 1917 and 1924.

Drummond, J. *Philo Judaeus*. London. 1888.

Stanton, V. H. *The Jewish and the Christian Messiah*. Edinburgh. 1886.

Montefiore, C. G. *Rabbinic Literature and Gospel Teachings*. London. 1930.

Klausner, J. *Jesus of Nazareth*. New York. 1925; 2nd ed. 1929.

Guignebert, C. *The Jewish World in the Time of Jesus*. London. 1939.

Moore, G. F. *Judaism*. Three vols. Oxford. 1927-30.

Schechter, S. *Studies in Judaism*. 1st and 2nd Series. London. 1896, 1908.

Montefiore, C. G., and Loewe, H. *A Rabbinic Anthology*. London. 1938.

Charles, R. H. *Apocrypha and Pseudepigrapha of the Old Testament*. Two vols. Oxford. 1913.

Schürer, E. *History of the Jewish People in the Time of Jesus Christ*. Five vols. and Index. Edinburgh. 1890-1.

## VII. COMPREHENSIVE STUDIES OF THE THEOLOGY OF THE NEW TESTAMENT

Taylor, V. *Jesus and His Sacrifice*. London. 1937.
*The Atonement in New Testament Teaching*. London. 1940.
*Forgiveness and Reconciliation: A Study in New Testament Theology*. London. 1941.

Rawlinson, A. E. J. *The New Testament Doctrine of the Christ*. London. 1926.

Du Bose, W. P. *The Soteriology of the New Testament.* New York. 1892.

Bell, G. K. A. and Deissmann, D. A. edd. *Mysterium Christi.* London. 1930.

Thornton, L. S. *The Common Life in the Body of Christ.* London. 1942.

Stevens, G. B. *The Theology of the New Testament.* Edinburgh. 1918.

Weiss, B. *Biblical Theology of the New Testament.* Two vols. Edinburgh. 1882, 1883.

Beyschlag, W. *New Testament Theology.* Two vols. Edinburgh. 1895.

## VIII. THE SYNOPTIC GOSPELS

Tasker, R. V. G. *The Nature and Purpose of the Gospels.* London. 1944.

Richardson, A. *The Gospels in the Making.* London. 1938. *The Miracle Stories of the Gospels.* London. 1941.

Burkitt, F. C. *The Earliest Sources for the Life of Jesus.* Boston. 1910. New ed. London. 1922. *The Gospel History and its Transmission.* Edinburgh. 1906; 3rd ed. 1911.

Crum, J. M. C. *The Original Jerusalem Gospel.* London. 1927.

Burney, C. F. *The Poetry of Our Lord.* Oxford. 1926.

Harnack, A. *Sayings of Jesus.* London. 1908.

Ogg, G. *The Chronology of the Public Ministry of Jesus.* Cambridge. 1940.

Redlich, E. B. *Form Criticism: its Value and Limitations.* London. 1939.

Easton, B. S. *The Gospel before the Gospels.* London. 1928.

Filson, F. V. *Origins of the Gospels.* New York. 1938.

Taylor, V. *The Formation of the Gospel Tradition.* London. 1933.

Dodd, C. H. *History and the Gospel.* London. 1938.

Lightfoot, R. M. *History and Interpretation in the Gospels.* London. 1935.

*Locality and Doctrine in the Gospels.* London. 1938.

Montefiore, C. G., *The Synoptic Gospels.* 2nd ed. London. 1927.

Streeter, B. H. *The Four Gospels.* London. 1924.

Sanday, W. and others. *Oxford Studies in the Synoptic Problem.* Oxford. 1911.

Hawkins, Sir J. C. *Horae Synopticae.* Oxford. 1899; 2nd ed. 1909.

Dibelius, M. *From Tradition to Gospel.* London. 1934.

Stanton, V. H. *The Gospels as Historical Documents.* Vols. I and II. Cambridge. 1903-10.

## IX. THE LIFE OF JESUS

Sanday, W. *Outlines of the Life of Christ.* 2nd ed. Edinburgh. 1906.

Gardner-Smith, P. *The Christ of the Gospels.* Cambridge. 1938.

Headlam, A. C. *Life and Teaching of Jesus the Christ.* London. 1923.

Mackinnon, J. *The Historic Jesus.* London. 1931.

Strachan, R. H. *The Historic Jesus in the New Testament.* London. 1931.

Dale, R. W. *The Living Christ and the Four Gospels.* London. 1890; 2nd ed. 1890.

Denney, J. *Jesus and the Gospel.* London. 1908.

Forsyth, P. T. *The Person and Place of Jesus Christ.* London. 1909.

Bousset, W. *Jesus.* London. 1906.

Bacon, B. W. *The Story of Jesus.* London. 1928.

Manson, W. *Jesus the Messiah.* London. 1943.

Warschauer, J. *The Historical Life of Christ.* London. 1927.

Sanday, W. *The Life of Christ in Recent Research*. Oxford. 1907.

Schweitzer, A. *The Quest of the Historical Jesus*. London. 1910.

Drews, A. *The Christ Myth*. London. 1910.

*The Witnesses to the Historicity of Jesus*. London. 1912.

Couchoud, P. L. *The Enigma of Jesus*. London. 1924.

Goguel, M. *Life of Jesus*. London. 1933.

Guignebert, C. A. E. *Jesus*. London. 1935.

Dibelius, M. *Gospel Criticism and Christology*. London. 1935.

## X. THE TEACHING OF JESUS

Gore, Charles. *The Sermon on the Mount*. London. 1896.

Marriott, H. *The Sermon on the Mount*. London. 1925.

Lagrange, M. J. *The Gospel of Jesus Christ*. London. 1938.

Latham, H. *Pastor Pastorum*. Cambridge. 1904.

Clutton-Brock, A. *What is the Kingdom of Heaven?* London. 1919.

Anderson Scott, C. A. *New Testament Ethics*. Cambridge. 1930.

Cadoux, C. J. *The Historic Mission of Jesus*. London. 1941.

Dougall, L. and Emmet, C. W. *The Lord of Thought*. London. 1922.

Stevens, G. B. *The Teaching of Jesus*. New York. 1901.

Curtis, W. A. *Jesus Christ the Teacher*. Oxford. 1943.

Scott, E. F. *The Ethical Teaching of Jesus*. London. 1924.

*The Kingdom and the Messiah*. Edinburgh. 1917.

*The Kingdom of God in the New Testament*. London. 1931.

Otto, R. *The Kingdom of God and the Son of Man*. London. 1938.

Grant, F. C. *The Gospel of the Kingdom*. London. 1940.

Easton, B. S. *Christ in the Gospels*. London. 1930.

Muirhead, L. A. *The Eschatology of Jesus*. London. 1903.

Manson, T. W. *The Teaching of Jesus*. Cambridge. 1931;
2nd ed. 1935.

Moffatt, J. *The Theology of the Gospels*. London. 1912.

Bruce, A. B. *The Kingdom of God*. Edinburgh. 1889.
*The Parabolic Teaching of Christ*. London. 1882.

Cadoux, A. T. *The Parables of Jesus*. London. 1930.

Dodd, C. H. *The Parables of the Kingdom*. London. 1935.
*The Gospel in the New Testament*. London. 1926.

Smith, B. T. D. *The Parables of the Synoptic Gospels*.
Cambridge. 1937.

Du Bose, W. P. *The Gospel in the Gospels*. London. 1906.

Seeley, Sir J. R. *Ecce Homo*. London. 1866; 5th ed. 1866.

Harnack, A. *What is Christianity?* London. 1901; 3rd ed.
1904.

Bultmann, D. R. *Jesus and the Word*. London. 1935.

Hodgson, L. *And was made Man*. London. 1928.

Grandmaison, L. de. *Jesus Christ, His Person, His Message,
His Credentials*. Three vols. London. 1930-4.

Lebreton, J. *The Life and Teaching of Jesus Christ our Lord*.
Two vols. London. 1935.

Wendt, H. H. *The Teaching of Jesus*. Two vols. Edinburgh. 1892.

## XI. THE PAULINE EPISTLES IN GENERAL

Nock, A. D. *St. Paul*. London. 1938.

Badcock, F. J. *The Pauline Epistles and the Epistle to the
Hebrews in their Historical Setting*. London. 1937.

McNeile, A. H. *New Testament Teaching in the Light of
St. Paul's*. Cambridge. 1923.
*St. Paul: His Life, Letters and Christian Doctrine*.
Cambridge. 1920.

Goudge, H. L. *The Mind of St. Paul as illustrated by his
Second Epistle to the Corinthians*. London. 1911.

Garvie, A. E. *Studies of Paul and His Gospel*. London.
1911.

Gardner, P. *The Religious Experience of St. Paul*. London. 1911.

Findley, G. G. *The Apostle Paul: a Sketch of the Development of his Doctrine*. London. 1891.

Anderson Scott, C. A. *Christianity according to St. Paul*. Cambridge. 1927.

Machen, J. G. *The Origin of Paul's Religion*. London. 1921.

Morgan, W. *The Religion and Theology of Paul*. Edinburgh. 1917.

Stevens, G. B. *The Pauline Theology*. New York. 1892; rev. ed. 1898.

Prat, F. *The Theology of St. Paul*. Two vols. London. 1926.

Sabatier, A. *The Apostle Paul*. London. 1891.

Wrede, W. *Paul*. London. 1907.

Scott, R. *The Pauline Epistles. A Critical Study*. Edinburgh. 1909.

Shaw, R. D. *The Pauline Epistles*. Edinburgh. 1903.

Thackeray, H. St. J. *The Relation of St. Paul to Contemporary Jewish Thought*. London. 1900.

Schweitzer, A. *St. Paul and his Interpreters*. London. 1912.

*The Mysticism of Paul the Apostle*. London. 1931.

Kennedy, H. A. A. *St. Paul and the Mystery Religions*. London. 1913.

*The Theology of the Epistles*. London. 1919.

Bacon, B. W. *Jesus and Paul*. London. 1921.

Knowling, R. J. *The Testimony of St. Paul to Christ viewed in some of its Aspects*. London. 1905.

*The Witness of the Epistles*. London. 1892.

Lake, Kirsopp. *The Earlier Epistles of St. Paul*. London. 1911.

Deissmann, A. *St. Paul*. London. 1912; 2nd ed. 1926.

Du Bose, W. P. *The Gospel according to St. Paul*. New York. 1907.

Baur, F. C. *Paul, the Apostle of Jesus Christ*. London. 1873.

Knox, W. L. *St. Paul and the Church of Jerusalem.* Cambridge. 1925.
*St. Paul and the Church of the Gentiles.* Cambridge. 1939.
Pfleiderer, O. *Paulinism.* Two vols. London. 1877.


## XII. GENERAL BOOKS ON THE EARLY CHURCH

Wand, J. W. C. *First Century Christianity.* Oxford. 1937.
Hamilton, H. *The People of God.* (Vol. II.) Oxford. 1912.
Hort, F. J. A. *The Christian Ecclesia.* London. 1897.
*Judaistic Christianity.* Cambridge. 1894.
Gore, C. *The Church and the Ministry.* London. 1882; new ed. rev. by C. H. Turner 1919.
Flew, R. N. *Jesus and His Church.* London. 1938.
Johnston, G. *The Doctrine of the Church in the New Testament.* Cambridge. 1943.
Bartlet, J. V., and Carlyle, A. J. *Christianity in History.* London. 1917.
Bartlet, J. V. *The Apostolic Age.* Edinburgh. 1900.
Bardy, G. *The Church at the End of the First Century.* London. 1938.
Ramsay, Sir W. M. *The Church in the Roman Empire.* London. 1893.
Sanday, W. *The Primitive Church and Reunion.* Oxford. 1913.
Lindsay, T. M. *The Church and the Ministry in Early Centuries.* London. 1902.
McGiffert, A. C. *A History of Christianity in the Apostolic Age.* Edinburgh. 1897.
Swete, H. B. (Editor). *Essays on the Early History of the Church and Ministry.* London. 1918; 2nd ed. 1921.
Mackinnon, J. *The Gospel in the Early Church.* London. 1933.
*The Rise and Growth of the Early Church.* London. 1936.

Ropes, J. H. *The Apostolic Age in the Light of Modern Criticism*. London. 1906.

Dodd, C. H. *The Apostolic Preaching and its Development*. London. 1936.

Wernle, P. *The Beginnings of Christianity*. Two vols. London. 1903-4.

Lebreton, J., and Zeiller, J. *The History of the Primitive Church*. Vol. I. London. 1942.

Lietzmann, H. *The Beginnings of the Christian Church*. Vol. I. London. 1937.

Weiss, J. *The History of Primitive Christianity*. Two vols. London. 1937.

Wordsworth, J. *The Ministry of Grace*. London. 1901.

Moberly, R. C. *Ministerial Priesthood*. London. 1897.

Harnack, A. *The Constitution and Law of the Church in the First Two Centuries*. London. 1910.
*The Expansion of Christianity in the First Three Centuries*. London. 1904; 2nd ed. 1908.

Hatch, E. *The Organization of the Early Christian Churches*. 3rd ed. London. 1888.

Bartlet, J. V. *Church Life and Order during the first four Centuries*. Oxford. 1943.

von Dobschütz, E. *The Apostolic Age*. London. 1909.
*Christian Life in the Primitive Church*. London. 1904.

Carrington, P. *The Primitive Christian Catechism*. Cambridge. 1940.

Streeter, B. H. *The Primitive Church*. London. 1929.

Pfleiderer, O. *Primitive Christianity*. Four vols. London. 1906-11.

## XIII. COMMENTARIES

### A

Commentaries on the New Testament in one volume
*A New Commentary on Holy Scripture*. Edited by C. Gore
H. L. Goudge, A. Guillaume. London. 1928.

*A Commentary on the Bible*. Edited by A. S. Peake. Edinburgh. 1919.

*The Abingdon Commentary*. Edited by F. C. Eiselen, E. Lewis, D. G. Downey. New York. 1929.

## B

Series of Commentaries on all, or nearly all, the books of the New Testament, in separate volumes.

*The Clarendon Bible*. Oxford.

*The Century Bible*. Edinburgh.

*The Cambridge Bible for Schools and Colleges*. Cambridge.

*The Cambridge Greek Testament for Schools and Colleges*. Cambridge.

*The Westminster Commentaries*. London.

*The Moffatt New Testament Commentary*. London.

*The Expositor's Greek Testament*. (5 vols.) London.

*The International Critical Commentary*. Edinburgh.

## C

Commentaries and other works on the Four Gospels and on the Acts of the Apostles, which are not included in the series mentioned in Section B.

### ST. MATTHEW'S GOSPEL

*Commentaries:*

McNeile, A. H. *The Gospel according to St. Matthew*. London. 1915.

Plummer, A. *An Exegetical Commentary on the Gospel according to St. Matthew*. London. 1909; 3rd ed. 1911.

*Other Works:*

Bacon, B. W. *The Sermon on the Mount*. London. 1902. *Studies in Matthew*. London. 1930.

Pallis, A. *A Few Notes on the Gospels according to St. Mark and St. Matthew*. Liverpool. 1903.

# APPENDIX B

## ST. MARK'S GOSPEL

*Commentaries:*

Menzies, A. *The Earliest Gospel*. London. 1901.

Lowrie, W. *Jesus according to St. Mark*. London. 1929.

Bacon, B. W. *The Beginnings of Gospel Story*. New Haven. 1909.

Allen, W. C. *The Gospel according to St. Mark*. London. 1915.

Swete, H. B. *The Gospel according to St. Mark*. London. 1898; 3rd ed. 1909.

*Other Works:*

Bennett, W. H. *The Life of Jesus according to St. Mark*. London. 1914.

Bacon, B. W. *The Gospel of Mark: its Composition and Date*. New Haven. 1925.

*Is Mark a Roman Gospel?* Cambridge. 1919.

Thompson, J. M. *Jesus according to St. Mark*. London. 1909.

Turner, C. H. 'Studies in the Gospel of Mark'. Published in the *Journal of Theological Studies*. 1925-8.

Crum, J. M. C. *St. Mark's Gospel*. Cambridge. 1936.

Cadoux, A. T. *The Sources of the Second Gospel*. London. 1935.

## ST. LUKE'S GOSPEL AND THE ACTS OF THE APOSTLES

*Commentaries:*

Wright, A. *The Gospel according to St. Luke in Greek after the Westcott and Hort Text*. London. 1900.

Easton, B. S. *The Gospel according to St. Luke*. New York 1926.

Creed, J. M. *The Gospel according to St. Luke*. London 1930.

Rendall, F. *The Acts of the Apostles in Greek and English* London. 1897.

Page, T. E. *The Acts of the Apostles*. London. 1918.

Furneaux, W. M. *Acts. A Commentary for English Readers.* Oxford. 1912.

*Other Works:*

Ramsay, Sir W. M. *The Bearing of Recent Discoveries on the Trustworthiness of the New Testament.* London. 1915.

*Luke the Physician.* London. 1908.

*St. Paul the Traveller and the Roman Citizen.* London. 1895; 14th ed. 1929.

Harnack, A. New Testament Studies. London. 1907-12.

*The Acts of the Apostles.*

*The Date of the Acts and Synoptic Gospels.*

*Luke the Physician.*

Hobart, W. K. *The Medical Language of St. Luke.* Dublin. 1882.

Chase, F. H. *The Credibility of the Book of the Acts of the Apostles.* London. 1902.

Taylor, V. *Behind the Third Gospel.* Oxford. 1926.

MacLachan, H. *St. Luke, The Man and His Work.* Manchester. 1920.

Knox, W. L. *St. Paul and the Church of Jerusalem.* Cambridge. 1925.

Cadbury, H. J. *Style and Method of St. Luke.* Harvard. 1919.

*The Making of Luke-Acts.* London. 1927.

Selwyn, E. C. *St. Luke the Prophet.* London. 1901.

Torrey, C. C. *The Composition and Date of Acts.* Cambridge. [U.S.] 1916.

Clark, A. C. *The Acts of the Apostles.* Oxford. 1933.

Jackson, F. J. Foakes, and Lake, K. *The Beginnings of Christianity.* (5 vols.) 1920-33.


ST. JOHN'S GOSPEL

*Commentaries:*

Westcott, B. F. *The Gospel according to St. John.* Two vols. London. 1908.

Hoskyns, Sir E. C., Bart. *The Fourth Gospel*. Two vols. London. 1940; 2nd. ed. 1947.

*Other Works:*

Redlich, E. B. *An Introduction to the Fourth Gospel*. London. 1939.

Murray, J. O. F. *Jesus according to St. John*. London. 1936.

Holland, H. S. *The Philosophy of Faith and the Fourth Gospel*. London. 1920.

Gardner, P. *The Ephesian Gospel*. London. 1915.

Charnwood, Lord. *According to St. John*. London. 1925.

Garvie, A. E. *The Beloved Disciple*. London. 1922.

Broomfield, G. W. *John, Peter, and the Fourth Gospel*. London. 1934.

Richmond, W. *The Gospel of the Rejection*. London. 1906.

Drummond, J. *An Enquiry into the Character and Authorship of the Fourth Gospel*. London. 1903.

Robinson, J. A. *The Historical Character of St. John's Gospel*. London. 1908; 2nd ed. 1929.

Smith, P. V. *Historical Importance of the Fourth Gospel*. London. 1926.

Swete, H. B. *The Last Discourse and Prayer of Our Lord*. London. 1913.

Lowrie, W. *The Doctrine of St. John*. London. 1899.

Strachan, R. H. *The Fourth Gospel*. London. 1917. *The Fourth Evangelist, Dramatist or Historian?* London. 1925.
*The Fourth Gospel: its Significance and Environment*. London. 1941.

Scott, E. F. *The Fourth Gospel: Its Purpose and Theology*. Edinburgh. 1906.

Sanday, W. *The Criticism of the Fourth Gospel*. Oxford. 1905.

Jackson, H. L. *The Problem of the Fourth Gospel*. Cambridge. 1918.

Gardner-Smith, P. *Saint John and the Synoptic Gospels*. Cambridge. 1938.

Howard, W. F. *The Fourth Gospel in Recent Criticism and Interpretation.* London, 1931.
*Christianity according to St. John.* London. 1943.

Nolloth, C. F. *The Fourth Evangelist.* London. 1925.

Carpenter, J. E. *The Johannine Writings.* London. 1927.

Schmiedel, P. W. *The Johannine Writings.* London. 1908.

Bacon, B. W. *The Fourth Gospel in Research and Debate.* London. 1910.

Burney, C. F. *The Aramaic Origin of the Fourth Gospel.* Oxford. 1922.

Sanders, J. N. *The Fourth Gospel in the Early Church.* Cambridge. 1943.

Bury, R. G. *The Fourth Gospel and the Logos Doctrine.* Cambridge. 1940.

Abbott, E. A. *Johannine Vocabulary.* London. 1905.
*Johannine Grammar.* London. 1906.

Stevens, G. B. *Johannine Theology.* London. 1894.

Lewis, F. W. *Disarrangements in the Fourth Gospel.* Cambridge. 1910.

Hore, F. R. *Original Order and Chapters of St. John's Gospel.* London. 1944.

Stanton, V. H. *The Gospels as Historical Documents.* Vol. III. Cambridge. 1920.

## D

Commentaries and Other Works on the Several Epistles of St. Paul, excluding the series of commentaries referred to in Section B.

### THE EPISTLE TO THE ROMANS

*Commentaries:*

Gore, C. *St. Paul's Epistle to the Romans.* Two vols. London. 1899, 1900.

Vaughan, C. J. *St. Paul's Epistle to the Romans.* London. 1859; 3rd. ed. 1870.

Jowett, B. *The Epistle of St. Paul to the Thessalonians, Galatians, Romans.* Two vols. London. 1855; 2nd ed. 1859.

Sadler, M. F. *The Epistle to the Romans.* London. 1888.

Beet, J. A. *A Commentary on St. Paul's Epistle to the Romans.* London. 1877; 9th ed. 1900.

Godet, F. *Commentary on St. Paul's Epistle to the Romans.* Edinburgh. 1888-9.

Liddon, H. P. *Explanatory Analysis of St. Paul's Epistle to the Romans.* London. 1893.

Benson, R. M. *An Exposition of the Epistle of St. Paul to the Romans.* London. 1892.

Lightfoot, J. B. *Notes on Epistles of St. Paul from Unpublished Commentaries.* London. 1895.

Barth, K. *The Epistle to the Romans.* Oxford. 1933.

*Other Works:*

Pelly, R. L. *Studies in the Epistle to the Romans.* London. 1917.

Hort, F. J. A. *Prolegomena to Romans and Ephesians.* London. 1895.

Pallis, A. *To the Romans.* Oxford. 1920.

## THE FIRST AND SECOND EPISTLES TO THE CORINTHIANS

*Commentaries:*

Sadler, M. F. *The First and Second Epistles to the Corinthians, with Notes.* London. 1889.

Beet, J. A. *A Commentary on St. Paul's Epistles to the Corinthians.* London. 1882.

Godet, F. *Commentary on St. Paul's First Epistle to the Corinthians.* Two vols. Edinburgh. 1886-7.

Stanley, A. P. *The Epistles of St. Paul to the Corinthians.* 4th ed. London. 1876.

Ellicott, C. J. *St. Paul's First Epistle to the Corinthians with Commentary.* London. 1887.

*Other Works:*

Rendall, G. H. *The Epistles of St. Paul to the Corinthians.*
London. 1909.

## THE EPISTLE TO THE GALATIANS

*Commentaries:*

Emmet, C. W. *St. Paul's Epistle to the Galatians.* (Readers'
Commentary.) London. 1912.

Ramsay, Sir W. M. *A Historical Commentary on St. Paul's
Epistle to the Galatians.* London. 1899.

Jowett, B. (See under the Epistle to the Romans.)

Ellicott, C. J. *St. Paul's Epistle to the Galatians.* London.
1854; 4th ed. 1867.

Lightfoot, J. B. *St. Paul's Epistle to the Galatians.* London.
1865; 10th ed. 1890.

*Other Works:*

Watkins, C. H. *St. Paul's Fight for Galatia.* London. 1914.

Macgregor, W. M. *Christian Freedom.* London. 1914;
new ed. 1931.

Askwith, E. H. *The Epistle to the Galatians.* London.
1899.

Murray, J. O. F. *A Fragment of Spiritual Autobiography.*
Cambridge. 1916.

Round, D. *The Date of St. Paul's Epistle to the Galatians.*
Cambridge. 1906.

## EPHESIANS

*Commentaries:*

Gore, C. *St. Paul's Epistle to the Ephesians.* London. 1898.

Synge, F. G. *St. Paul's Epistle to the Ephesians.* London.
1941.

Beet, J. A. *A Commentary on St. Paul's Epistles to the
Ephesians, Philippians, Colossians and to Philemon.*
London. 1890.

Ellicott, C. J. *St. Paul's Epistle to the Ephesians.* London. 1855; 5th ed. 1884.

Macpherson, J. *Commentary on St. Paul's Epistle to the Ephesians.* Edinburgh. 1892.

Robinson, J. A. *St. Paul's Epistle to the Ephesians.* London. 1903; 2nd ed. 1904.

*Other Works:*

Goodspeed, E. J. *The Meaning of Ephesians.* Cambridge. 1933.

### COLOSSIANS AND PHILEMON

*Commentaries:*

Beet, J. A. (See under the Epistle to the Ephesians.)

Ellicott, C. J. *St. Paul's Epistles to the Philippians, Colossians and Philemon.* 1857. 5th ed. London. 1888.

Lightfoot, J. B. *St. Paul's Epistles to the Colossians and Philemon.* London. 1875.

*Other Works:*

Moule, H. C. G. *Colossian Studies.* London. 1898.

### THE EPISTLE TO THE PHILIPPIANS

*Commentaries:*

Beet, J. A. (See under the Epistle to the Ephesians.)

Lightfoot, J. B. *Philippians.* London. 1868; new ed. 1879.

### THE FIRST AND SECOND EPISTLES TO THE THESSALONIANS

*Commentaries:*

Milligan, G. *St. Paul's Epistles to the Thessalonians.* London. 1908.

Jowett, B. (See under the Epistle to the Romans.)

Ellicott, C. J. *St. Paul's Epistles to the Thessalonians.* London. 1858; 4th ed. 1880.

Plummer, A. *Commentary on St. Paul's First Epistle to the Thessalonians*. London. 1918.
*Commentary on St. Paul's Second Epistle to the Thessalonians*. London. 1918.

*Other Works:*
Kennedy, H. A. A. *St. Paul's Conception of the Last Things*. London. 1904.
Bousset, W. *The Anti-Christ Legend*. London. 1896.

### THE PASTORAL EPISTLES

*Commentaries:*
Ellicott, C. J. *The Pastoral Epistles of St. Paul*. 1856; 5th ed. London. 1883.
Plummer, A. *The Pastoral Epistles*. (The Expositor's Bible.) London. 1907.
Liddon, H. P. *Explanatory Analysis of I Timothy*. London. 1897.
Parry, R. St. J. *The Pastoral Epistles*. Cambridge. 1920.
Falconer, R. *The Pastoral Epistles*. Oxford. 1937.

*Other Works:*
Harrison, P. N. *The Problem of the Pastoral Epistles*. Oxford. 1921.

### E

Commentaries and Other Works on the Remaining Books of the New Testament, excluding the series of commentaries mentioned in Section B.

### THE EPISTLE TO THE HEBREWS

*Commentaries:*
Rendall, F. *Hebrews, Greek and English, with Notes*. London. 1883.
Westcott, B. F. *The Epistle to the Hebrews*. London. 1889.

# APPENDIX B

*Other Works:*

Nairne, A. *The Epistle of Priesthood.* Edinburgh. 1913.

Peake, A. S. *Heroes and Martyrs of Faith.* London. 1910.

Vaughan, C. J. *Heroes of Faith, Lecture on the 11th Chapter of Hebrews.* London. 1876.

Milligan, G. *Theology of the Epistle to the Hebrews.* Edinburgh. 1899.

Dale, R. W. *Jewish Temple and Christian Church.* London. 1865; 2nd ed. 1871.

Bruce, A. B. *The Epistle to the Hebrews.* Edinburgh. 1899.

Du Bose, W. P. *High Priesthood and Sacrifice.* London. 1908.

Scott, E. F. *The Epistle to the Hebrews.* Edinburgh. 1922.

## THE TWO EPISTLES OF ST. PETER

*Commentaries:*

Masterman, J. H. B. *The First Epistle of Peter.* London. 1900.

Robson, E. I. *Studies in the Second Epistle of St. Peter.* Cambridge. 1915.

Hort, F. J. A. *The First Epistle of St. Peter.* (i. 1-ii. 17 only. Greek text, with introductory lecture, commentary, and additional notes.) London. 1898.

Mayor, J. B. (See under the Epistle of Jude.)

Selwyn, E. G. *The First Epistle of St. Peter.* London. 1946.

## THE JOHANNINE EPISTLES

*Commentaries:*

Gore, C. *The Epistles of St. John.* London. 1920.

Westcott, B. F. *The Epistles of St. John.* London. 1883; 2nd ed. 1885.

## THE EPISTLE OF JAMES

*Commentaries:*

Smith, H. Maynard. *The Epistle of S. James.* Oxford. 1914.

228

Dale, R. W. *The Epistle of James and other Discourses.* London. 1895.

Hort, F. J. A. *The Epistle of St. James.* (A Fragment. Greek text, with introduction, etc.) London. 1909.

Mayor, J. B. *Epistle of James.* London. 1892. 3rd ed. 1913.

*Other Works:*

Rendall, G. H. *The Epistle of James and Judaic Christianity.* Cambridge. 1927.


## JUDE

*Commentary:*

Mayor, J. B. *The Epistle of St. Jude and the Second Epistle of St. Peter.* London. 1907.


## THE REVELATION OF ST. JOHN

*Commentaries:*

Hort, F. J. A. *The Apocalypse of St. John I-III.* London. 1908.

Beckwith, C. L. *The Apocalypse of John.* New York. 1919.

Swete, H. B. *The Apocalypse of St. John.* London. 1906.

*Other Works:*

Kiddle, M. *The Revelation of St. John.* London. 1940.

Ramsay, Sir W. M. *The Letters to the Seven Churches of Asia.* London. 1904.

Burkitt, F. C. *Jewish and Christian Apocalypses.* London. 1914.

Charles, R. H. *Studies in the Apocalypse.* Edinburgh. 1913. *Lectures on the Apocalypse.* London. 1922.

Peake, A. S. *The Revelation of St. John.* London. 1919.

Carrington, P. *The Meaning of Revelation.* London. 1931.

Maurice, F. D. *Lectures on the Apocalypse.* Cambridge. 1861.

## APPENDIX B

Selwyn, E. C. *The Christian Prophets and the Prophetic Apocalypse*. London. 1900.

Workman, H. B. *Persecution in the Early Church*. London. 1906.

Scott, E. F. *The Book of Revelation*. London. 1939.

# An Index of References

# AN INDEX OF REFERENCES

# AN INDEX OF REFERENCES

# AN INDEX OF REFERENCES

# AN INDEX OF REFERENCES